DEVELOPMENT CENTRE STUDIES

CHANGING APPROACHES TO POPULATION PROBLEMS

by

Margaret Wolfson

DEVELOPMENT CENTRE
OF THE
ORGANISATION FOR ECONOMIC CO-OPERATION AND DEVELOPMENT
in co-operation with
THE WORLD BANK

The Organisation for Economic Co-operation and Development (OECD) was set up under a Convention signed in Paris on 14th December 1960, which provides that the OECD shall promote policies designed:
— to achieve the highest sustainable economic growth and employment and a rising standard of living in Member countries, while maintaining financial stability, and thus to contribute to the development of the world economy;
— to contribute to sound economic expansion in Member as well as non-member countries in the process of economic development;
— to contribute to the expansion of world trade on a multilateral, non-discriminatory basis in accordance with international obligations.

The Members of OECD are Australia, Austria, Belgium, Canada, Denmark, Finland, France, the Federal Republic of Germany, Greece, Iceland, Ireland, Italy, Japan, Luxembourg, the Netherlands, New Zealand, Norway, Portugal, Spain, Sweden, Switzerland, Turkey, the United Kingdom and the United States.

The Development Centre of the Organisation for Economic Co-operation and Development was established by decision of the OECD Council on 23rd October 1962.

The purpose of the Centre is to bring together the knowledge and experience available in Member countries of both economic development and the formulation and execution of general policies of economic aid; to adapt such knowledge and experience to the actual needs of countries or regions in the process of development and to put the results at the disposal of the countries by appropriate means.

The Centre has a special and autonomous position within the OECD which enables it to enjoy scientific independence in the execution of its task. Nevertheless, the Centre can draw upon the experience and knowledge available in the OECD in the development field.

*
* *

CONTENTS

3

CONTENTS

PREFACE

It gives me a special pleasure to introduce this book, which was sponsored jointly by the Development Centre and the World Bank. The study reviews the changes that have taken place within only a few years in our thinking about a particularly elusive aspect of development—namely, problems of population.

The period since the World Population Conference at Bucharest in August 1974 has seen striking changes in our understanding of these problems. At the time of the Conference, with its much-publicized and loudly-contested debate, it seemed that there was a profound, perhaps irreconcilable difference of opinion as to the true nature of the problems involved, and, hence, as to the means of dealing with them. As it has turned out, the very dissentions of Bucharest have proved of inestimable value. They were a revelation—to governments and to ordinary citizens alike—of the immediacy of population problems for the world as a whole and for themselves. And they have enabled all of us to grasp better the real issues that are at stake.

As this book shows, perceptions of what constitutes a population problem are very different now from those most commonly held in the 1960s and early 1970s. It is now understood that "population" is not solely a matter of fertility or rate of growth but covers a much wider range of problems than we had suspected before. It is also understood that to solve these problems, indirect approaches may be as important as the direct, and measures to tackle causes as much needed as those to cope with consequences.

Today, we not only understand that population must be linked with development, but we recognise that this interrelation is, indeed, basic to efforts to solve our population problems. It is significant that whereas at Bucharest the issue of population *versus* development split international opinion into two bitterly opposed ideological camps, four years later, when representatives from developing countries and donor agencies discussed these same issues at the OECD in Paris, the dual approach of population *and* development had become the accepted wisdom, and was felt to require no further re-statement.

In May 1978, the Development Centre, in collaboration with the Development Assistance Committee of the OECD and the World Bank, organised a meeting to consider the findings of this book, and in particular, their implications for population assistance. The meeting was attended by policy-level representatives from twelve developing countries, the heads of the population assistance agencies, and representatives of those DAC Member countries which have bilateral population assistance programmes. Their endorsement of the conclusions of the book, and specifically, of the concept that population problems depend in part for their solution on improving the condition of people's lives, could hardly have been in greater contrast to the violent controversies of Bucharest.

It is today widely held that the provision of a good life for all classes of society should be a major goal of development policy. We have now also learnt that by helping to meet people's basic human needs, we are at the same time helping to deal with population problems. The relation of improved economic and social conditions to such problems as high infant mortality, uncontrolled urban growth, or massive unemployment among the young, needs no underlining. In particular, governments have begun to realise that the social status, education and earning opportunities of women play a fundamental part in determining family size. The great change since Bucharest is that we now recognise that people's fertility behaviour is very much a function of the circumstances in which they live. Even in those countries, therefore, where the major population problem is the high rate of natural increase, the solution is to be found through overall development strategies, as well as through specific population programmes.

In the period since Bucharest, we have begun to search for ways in which these new concepts of population and development can best be given practical effect. In particular, we need to translate these broad concepts into actual development policies and devise the institutional structures needed to carry them out. Many difficult and far-reaching questions are immediately opened up: how should the direct and the indirect approaches be organised so that they will be mutually supportive? What structures are needed? And how can development assistance best contribute to these diverse purposes? These are questions in which the international community and developing countries are now increasingly focusing their attention. We are all seeking for solutions, but we are still very much at the learning phase.

The present book poses these questions—some of them directly, others by implication, in its analysis of the way developing countries and aid agencies are now trying to deal with population problems. The analysis is based on a review of the population policies of twelve developing countries in different regions of the world and of the major agencies providing population assistance, all of which were visited for direct discussions.

In this work, we are greatly indebted to the generous collaboration of the World Bank. Their counsel, their wide-ranging personal contacts, and their financial assistance made possible the extensive series of visits world-wide that has enabled us to see at first-hand some of the problems involved and get the views of the people responsible for their solution. I would like to express my appreciation to Dr. Kanagaratnam, Director of the Population Projects Department of the World Bank, and to his staff, not only for their financial participation in this study, but also for their unstinting help to the Development Centre and to the author during the whole period that the study was under way.

Professor Louis SABOURIN,
President, OECD Development Centre
Paris, October 1978

6

INTRODUCTION

When the World Population Conference came to a close on 31st August 1974, it seemed to many of the four thousand or so delegates, observers, journalists, etc., who had filled Bucharest for that turbulent week, that a whole generation of thinking about population policy had come to a close with it. Among much of the donor community, in particular, there was a feeling that the Conference had resulted in a public repudiation of family planning as the main solution of population problems, and that henceforward the attitude of the Third World towards population problems would be dominated by the slogan "Development is the best contraceptive".

A few weeks after Bucharest, the Development Assistance Committee (DAC) of the Organisation for Economic Co-operation and Development (OECD), having heard an oral report on the Conference from an observer from the OECD Development Centre, raised the question of what the results of Bucharest were likely to be once the rhetoric of the debates had died down and, in particular, what were the implications for population assistance. It was accordingly suggested that the Development Centre might undertake a study to find out how the different agencies providing population assistance were proposing to respond to the Conference in their respective aid programmes. Shortly afterwards, the World Bank suggested that it associate itself with the Development Centre as co-sponsor of the study.

The present report is the result of this collaboration. The participation of the World Bank has enabled the Development Centre to extend the scope of the enquiry beyond that originally envisaged in response to the request of the DAC, and to try to discover how developing countries, as well as aid agencies, were thinking about population problems and, as a consequence, about population assistance, in the "post-Bucharest era".

It was decided that the work should start at the end of 1975, after the UN and the UN Fund for Population Activities (UNFPA) had completed their series of Regional Consultative Conferences that were a follow-up to Bucharest, and a Committee of Experts had discussed their results. The study was completed at the end of 1977, that is to say, some three and a quarter years after Bucharest, a period sufficiently long for any real changes in attitudes that may have ensued to be already discernable.

The work has covered direct discussions in twelve developing countries and with a large number of population assistance agencies[1]. In choosing the countries to be visited, it was felt that the prime consideration should be the interest that they presented for population assistance. The agencies providing population assistance were concerned to know what changes, if any, were taking place in

---

1. The interviewing started in the summer of 1976 and continued to the end of the year. The country chapters and the agency pieces were mostly written in 1977, and have since been up-dated in collaboration with officials of the country or agency concerned. As far as possible they describe the situation as at June 1978.

the policies and programmes of the countries to which they were already giving such aid, what new "clients" were likely to be coming up and what new form population assistance might need to take in the future. At the same time, we were careful not to identify a "national population policy" as being synonomous with the desire to reduce population size (an association which would, in itself, be contrary to the "message" of Bucharest). We have accordingly included some countries whose governments are interested in promoting family planning services for their citizens for reasons other than population control.

It was decided that in Asia where, in terms of sheer numbers, the problems caused by population increase are the most acute, four countries should be visited. These were India, a sub-continent plagued by massive poverty, where, after over 20 years of publicly-sponsored family planning programmes, the problem of runaway population growth looked as intractable as ever; the Republic of Korea, a "modern" developing country, and one of family planning's classical success stories; Thailand, a country that had come to adopt a national population policy relatively recently, but where it seemed that the people were particularly responsive to family planning; and the Philippines, where the Government had adopted a national population policy at about the same time as Thailand, but where the problem was of much greater urgency.

In Latin America, three countries were chosen; Brazil, a vast and wealthy country whose publicly-announced volte-face at Bucharest in favour of the principle of individual freedom to decide the number of children desired was one of the highlights of the Conference; Mexico, a country well along the road to modernisation, which had decided on a policy of fertility limitation shortly before Bucharest; and to complete the spectrum, Bolivia, a largely traditional agricultural country with a very high rate of population growth, where the official stance had been resolutely against family planning. The interest in this latter case was to see whether since Bucharest there had been any signs of a softening of this attitude.

In Africa, the three countries chosen were: Kenya, the first sub-Saharan country to adopt a national policy to limit population growth; Tanzania, where there was no official population policy but where the Government was concerned that families should have no more children than they could properly care for; and Zaire, the largest and most populous country in Central Africa, which has a special kind of population policy designed not to limit population growth, but to tackle the problems of infant mortality, abortion and sterility.

To complete the global representation, one Maghreb country was selected and one in the Middle East; namely Tunisia, a small country with a national population policy and well established population programme, and Egypt, an Arab country trying to restrain its galloping population growth.

Selection of the aid agencies was more straightforward, the chief criterion being the scale of assistance. In the case of DAC Members, countries were not included if their population assistance was given almost entirely through multilateral channels; in the case of the Specialised Agencies of the United Nations, their population activities have not been reviewed separately (except for the World Bank), but are included in the review of the UNFPA. Of the specialist, non-governmental population institutions, some of those with whom we had direct discussions are not reviewed individually, but what we learnt from the interviews that they were kind enough to give to us has provided valuable additional insights, which we have drawn on in the Overview chapter presenting some reflections on the study's general findings.

We were not expecting that these discussions would establish causal relationships between the Bucharest Conference and any changes that may have come about since. Our purpose was to discover whether the approach to population problems in the developing countries[2] had changed since Bucharest and, if so, whether such changes as had occurred were in line with the general spirit of the Bucharest Conference and the World Population Plan of Action that had issued from it, and whether the principal agencies that provide population assistance were showing a similar evolution.

The World Population Plan of Action is, of course, a political consensus document. An attentive reading of its 109 paragraphs offers justification for several different "population approaches" and yet more definitions of "population activities". We have accordingly tried to distil from the Plan a certain "spirit of Bucharest" that has come to be generally recognised as the "message" of the Conference.

It is perhaps paragraphs 31 and 32, in particular, that provide the most practical working guide for further population programmes[3] in the countries reviewed in this book. We have accordingly tried to use these as our guide for the purpose of this study.

It should be stressed that in reviewing current population policies and programmes of the countries and agencies that have collaborated with us in this study, it was not the intention to make any evaluation of either the desirability of the policies nor the effectiveness of the programmes. The purpose was simply to identify what these policies and programmes were, in order to try and find out whether, consciously or unconsciously, they now reflected some of the principal approaches associated with Bucharest—in other words, whether Bucharest had made any real difference.

This question is considered in the following chapter, which attempts to give an overview of the results of the discussions held in the twelve countries and with population assistance agencies.

The views set out in that chapter are, of course, based solely on the situation of the particular developing countries visited in the course of the study. They do not purport to be necessarily valid also for other countries whose population problems and policies for dealing with them may be different.

The opinions expressed in the Overview chapter and in those that follow on the individual countries and agencies are solely those of the author of this book and of the consultants who collaborated with her in the task of interviewing. They are not necessarily shared by either the World Bank or the Development Centre of the OECD.

---

2. Since the concern of this work is with policies and programmes, the discussions were held with senior officials of developing country governments, heads of universities and other relevant institutions. It was not within the scope of the study to investigate *popular* attitudes to questions of family size, family planning, etc.

3. Set out in an annex directly after this Introduction.

EXTRACTS FROM THE WORLD POPULATION PLAN
OF ACTION (WPPA)

Paragraph 31

"It is recommended that countries wishing to affect fertility levels give priority to implementing development programmes and educational and health strategies which, while contributing to economic growth and higher standards of living, have a decisive impact upon demographic trends, including fertility. International co-operation is called for to give priority to assisting such national efforts in order that these programmes and strategies be carried into effect."

Paragraph 32

"While recognizing the diversity of social, cultural, political and economic conditions among countries and regions, it is nevertheless agreed that the following development goals generally have an effect on the socio-economic context of reproductive decisions that tend to moderate fertility levels:

a) The reduction of infant and child mortality, particularly by means of improved nutrition, sanitation, maternal and child health care, and maternal education;

b) The full integration of women into the development process, particularly by means of their greater participation in educational, social, economic and political opportunities, and especially by means of the removal of obstacles to their employment in the non-agricultural sector wherever possible. In this context, national laws and policies, as well as relevant international recommendations, should be reviewed in order to eliminate discrimination in, and remove obstacles to, the education, training, employment and career advancement opportunities for women;

c) The promotion of social justice, social mobility and social development, particularly by means of a wide participation of the population in development and a more equitable distribution of income, land, social services and amenities;

d) The promotion of wide educational opportunities for the young of both sexes, and the extension of public forms of pre-school education for the rising generation;

e) The elimination of child labour and child abuse and the establishment of social security and old-age benefits;

f) The establishment of an appropriate lower limit for age at marriage."

POPULATION PROGRAMMES SINCE BUCHAREST:
SUMMARY AND CONCLUSIONS

BUCHAREST AND AFTER: THE FIRST REACTIONS

1. Bucharest brought to the fore the enormous complexity of the population issue. It revealed that every country has its own "population problems" and even those countries concerned about the problem of rapid population growth repudiated family planning as the sole solution in favour of a broader development effort and an "attack on poverty". The "message of Bucharest" was thus primarily a message to donors.

2. As it turned out, among developing countries, Bucharest seems to have resulted not in a repudiation of population policies, but, in the case of governments already committed to limiting population growth, in a legitimising and strengthening of them. Although there have been few new converts to population policy, some governments, concerned about other population problems (e.g. infant mortality, morbidity) have sought to introduce family planning as a health measure.

3. Among the donor community, although in a few cases the immediate reaction was a reaffirmation of family planning and the direct approach, most donors have come to modify their initial stance to a greater or lesser degree. There has been a genuine desire to adapt to changing situations and needs, and most of the principal donors of population assistance have undertaken major reappraisals of requirements and of how their programmes should be adjusted to meet them.

CHANGING APPROACHES TO POPULATION PROBLEMS

4. Family planning is wanted as much as ever. There is, however, a perceptible change in approach. Developing countries are increasingly stressing:
   a) the *human rights* aspect (the individual's right to decide the size and spacing of his family, and as a corollary, the government's obligation to provide the knowledge and the means); and
   b) the *family welfare* aspect (responsible parenthood and smaller family size).

This may be part genuine social philosophy, part packaging. Either way, it suggests that for donors to insist as in the past on the macro-economic aspect of overall population growth would often be inappropriate and may even prove to be counter-productive.

5. At the same time as they press family planning and fertility reduction, developing countries have broadened significantly the range of problems to which the national population policy should be addressed. In those countries in particular, where economic progress is badly outpaced by population growth, governments now seem to feel that family planning alone is not enough and it is

11

necessary to tackle also the determinants of fertility. Governments also are beginning to include as objectives of their population policy the adverse *consequences* of high fertility, for example the drift to the towns, some of which present problems of more immediate urgency than that of checking the population growth that caused them.

6. This new wide concept of population policy offers donors a disconcertingly broad spectrum of possible objectives. Among the *determinants* of fertility are not only nutrition, sanitation, health, but also education, the position of women, employment, social security, redistribution of income and indeed, the possibility of aspiring to a better life. Among the consequences of high fertility are urban growth, rural exodus, unemployment and migration. This raises a basic question of what *is* a "population activity". Is it whatever any particular developing country feels that it is? Or what any particular donor considers eligible for population assistance funding?[1]

7. Many donor agencies recognise these various social problems as part of the overall objective of meeting "basic human needs". Few are prepared to include them as part of their population assistance (although they may include them under other headings of assistance) with the exception of certain activities whose close relationship to fertility is well accepted (health, nutrition, and now increasingly, the status of women), and then usually as part of a package, in association with family planning. Only a very few donors have so far been prepared (experimentally) to support these activities *without the family planning element* as part of their population assistance.

8. Many developing country governments, however, particularly those with well-established population programmes, realise that they must pay increasing attention to the *demand* side (they recognise that their programmes have already creamed off a large part of the ready family planning acceptors and that the problem of gaining new acceptors—and of keeping them—is going to become harder). The donors are prepared to help build up demand by the *direct* method, i.e. by persuasion (IEC)[2], and by fostering greater community participation. Indirect approaches, however, which might provide "alternative ways in" to encouraging family planning acceptance, say by offering family planning in association with other more popularly-felt needs, are only just beginning to figure in population assistance programmes—perhaps largely because the developing countries have not often asked for them.

CHANGING PROGRAMME STRATEGIES

9. Despite the Bucharest call for development approaches, family planning remains the prime strategy for implementing population policies. Developing country governments and private population agencies are making new efforts to make their programmes more accessible, more attractive and more efficient.

10. These imply a number of changes in the way family planning services are to be delivered. Specifically, these include:

    a) the association of family planning with the public health services and, in particular, maternal and child health care;

---

1. This question, clearly, has different implications for donors who provide assistance for all forms of development than for those who have specialised in what has hitherto been regarded as the population field. For the former, it is largely a matter of internal organisation; for the latter, it is a question of how far they should, or can effectively, operate in areas beyond what they have hitherto considered as their boundaries.

2. Information, Education and Communication.

b) a drive to extend the coverage of both family planning and health care in the rural areas;

c) greater use of para-medical personnel to reduce dependence on doctors and clinics;

d) a move to involve the local community in the distribution of contraceptive supplies (CBD), in family planning motivation and follow-up, and in preventive health care;

e) making available a wider range of contraceptive methods;

f) increasing interest in sterilisation as the terminal form of population limitation;

g) more systematic use of incentives and disincentives to promote sterilisation and the small family norm.

Many of these activities postulate a substantial and continuing aid input for infrastructure, equipment and training.

11. Population education to create awareness of the societal and family implications of population growth has made considerable progress since Bucharest (it even commends itself to some countries which do not have national population policies). The donor community has supported these activities at the creative and experimental stages. Once the programmes are established, the problem will be to induce governments to finance them as a regular budgetary undertaking—*and* to build up the educational system and school attendance so as to provide a valid vehicle.

12. The need for integrated approaches to population and development (implicit in the World Population Plan of Action—WPPA) is accepted in principle by most developing country governments and also by the donors. Since Bucharest, several governments have tried to strengthen the administrative machinery intended to co-ordinate population with development policies in other sectors, and some countries have initiated programmes intended to introduce integrated approaches to population and development activities at the level of local government. In practice, however, integrated approaches are proving difficult to organise: long-standing habits of sectoral thinking in both programme countries and aid agencies tend to be reinforced by bureaucratic structures, and vice-versa. Multisectoral approaches, therefore, do not come naturally. However, some donors are trying to insert "population components" into their development projects in other sectors. Others are trying to assess in advance the likely population "impact" of *proposed* development projects in other sectors—a subtle and difficult exercise.

13. Population research has been particularly responsive to the changing approaches since Bucharest. While research into the bio-medical aspects of fertility remains important, there has been an increase of research into the socio-economic aspects of population, and particularly into the complex inter-relationship between fertility, development and human motivation.

SOME IMPLICATIONS FOR AID

14. In terms of requests for aid, the post-Bucharest scene has turned out to be much less different than expected. There has been not a slackening but a considerable increase in the demand for "population assistance" activities of the classical pre-Bucharest type. The donors have responded with an increased volume of aid for population and some new arrangements for providing it (e.g. co-financing).

15. The developing countries are for the most part greatly in favour of "self-reliance" in the determination of national population policy, in the selection

13

of programme priorities and in research. There is increasing desire also for self-reliance through local production of contraceptive material and supplies (which most donors, though not all, encourage). As regards foreign aid for population programmes, however, the situation varies widely, as in the past. Some developing country governments are still predicating their national population programmes on the continuance of generous aid support, others look to aid primarily as a source of funding for special efforts of programme expansion, for innovative and high-risk projects, and sometimes also for its valuable catalytic effect.

16. Faced (somewhat to their surprise) with an increased demand for population assistance (largely old-style), donors have reacted by introducing a new coherence into their choice of programme countries. Differing criteria seem to be employed—countries most in need of help, countries where the national population problem is most serious, etc.—but sometimes cutting across these categories is the simple desire to direct the aid effort to where it will have the most impact.

17. Contrary to expectations (or perhaps fears?), Bucharest has not blurred the distinction between "population activities" and "development activities" to any considerable extent. Some developing countries may have broadened their definition of their national population policy to include problems of population structure, geographical distribution and even social characteristics, but they do not generally request population funding except for the usually-accepted population/family planning elements.

18. The small percentage of total official development assistance (ODA) going to population assistance activities has remained roughly unchanged (although the absolute amount has increased), and it continues to be applied very largely, as before Bucharest, to activities that are considered likely to affect the population factor *directly*. Certainly, there is increasing variety and imagination in the design of such activities. There are also occasional activities which include both population *and* development components. As yet, however, there seem to have been few attempts to apply population and other development activities in a mutually supportive or "multiplicative" relationship.

19. The message of Bucharest (population *and* development) was addressed to the whole of the international community. The population assistance donors, certainly, are doing their best to respond. But it is perhaps from the *rest* of development activities that the real leverage on the population factor may come. So far, there has been conspicuously little interest in population from other sections of the international community, whether in international fora, donor agency programmes, or even sometimes, in the national economic and social programmes of the developing countries themselves.

20. One way of bridging this continuing dichotomy may be through the growing interest in "basic human needs". Although the advocates of a "basic needs strategy" often do not mention the population implications, the principal elements in that strategy and the factors held to be the important determinants of fertility, in fact, very largely coincide.

14

OVERVIEW

I. BUCHAREST AND AFTER: INITIAL REACTIONS

In looking for reflection of the "ideas of Bucharest" in the subsequent policies and programmes of individual countries, it is perhaps useful to keep in mind the fact, obvious but easily over-looked, that these ideas did not spring forth fully-grown from the heat of the Conference debates. They had a well-established parentage. On the one side was the whole series of re-examinations at international level, set in train by the United Nations Second Development Decade, of world development problems and, in particular, of the relationship between the developed and the developing world[1]; on the other was the experience of the countries participating in the Conference, who brought to it the philo-sophies that were already guiding their approaches to population problems and the strategies by which they were seeking to solve them.

It was not, therefore, the developing countries but the population assistance agencies who came to look upon Bucharest as a watershed which would change the whole course of thinking about population from that time on. Because of its own preoccupation with the dangers of continuing rapid population growth, the donor community in the period before Bucharest tended to assume that developing countries would naturally see the "population problem" in the same light. It is one of the important contributions of Bucharest, and in particular of the World Population Plan of Action (WPPA) with its remarkably compre-hensive range of topics, that it is now beginning to be understood that individual developing countries have different perceptions of their respective "population problems". At the same time, Bucharest represented a public and unequivocal repudiation of family planning as *the* solution to the problem of population growth. For much of the donor community, the shock was the greater because even many governments with well-established national population policies and family planning programmes joined the chorus of rejection.

Among the developing countries, few seemed to consider the Bucharest Conference or the World Population Plan of Action as a sudden revelation or even as a source of particularly new ideas. Their attitude, judged by the comments made two or three years later by some of the officials of the countries visited in the course of this study, seems to have ranged from disappointment that the World Population Plan of Action was not stronger (no overall targets for reduction of population growth—Thailand), to regret that the urgency of the population problem had been overlaid with other considerations (the Republic of Korea), through a certain satisfaction ("it only expresses what we were already doing"—Tunisia, the Philippines), to a practical "it gave us a useful mandate for what we were wanting to do" (Mexico). In other countries, officials expressed

---

1. In particular, the Sixth Special Session of the UN (May 1974) which resulted in the Declaration of a New International Economic Order.

15

gratification at the international endorsement given to their government's own approaches (Egypt), social philosophies (Tanzania), special population preoccupations (Zaire)[2], or political attitudes (Bolivia).

There is no doubt that the Conference as an event, taken together with the four international symposia that preceded it and the five Regional Consultative Conferences that followed it, gave a new importance and political sanction to population issues. Apart, however, from Brazil's[3] declaration in favour of the human right of the individual to determine the size and spacing of his family, few other countries have since come forward as recruits to the cause of limiting population growth. Nonetheless, some countries, not concerned about overall population size, have shown interest in introducing family planning as a health measure. In the wake of Bucharest, the Government of Bolivia made a brief move in this direction, until political pressures forced it to retreat[4].

In those countries which already had policies to control population growth, Bucharest, contrary to what might have been expected at the time, has been followed by a general strengthening of official commitment. The countries reviewed here which have national population programmes have all intensified their efforts to hasten fertility decline. Their governments have increased budgetary allocations for population activities, set new and more rigorous demographic targets as part of the national development plan, and announced new programmes of family planning together with a variety of other measures intended to help realise these targets[5].

The donor community for its part, in its immediate reactions to Bucharest, seems to have adopted varying positions. The largest donors of population assistance—US AID, UNFPA and the World Bank—either explicitly or implicitly reaffirmed their previous policies. The smaller bilateral donors, for the most part, tended to retreat into the safer anonymity of multilateral channels. The foundations and specialised population assistance agencies, in some cases came out squarely in favour of the development approach, while others prudently kept counsel, pending further consideration. Subsequently, however, and indeed fairly quickly, nearly all donor agencies, both the specialist population agencies and the donors of development assistance, have come to take a broader approach to population problems.

Following Bucharest, a strikingly large number of the principal donors of population assistance have undertaken a *major review* of their respective population assistance activities for the purpose of re-examining needs and re-

---

2. Zaire was one of the very few countries participating at the Bucharest Conference which did not make any official statement.

3. Brazil is a special case because of the vast size and diversity of the country: the Federal Government has left the determination of population policy to the individual State Governments.

4. The Government of Bolivia sees its population problem not in terms of overall numbers—it would welcome a *larger* population in the interests of the economy and defense—but in the badly skewed geographic distribution of the population and continuing drain of manpower through emigration. At the same time, it is concerned at the high infant mortality and morbidity.

5. Only two countries would seem to have had some initial reluctance about setting official targets for population limitation (possibly reflecting a certain unease on the part of the government at declaring a national policy aimed at reducing population growth). Kenya had included population in its development plans to the extent of drawing attention to the adverse effects of the high growth rate on development prospects (it is one of only seven African countries to have done so), but did not announce target figures for population reduction until 1975 (nine years after the introduction of a national family planning programme); and Mexico has set targets only very recently (1977, four years after the introduction of the national programme).

defining their priorities (viz., the World Bank and the Government of Japan, in consultation with outside advisors, UNFPA, the Population Council, IPPF, US AID and SIDA, by means of in-house reviews)[6]. These "introspection exercises", as Carmen Miro calls them[7], attest to the sincerity of the donor community's desire to adjust its assistance in the population field to the requirements of a changing situation.

II. CHANGES IN THE APPROACH TO POPULATION PROBLEMS

In adopting national policies to limit the rate of population increase, the prime consideration of developing country governments was to keep demographic growth commensurate with the country's economic possibilities. President Bourguiba of Tunisia, long one of the most consistent, determined and out-spoken Heads of State on the necessity for limiting population growth, had no hesitation in declaring publicly: "En instituant le 'planning familial', notre principal souci a été d'assurer l'équilibre entre l'augmentation de la population et l'accroissement du revenu national. Pour qu'ils aient le même rythme de croissance, il était nécessaire de *planifier la natalité en même temps que la production*." ("In introducing 'family planning', our prime concern was to achieve a balance between population increase and the growth of the national income: in order that they should both proceed at the same rate, it was necessary to *plan births* as well as production.") Gradually, however—and certainly the process began before Bucharest—there has been a change in countries' perception of the *nature* of the population problem. As development philosophy has moved away from the earlier confidence in economic growth and the expectation of the "trickle-down effect", thinking about population as a factor in the development process has been evolving also. In particular, as social progress has come to be considered as being equally if not more desirable than economic growth, it was natural that the "population problem" should cease to be thought of as primarily a matter of numbers.

FAMILY PLANNING, HUMAN RIGHTS AND FAMILY WELFARE

A noticeable development since Bucharest has been the increasing emphasis on the implications of high fertility at the micro-level—for the individual and the family. There seems to be a growing recognition among both developing countries and aid agencies[8] that "development" should be "for people", and, in particular, that "population" is "about people". The result is that governments still want to spread the practice of family planning, but there is now a new and subtle change in the motivation.

The fact that Brazil, a pronounced champion of pronatalist population policies up to the very eve of the Conference, announced at Bucharest that it accepted the *human right* of the individual to determine the desired size of his family and of the State to provide the necessary knowledge and means is

---

6. Other donors have also reviewed their population assistance activities during this period, but in the context of overall assistance policies.

7. Paper submitted to the Bellagio Conference, June 1977.

8. Viz. some of the speeches made by Mr. McNamara, the President of the World Bank.

perhaps indicative of the current trends in political thinking[9] Developing country governments today are increasingly taking the view that family planning is necessary not only in the interests of controlling national population growth, but also to enable the individual to exercise the right of choice as to the number and spacing of his children.

If the human rights aspect of family planning is perhaps an abstraction, to be made much of or not by governments as may be convenient, it leads straight to another that is much more concrete, namely the *health and welfare of the family*. There is a growing belief that parents should have the right to decide the size of their family in the light of their own possibilities of *caring* for their children and of giving them a decent start in life. The idea of human rights thus imperceptibly shades into that of *family welfare*.

A concern for "family welfare" has been the reason given for the introduction of official family planning programmes by governments whose policy as regards overall population growth was either pro-natalist (Bolivia) or largely indifferent (Tanzania and Zaire).

Increasingly, this concern has come to be voiced also by governments whose policy is avowedly anti-natalist and which introduced family planning programmes for that reason. As President Bourguiba openly acknowledged shortly after Bucharest, the notion of family welfare provides an ideological justification for "birth control": "La conciliation de l'idée de la régulation des naissances avec le 'droit' proclamé par la Conférence de Bucarest... de l'épanouissement familial" ("Harmonisation of the notion of controlling births with the 'right' proclaimed by the Bucharest Conference, of family welfare").

In Tunisia, the official family planning programme is now called the Family Welfare Programme. Kenya also has a Family Welfare Programme, covering both the family planning programme and a health development plan. In India, significantly, one of the first acts of the new Government that took over after Mrs. Ghandi had been defeated at the polls—in part because of popular resistance to the official family planning campaign—was to change the name of the Ministry of Health and Family Planning to Ministry of Health and Family Welfare.

Unavoidably, the question arises as to what extent these changes of nomenclature indicate a genuine change of approach, or are merely "packaging". There is probably an element of both. The advantage of promoting family planning in the welfare context is undeniable. At the same time, slogans such as that of the Planned Parenthood Federation of Korea's "Stop at two and bring them up well", or the call of the Mexican Government for "responsible parenthood" neatly bring together the demographic considerations of the State and the concern of parents for their children.

The "responsible parenthood" approach to the family planning message is, of course, not new[10]. In Africa, health and welfare are the only considerations

---

9. The Second Brazilian Plan (1975) nonetheless clearly states the macro-economic reasons for limiting population growth: "In practice, it is appropriate that the rate of demographic increase be inferior to the rate of employment increase, in order to allow a reduction in the degree of under-utilisation of the labour force and a certain degree of income redistribution in favour of the working classes".

10. This has always been the Western motivation for family planning, but it has not until now been the inspiration for official family planning programmes in developing countries to any considerable extent.

18

which make family planning acceptable, and in Kenya, Tanzania and Zaire[11] the family planning message has been based for a decade on the theme that fewer children and/or spaced births mean a healthier, happier and more prosperous family. The same message is now increasingly being used in other parts of the world. In the Republic of Korea, Mexico, the Philippines, Thailand, and Tunisia, for example, the programmes of population education and communication are taking this same welfare approach.

One of the principal new developments in the period since Bucharest is governments' acceptance of the implications of this message for social policy. A policy of family welfare, in effect, implies obligations not only on parents, but also on the State. If couples are to limit the number of their children so that they can exercise "responsible parenthood", i.e. "put the emphasis on caring for children and the ability to bring them up properly"[12] it also requires that they should have the effective possibilities for doing so within reasonable reach.

The family welfare approach thus joins with the growing concern of governments with social progress. The family welfare message, oriented, as is increasingly the case today, towards such considerations as the health of the mother and the child, the financial burden on the father, the possibilities for better nutrition, housing and education attendant on smaller families, in order to be convincing, needs to be backed by measures to make the conditions of better health, education, etc. actually available. The concept of "family welfare", in fact, if carried to its logical conclusion, implies the satisfaction, not only of the need for family planning and better health, but for the whole range of what are now generally considered as "basic human needs".

From the point of view of aid, the present trend towards the family welfare approach may have important presentational implications. For donors to continue to insist, as they have done in the past, on the dangers inherent in overall population growth, may in some countries (particularly in Latin America and in Africa) prove to be not only unwelcome but even counter-productive. Support for some of the other aspects of "family welfare" might be a good way for donors to gain credibility for their family planning efforts also.

PROGRAMMES TO TACKLE THE DETERMINANTS OF FERTILITY

At the same time as they are promoting family planning, developing countries have broadened significantly the range of problems to which they feel the national population policy should be addressed. In those countries, in particular, where the gap between population growth and the absorptive capacity of the economy is growing ever wider, there is increasing realisation that family planning alone is not enough and that it is necessary to tackle also the determinants of fertility behaviour. From an initial concern with the effect of population on development, some countries are now becoming concerned with the effects of *development* on *population,* and thence with the necessity to influence those particular development factors that are thought to affect population most directly.

This shift in the approach to population problems certainly pre-dated Bucharest, but it has since been gaining considerably in strength. When the

---

11. For the Government of Zaire, family welfare is the whole purpose of its national population policy of "Desired Births". It sees Zaire's population problems as overfrequent births, induced abortions, sickness, etc., and the dangers that they imply for the next generation: "Ceux qui ont beaucoup d'enfants et peu de moyens risquent de les voir souffrir d'un développement physique et moral insuffisant" ("Those who have many children and few means are likely to see their children develop inadequately both in body and spirit") - Speech of President Mobutu, 5th December, 1972.
12. President Nyerere in his speech to the TANU Conference at Arusha, January 1967.

Head of the Indian Delegation to the Bucharest Conference declared that "our real enemy is poverty", he was not only making a political statement, he was describing India's population problem in terms of its fundamental causes as the Government had come to understand them.

As history was shortly to show, the drama for India was that the Government was suddenly panicked into short-term and drastic solutions. The experience of certain Indian States had already demonstrated the relevance to fertility patterns of factors such as the level of literacy, the position of women, nutrition, equality of income distribution, etc.[13], but to try to improve these conditions nationwide would inevitably be a very long-term and costly process. The Government of Mrs. Ghandi accordingly made the decision that it could not after all wait for the "frontal attack on the citadels of poverty" that had been bravely promised in the Fifth Five-Year Plan, and must instead go out for direct and massive population "control". As Mrs. Ghandi herself put it "the percolation effect (of development) will take too long"[14].

A number of other countries, however, seem prepared to give the "percolation effect" a try—not in substitution for family planning, but in support of it—as a means of building up new *demand*. Thus, in Egypt, the Board for Population and Family Planning has identified nine variables as necessary to raise the standard of living and bring down the birth rate (the two objectives being seen as inter-linked) viz.: raising the socio-economic standards of the family; education, and particularly vocational and functional education; women's employment; mechanisation of agriculture; industrialisation, particularly in rural areas; reduction of infant mortality; improved social security; information and education; and family planning as part of improved social services generally. That family planning is placed last on this list may denote an order of logic rather than of priorities: family planning still occupies an important place in the Egyptian population programme. Nevertheless, the thrust of the attack as thus defined has moved from sole reliance on the direct family planning approach to the indirect one of socio-economic development.

Population policy in the Philippines seems to be moving in the same direction. A country where completed family size is one of the highest in the world, it was a logical progression on the part of the Philippines Commission on Population to go from motivational activities designed to encourage people to have smaller families, to activities designed to influence the factors that are at the origin of their desire for large families. Beginning with programmes to reduce mortality and morbidity rates (and social research into the complex problem of fertility motivation and its determinants), population policy in the Philippines is increasingly concerned with the transformation of those determinants.

In both Egypt and the Philippines, the family planning approach and the development approach exist side by side. In fact, this is the situation today in most countries with national population programmes. The particular interest of the "development" initiatives that have been tried in these two countries is the fact that they are seeking to change the *totality* of the presumed determinants

---

13. The most striking and frequently-cited illustration of these inter-relationships is the situation of the State of Kerala, where average fertility is among the lowest in India. Despite a generally low economic level, Kerala has higher rates of nutrition, female literacy and equality of income distribution than can be found in most other Indian States.

14. Address to the 31st Joint Conference of the Association of Physicians, New Delhi, 27th January 1976.

of fertility[15], or at least a very large portion of them, while other countries take a less ambitious approach, preferring to limit their efforts to selected factors thought to be particularly relevant.

The most generally recognised factors are those set out in the following statement by the new Government of India[16]. In outlining its new version of the National Family Planning Programme, President Reddy, declared: "Family planning will be pursued vigorously... as an integral part of a comprehensive package covering education, health, maternity and child care, free welfare, women's rights and nutrition". The governments of countries as diverse as Mexico, Thailand and the Republic of Korea, would in principle probably endorse a similar package. In practice, however, these various elements are only just beginning to play a recognised part in governments' actual population programmes.

The factor that receives most attention is the obviously related one of health. The link between high fertility and high infant mortality has long been recognised. [Cf. President Mobutu, announcing the start of the "Desired Births" policy in Zaire: "... un couple qui voulait cinq enfants était amené à en avoir dix ou quinze, espérant qu'il y en aurait au moins cinq qui survivraient" ("a couple who wanted five children would need to have ten or fifteen in the hope that at least five would survive").] While this problem is particularly acute in African countries, in other parts of the world similarly, in Egypt, in Bolivia, in India, or in any developing country where large parts of the population live in highly insanitary conditions and are deprived of even elementary health care, the scourge of high infant mortality is both a recurring personal tragedy and an incentive to continued high fertility.

Gradually, therefore, governments with population programmes have come to see that family planning is unlikely to make much progress among poor communities unless it is associated with *maternal and child health care*. Since Bucharest, there has been a much more determined effort to link family planning with MCH services and to make the two more widely available in the rural areas and to the urban poor. In part, this move is a function of the greater concern with welfare, and in part, it is hoped that it will lead eventually to a decline in the number of births.

Another factor which is receiving increased attention is the position of women. *Improvement in the status of women* in developing countries is seen as a "human right" and at the same time as a likely means of reducing fertility. Countries where the situation and life-style of women are as widely different as, for example, India, the Republic of Korea, Mexico and Tunisia, are all now actively seeking to give women enhanced social status. They thereby hope not only to redress the inherited results of century-old traditions of male superiority but to offer new possibilities of occupation and social prestige as alternatives to the customary early marriage and motherhood. India has passed legislation raising the minimum age for marriage for both men and women; the Republic of Korea (traditionally a very strongly male-dominated society) has passed laws giving women a new, independent status within the family and in regard to inheritance; Tunisia has modified its marriage laws. Other countries are making similar moves.

So far, some of these initiatives have not got much beyond the stage of enabling legislation. However, they represent a start, and are often actively

---

15. When the Philippines Population Commission first launched the programme in question, they called it, significantly, "Total Integrated Development Approach". They subsequently modified considerably the whole scope of the undertaking.
16. Address to Parliament two weeks after the elections (March 1977).

supported by the (private) family planning associations of the country concerned, and by the donors of aid. There are occasional experimental projects to provide functional literacy or special employment possibilities for girls (also often supported by population assistance), but usually they are on a small pilot scale. Attempts to transform the traditional life-style of women in developing countries on any large scale, inevitably involve major programmes in the fields of education, rural development, employment, etc., which the population assistance donors are less likely to consider part of their population "mandate".

One activity that the donors have proved very willing to include as part of their population projects is improvement of *nutrition,* particularly programmes designed to improve the standard of nutrition for vulnerable target groups. There is also a growing appreciation of the importance of nutrition education. Overall, however, with the exception perhaps of the large programmes provided by CARE, most of the nutrition activities related to population projects seem to have been experimental and on a pilot scale. (Perhaps the practical difficulties of cost, distribution, storage, etc., and the longer-term problems involved in changing dietary habits and crop patterns are still too daunting for large-scale efforts?) It is possible that the 1979 Conference of the International Year of the Child will bring fresh attention to this aspect of population problems.

Another of the factors on the Indian President's list that is beginning to make progress in a number of countries is "social welfare" (i.e. *social security),* (e.g. the Republic of Korea, the Philippines). Governments are beginning to recognise that an important motive for having large families is people's need to ensure support for their old age. However, the goal of making the mass of the rural and urban poor largely independent of their children for support is still a long way off for most developing countries. And again, it raises the question of whether such programmes, even if their relevance to family size is well recognised, can reasonably form part of "population assistance"?

THE CONSEQUENCES OF HIGH FERTILITY

A number of governments are beginning to include as part of the national population policy not only the determinants of high fertility, but also the consequences. In many developing countries, the consequences of rapid population growth are now posing problems of more immediate urgency even than that of curbing the high birth rates that gave rise to them. The continuing rural exodus, caused by pressure of population on the land, has led to massive problems of mushrooming urban growth, unemployment and emigration of manpower. These are potentially explosive political problems, and governments naturally give them very high priority. That many countries consider them as aspects of the "population problem" gives to population policy and planning a broad new social and environmental dimension.

Three countries so far have firmly included these problems in their official definition of the scope of the national population policy. In Mexico, the General Law on Population (1973) specifies that the national population policy, should deal not only with population size, but also with structure, dynamics and distribution. Egypt, since 1975, has a similar formulation. The Republic of Korea (1976) redefined its population policy to cover not only reduction of fertility, population education and improving the position and employment prospects of women, but also dispersal of large urban populations, and migration on a planned basis. All three countries have policies to create new poles of economic growth and settlement to relieve the mounting population pressure on the capital and other large cities. At the same time, they are making efforts to upgrade the

22

quality of rural life (by improvement of infrastructure, health and educational facilities, etc.) in the hope of reducing the urban drift. (Cf. Egypt's policy of "Regeneration of the Egyptian Village"). A number of other countries have similar programmes but do not include them as part of the national population policy.

Some countries extend the scope of the national population policy to cover also *migration,* both internal and external, a problem which continues to grow with the steadily mounting numbers of young people entering the labour market[17]. Thus, in Mexico, it is the National Population Council which is preparing plans to try and exercise some control over the large-scale emigration of Mexicans to the United States and the big cities. In the Republic of Korea, the task of planning emigration is considered a high priority population objective[18]. Tunisia also looks to controlled emigration of part of its labour force as a means of dealing with the problem of unemployment, though in this case, the Government does not consider this as part of "population" policy.

The country that may be considered as having the most comprehensive set of policies intended to cover all aspects of the population is Tanzania. While officially unconcerned about the size of the population (though, in fact, it is worried that the population is growing faster than the absorptive capacity of the economy), the Government of Tanzania is very much concerned about the "quality" of life, the high morbidity and mortality, and the geographical distribution of the population. The whole development purpose is directed to improving the standard of living, the health programmes (including family planning) aim to extend the life span and raise the general level of health, and the programme of "villagisation" is intended to regroup the whole of the rural population in new village settlements.

Tanzania is perhaps a special case. The Government of Tanzania does not consider these various objectives as constituting a "population policy". Indeed, the Government has no declared population policy at all. However, the fact that some other countries are now widening their concept of population policy to include many of the determinants and some of the consequences of high fertility is presenting the donors of population assistance with something of a dilemma.

The range of possible "population" activities has now become disconcertingly wide. Indeed, the question now arises—*what is a "population activity"?* Is it whatever any particular country says it is? If the Republic of Korea includes the dispersal of economic activity and urban settlements in the official scope of its population policy, does that make this objective a "population activity"? Is a nutrition project or a women's employment project a population activity because it may have an eventual effect on fertility? Or only if it is undertaken primarily with this effect in view? Clearly, there is no straight answer.

The response of the donor agencies has tended to be conservative. Few, if any, would consider as eligible for "population assistance", as wide a spectrum of social activities as that encompassed by the population policies of the Governments of the Republic of Korea or Egypt, or for that matter, the World Population Plan of Action. (Most donors would agree with Halvor Gille of the UNFPA that the definition of a population activity is not the whole range of subjects covered by the World Population Plan of Action.) In particular, not

---

17. The World Population Plan of Action devotes 12 paragraphs (51-62) to this subject.
18. In the Republic of Korea, a sizeable proportion of emigrants are intellectuals and highly-qualified personnel.

many donors are prepared to include the *consequences* of fertility as legitimate objectives of population assistance, although they may be prepared to assist them under other programmes.

In respect of the *determinants* of fertility, donors' responses have been more flexible. Although the prime concern of population assistance remains the reduction of fertility, it has gradually come to be recognised by some donors as well as by developing country governments that in order to achieve this goal, it may be necessary to try to influence the *demand* for family planning as well as to provide the supplies. It is this issue of demand versus supply (or indirect versus direct approaches) that lay at the heart of the Bucharest controversy.

Donors, of course, have taken varying positions. At one extreme is the view of US AID. This maintains that developing countries have a large unsatisfied demand for family planning and that, further, a readily available supply of family planning services and material will create its own demand. The main thrust of US AID's population assistance, therefore, has been on the supply side. The Bucharest debate has not resulted in any substantial change and US AID continues to be the developing countries' principal source of contraceptive supplies, although it now supports increasingly varied methods of delivery.

At the other end of the spectrum, perhaps the most dramatic "conversion" to the broader "development" approach was that of the Population Council, a specialist "population" body, which took a policy decision to move away from its initial prime concern with fertility reduction to include work on both the determinants and the consequences of fertility. The IPPF, another veteran "family planning" body has also been moving further in the direction of the determinants of fertility (e.g. nutrition, women, youth). Among the bilaterals, a particularly broad view is that taken by SIDA, which, for example, is currently including in its population assistance, activities connected with the International Year of the Child.

Other donors take positions somewhere in between. On the whole, the "non-population" activities that most readily commend themselves to donors as qualifying for population assistance are those whose close relationship to fertility is well accepted, namely maternal and child health care, nutrition, and recently, also, improvement of the position of women. In most cases, the projects are designed as a package in association with a family planning component. Only a few donors so far have (experimentally) been prepared to support these activities *without* the family planning component, as part of their population assistance. In most cases, even when the activities are generally recognised as having an important bearing on fertility, donors tend not to think of them as "population activities" but to support them under other social development programmes.

Although donors are usually very willing to help build up demand for family planning by direct methods—i.e. by *persuasion* (information, education and communication) and by fostering greater *community involvement,* they have so far done relatively little in the way of *indirect approaches.* One reason perhaps is that there has been very little demand from the developing countries, and in the absence of specific requests, donors hesitate to "push" their own ideas. By this reticence, however, it is possible that donors are missing valuable opportunities. For those donors in particular who hesitate to intervene directly in the population field, indirect approaches such as women's projects, etc. could offer interesting "alternative ways in" to "population", by helping to create the conditions which are favourable to fertility decline (and which will lead to increased demand for family planning).

III. CHANGING PROGRAMME STRATEGIES

FAMILY PLANNING

If in the immediate aftermath of Bucharest, it seemed that the outcome of the Conference was that the developing countries were largely rejecting family planning as the solution to the problem of over-rapid population growth, it is clear that this was a needless worry. Indeed, family planning is currently the subject of increasing interest, attention and resources on the part of developing country governments.

Of the twelve countries reviewed here, two (Bolivia[19] and Brazil) have only recently accepted the idea that family planning should be provided as a public service. In all the others, which already had national population policies, family planning is still the most important of their population strategies. The period since Bucharest has seen increased efforts on the part of governments and private family planning agencies to make their existing family planning programmes more efficient, more attractive and accessible to larger numbers of people.

Thus, Kenya and Zaire have taken new initiatives to invigorate a previously lagging Government programme. Thailand and Tunisia, where previous programmes have been limited in their effective outreach, have launched new plans to extend their coverage. Even in countries which have shown a particular interest in broader "development" approaches (e.g. Egypt), official family planning programmes are continuing alongside more innovative activities in more or less comfortable tandem.

One important reason for this intensification of effort is the realisation on the part of a growing number of governments that their population programmes have already "creamed off" a large part of the already predisposed potential family planning acceptors. In some cases (e.g. the Republic of Korea), the declines in the birth rates that followed the introduction of the national family planning programme have since been succeeded by flattening acceptance rates and falling continuation rates. Other countries (e.g. Thailand, Tunisia and the Philippines), although spared this latter development, have nonetheless become aware that in the last few years the task of attracting and keeping a growing number of the country's eligible couples to regular contraceptive practice is becoming increasingly difficult. It is this realistic appraisal of the situation that has led, on the one hand, as we have seen, to the interest in "new approaches" which seek to influence the *demand* for family planning and, on the other, to the search for ways in which the *supply* can be expanded and improved.

In the effort to improve the supply side, a number of new trends may be noted in the way that family planning services are being delivered. In many cases, these are not new approaches but are rather a strengthening and rationalisation of more sporadic initiatives that were already being tried before Bucharest.

The first trend, common to practically all the countries reviewed here, is one that we have already noted—namely the *association of family planning with health services* and, in particular, with *maternal and child health care*. Already before Bucharest, governments with population programmes had realised the advantages of linking family planning with MCH: the same facilities can be used to deliver both, and mothers seeking MCH care are likely to be receptive to family planning benefits. However, as governments have come to link family

---

19. In the case of Bolivia, the Government's rather tentative initiative proved more than the Church and certain influential political opinion was ready to accept.

planning with the national health services, the lack of health infrastructure in the rural areas[20] has further limited family planning delivery among the rural communities.

A second very important trend therefore, and one closely linked with the first, is towards providing *better family planning coverage in the rural areas*. Most family planning programmes begin in the towns[21] which is where the doctors and medical facilities are to be found, as well as the greatest concentration of population (urban communities are also usually less bound by traditional cultural patterns and thus are more receptive to the idea of limiting family size). Bringing family planning within effective reach of rural communities will involve an important input into infrastructure (construction of new facilities for both service and training, equipment, vehicles, etc.), and also a major effort of training of personnel at all levels. It also implies a considerable burden on government budgets but it is an area where foreign aid is accustomed and generally still willing to provide generous support.

A third trend, therefore, is a move to *reduce the dependence on doctors and clinics by making greater use of para-medical personnel*. It is gradually becoming recognised that rural health care in developing countries can only be provided by moving away from the conventional Western type health systems which were designed to provide curative medical services for a primarily urban and middle-class clientele[22], in favour of a pattern of health care more suitable for poor and often scattered rural communities. (It is perhaps the wide interest in the Chinese "bare-foot doctors" that is leading to the gradual rejection of the colonial heritage of Western standards of medicine.) Given the practical impossibility of providing fully-equipped and staffed hospitals all over the country, there is a growing emphasis on preventive health care and environmental hygiene and, as a corollory, on the use of para-medical and non-professional personnel to replace doctors for simple health functions.

This same tendency towards the "deprofessionalising" of some aspects of the work is seen in the delivery of family planning services. Most governments recognise that it is unrealistic to look to the medical profession to bring to the rural areas adequate primary health care or family planning services[23]. Doctors, generally, dislike rural practice and tend not to provide good service, particularly in family planning, which they have not been trained to consider part of their duties. Several countries are trying to get doctors more involved in family planning work (for example, India, by special training courses and financial bonuses, or Egypt, by giving family planning greater prominence in the medical training curriculum). The main trend, however, is increasingly to use nurses, nurse-midwives and auxiliary personnel to perform tasks for which fully-qualified physicians are not essential. One of the first countries to advance along these lines was Thailand where not only the Health Ministry but also the medical profession have taken an increasingly liberal view of the need to "deprofessionalize" family planning in order to extend it in the rural areas.

---

20. In Mexico, the effective delivery of family planning services had been greatly extended by the participation of the two major social security institutions. The problem of inadequate coverage of the rural areas, however, still remains.

21. An exception is the Republic of Korea, where the Government *began* its programme in the rural areas, on the assumption that the population of the fast-modernising towns would be able to obtain family planning services under private auspices.

22. Cf. the Mama Yemu Hospital in Kinshasa, with 1,800 beds, the biggest hospital in Africa, which, together with a few clinics, also in the capital, has a budget larger than that of all public health services in the rest of the country.

23. There are some exceptions: in Egypt so many thousands of doctors graduate each year that not even the bursting populations of the towns can provide a living for all of them. Tunisia anticipates a similar development.

In some countries, the health Ministries have decided to use the same personnel for basic health care and family planning work at the village level. The *"multi-purpose health worker"* (the solution favoured by India and the Philippines, for example) has obvious advantages: economy, greater acceptability of the family planning function if offered by someone of proven competence (and confidence) in other areas of health. Sometimes, however, the family planning interests are dubious about the desirability of this fusion of functions which they see as likely to result in diminution of the family planning effort.

A fourth trend and one of the most interesting developments in family planning activities in the post-Bucharest period, has been the increasing *involvement of the (non-professional) local community*. This has been inspired partly by the practical need to enlarge the numbers of people able to deliver family planning supplies and follow up on acceptances, partly to free qualified personnel for more specialised tasks, and partly also as a deliberate move to free family planning from the psychological and often physical constraints of association with doctors and clinics ("family planning is not an illness")[24].

One of the most successful forms of community participation in family planning is proving to be the distribution of contraceptives through a variety of non-professional channels. "Community-based distribution" (CBD) to extend the sources of contraceptive supply using elements of the regular social structure has had a striking and very rapid success. CBD may take the form of sale or free distribution. It is an area where non-government bodies are showing great ingenuity. The range of devices employed in Thailand, for example, to get condoms and oral pills delivered by canoe to the remoter villages and to link family planning with all sorts of local incentive schemes has been widely publicised. Other countries are fast catching up.

The participation of the local community in family planning activities generally has proceeded very fast in recent years. The much-admired model is the Korean Mothers' Clubs, which combine family planning motivation and contraceptive distribution and follow-up, with a variety of constructive local activities. Such arrangements (they are being experimented with increasingly in the other Asian countries) offer a number of advantages for the promotion of family planning practice. First, the basic group is small enough for the person responsible for distribution and record-keeping to follow up clients individually. (Since most countries which have had family planning programmes for any length of time now recognise that one of the major problems is not acceptances but the low continuation rates, this is, obviously, extremely important.) Secondly, there is the further psychological advantage of making family planning practice an accepted part of community life.

"Community participation" is not, of course, limited to rural communities. One of the particularly encouraging developments of recent years is the way in which the industrial sector is being mobilised to bring family planning (information and delivery) to particular groups of the community. The idea is certainly not new (in India and Tunisia, major industries and the railways have been helping to promote family planning for many years), but the practice is spreading remarkably. In the Philippines, industrial enterprises employing over 200 persons are compelled by law to include family planning with the health facilities they have to provide for their staff; in Tunisia, small enterprises are grouping together for this purpose; in the Republic of Korea, where family planning in industry is now starting together with health insurance (also a new development), some factories are directing the message particularly to the young *unmarried*

---

24. Statement made by Tunisian officials.

woman worker, etc. Thanks, in many countries, to the resourcefulness of the (private) national family planning association, as well as to the influence of the government, family planning now can count on such seemingly unlikely agents as sports groups (the Philippines), youth groups (India), the Party (Tanzania), the Army (Republic of Korea), the Border Police (Thailand), etc. Even in Bolivia, the Truck Drivers' Association was co-opted to assist in transporting contraceptive supplies. Most of these initiatives are still far from being organised on a nationwide scale, but they offer very promising leads.

A further move to make family planning more readily accessible to the general public is the growing number of *commercial sales outlets*. In Egypt, contraceptives can be bought not only in pharmacies but in coffee-shops, grocery stores and sweet stands. Even countries where the approach is more cautious ("contraceptive pills are not sweets"), are beginning to see the possibilities. Tunisia, for example (which has traditional Islam as well as the medical profession to consider), has passed legislation making the oral pill (government subsidised) available in all pharmacies on receipt of a once-only doctor's prescription.

A fifth trend in family planning approaches noticeable since Bucharest is the *progressive widening of the range of contraceptive methods offered*. Both government and private family planning associations are aware that unsatisfactory methods have in the past contributed to falling off in continuation rates. Many countries now (like the Philippines) pride themselves on their "cafeteria approach".

At the same time, there is an increasing emphasis on *sterilisation*. Not only in Asia, but in many other countries, there seems to be a feeling that the best method of contraception is the terminal one. There are some exceptions—in Tanzania, for example, sterilisation is not permitted. But elsewhere, governments are showing increasing interest not only in vasectomy, but in the possibilities of uncomplicated tubectomy, opened up by the new techniques of laparoscopy and "mini-laps".

In India, despite the resentment caused by the escalating degree of coercion that marked the sterilisation campaigns in the last 18 months of Mrs. Ghandi's Government, the new Government has reiterated its confidence in sterilisation as a major solution to India's population problem[25] (although stressing its voluntary nature). Significantly, the appeal of sterilisation as a method is growing also in countries where the problem of population growth is much less urgent and where other kinds of contraceptive methods are readily available. The Republic of Korea, for example, has just made it obligatory for all industrial enterprises above a certain size to subsidise the expenses of the (voluntary) sterilisation operation for both their male and female staff.

A final trend that may be noted is the *growing use of incentives*. It is no doubt due to the Indian experience that incentives for smaller family size have come to be associated in the public mind (particularly among some of the donor community) with sterilisation. Certainly in India, the range of possible incentives and disincentives was enormous, covering jobs, promotion, housing, permits for activities of all kinds (including sometimes education and food rations at subsidised prices), loans at lower interest rates, etc., and these did become linked to the Government's sterilisation campaign. Some of these (although without the coercive element) are still being applied. But other countries (for example, the Philippines, Thailand, the Republic of Korea) are now also offering various

---

25. Of a country-wide target of 10 million acceptors for *all* family planning methods set for 1977, voluntary sterilisation was to account for 4 million.

material advantages for smaller families (e.g. income tax benefits). There are also the beginnings of disincentives (family allowances, or maternity leave which stops after a certain number of children). From economic disincentives to implicit coercion is perhaps a thin line.

To most of these various trends in the delivery of family planning services, the response of the aid donors has been very positive. Expansion of health infrastructure, extension of MCH and family planning services in the rural areas, and more intensive use of para-medical personnel are all activities that fall within the generally accepted scope of population assistance. The major donors, particularly the World Bank, whose population assistance had traditionally included an important element of construction and equipment, have been very ready to help.

The donors have also proved very flexible in their support of a variety of sometimes very imaginative efforts to promote community participation in family planning. Thus, the IPPF, followed by a number of other donor agencies (notably US AID), see CBD as a particularly promising new development and have been providing substantial assistance. UNFPA has been supporting experimental efforts to promote family planning in industry, etc. In the case of CBD (and frequently family planning in industry also), it is aid that usually provides the contraceptives. Since it is difficult to envisage CBD as becoming wholly self-supporting, the question inevitably arises—will aid be needed indefinitely to keep these channels of distribution functioning efficiently? Certainly some degree of subsidy will be needed: to provide contraceptive supplies for *all* the eligible married women in the poorer income groups would be a formidable and, in many cases, a well-nigh impossible burden for the governments of many developing countries.

Some donors enthusiastically support the solution of sterilisation, although a few, particularly the smaller bilaterals, are resolutely opposed to it in principle and refuse to include it in their programmes. Others, however (notably US AID), have responded generously to the growing demand for the new types of tubectomy equipment and for help in training personnel in their use. Donors also have a mixed reaction to the use of aid funds for incentive payments (to both individuals and to the doctors performing sterilisation operations). On the whole, however, donors tend to welcome initiatives designed to widen acceptance of family planning, and are prepared to make substantial funds available for experimental approaches of various kinds as well as for the more traditional family planning activities.

POPULATION EDUCATION AND INFORMATION

Efforts designed to expand the demand for family planning through Information, Education and Communication (IEC) began well before Bucharest. Interest in the possibilities of well-tuned programmes of *persuasion* to create awareness of the population issue has, however, grown considerably over the past few years, and with it, experience in the more finely adjusted approaches and techniques.

Population education in school, begun in the early 1970s with technical advice from UNESCO, has caught the imagination of governments in a wide range of countries[26]. (It even commends itself to countries which do not have national population policies.) The idea of "creating a revolution in attitudes"[27]

---

26. One notable exception is Tanzania, where it is not allowed.
27. Phrase used in conversation with the author by the Director of the Tunisian Population Education Committee.

by subtly inserting through the normal school curriculum an appreciation of the social, economic, environmental, as well as health and family implications of population has great appeal. The country that has gone furthest in this area is the Philippines, which has an intensive programme of curriculum development and teacher training. Many other countries (for example, Egypt, Tunisia, Mexico, Thailand and Kenya) have also started to introduce it into schools at various levels. Although the preparation of curriculum material suited to particular cultural needs, and the training of teachers in its use, takes time, most countries are hoping eventually that population education will become a regular part of the country's educational system at all levels, starting with the kindergarten.

For most countries, the nub of the problem may well prove to be less the excellence of the teaching material and approach, than the coverage and efficiency of the national school system which is to deliver it. This obviously is something outside of the scope of population assistance—though it could perhaps be tackled if donor agencies were to co-ordinate more closely their aid for population with their aid programmes in other sectors. There is the further problem, a fear voiced by a number of countries, that aid support may be phased out before population education is fully established. Aid donors have been very helpful in the initial and preparatory stages of population education. In several countries, however, the aid projects will have reached their agreed term before the government's regular programme budgets are ready to take them over, and the projects are in danger of foundering unless aid funds continue to provide part of their recurring expenses.

Population information and communication out-of-school is an area where non-government bodies are often particularly effective. (They have the advantage of greater administrative flexibility and are in touch with different classes of society, groups and interests.) In several countries, the (private) national family planning association acts as the government's agent for family planning motivational activities (e.g. in Thailand, Republic of Korea, Tunisia)[28].

As to the methods employed to communicate the family planning message, there is enormous variety according to the characteristics and culture of the country. Thailand, for example, likes the mass media approach, as does Mexico, where transistor radios are ubiquitous. The Philippines are beginning to feel that direct, person-to-person communication is likely to be more effective. Tunisia is careful to keep the approach low-key ("pas de matraquage" - "no bludgeoning") and so on. Aid donors (notably UNFPA and the World Bank) have been generous and imaginative in support of these efforts. Projects range from supplies of audio-visual equipment, mobile cinema vans, etc., to encouragement of plays and other folk media efforts.

INTEGRATED APPROACHES

The need to integrate population activities with general development (implicit in the World Population Plan of Action) has now been accepted, at least in principle, by most developing countries and by most of the donors.

Already before Bucharest, in a number of countries, the adoption of a national population policy had been accompanied by the creation of a council at ministerial level to be responsible for the formulation of population policy and for overseeing the implementation of the national population programme.

---

28. This responsibility, together with training in family planning work, is sometimes becoming the principal function of the national family planning associations in countries where the Health Ministry is progressively taking over the clinics and delivery services originally started through private initiatives.

In Egypt, Kenya, Republic of Korea, Mexico, Thailand, Tunisia, for example, such bodies were established under the chairmanship of the Prime Minister or the Head of the Planning Office. In principle, they were well placed to give to population the highest national authority. In practice, however (the experience in each country was very similar), since population is not of high priority for most sector ministers, these councils met but rarely, if at all.

It marks a real step forward, therefore, that over the past few years, in each of these countries, the ministerial-level council has come to be supplemented by an executive sub-committee or similar body at sub-cabinet level, which does meet regularly and exercises a degree of effective co-ordination. In Egypt, Republic of Korea and Thailand, for example, these bodies, which have secretariats of high professional competence, function in the way recommended in the World Population Plan of Action[29] and make it their business to see that the nation's chief decision-makers are at least kept aware of the population issue and of how activities planned in other sectors may affect it.

Despite these efforts at the policy level, in practice, integration does not yet seem to have progressed very far.

There are, of course, many levels of integration. The association of family planning with health in a single service can, strictly speaking, be called "integration"; so can a multi-purpose health worker; so can a programme of population education in schools. Since Bucharest, however, "integrated approaches" usually have a much broader significance. The underlying assumption is that family planning has a better chance of being successful if it is allied to the satisfaction of other social needs. The problem is proving to be the translation of this concept into programme terms. Countries are examining various modalities. Pilot schemes and experimental projects are trying out different "mixes" of population and other activities in different structural arrangements. So far, few of these have gone beyond the experimental stage.

One example that is being tried out in several countries is a Japanese project which links family planning with parasite control and improved nutrition. The project is currently under way in Thailand, the Republic of Korea and the Philippines[30]. The basic idea is that by providing a service which will have immediately perceptible and appreciated results (curing people of parasites), a climate of confidence will be established which will increase the acceptability of family planning also.

In Egypt, a different form of integration is being tried. The idea is to "inject" a population element into all economic and social development activities at the local level. Described enthusiastically by one foreign observer as "an attempt to create a revolution by the Establishment", the idea is that a corps of specially-trained civil servants ("co-ordinators") will work with the existing local government structure so as to ensure that all local activities will be undertaken with due regard to their "population dimension"[31].

In general, however, integrated approaches are proving hard to organise. Since Bucharest, both developing country governments and most donor agencies have issued official statements asserting their conviction that problems of population can only be treated in their socio-economic context, and that accordingly,

---

29. Paragraph 25.
30. The Joint Parasite Control/Nutrition/Family Planning Project; the project covers also Indonesia, Malaysia and Taiwan. The initiative of the Japanese Organisation for International Co-operation in Family Planning (JOICFP), it is supported also with funding from IPPF and UNFPA.
31. The "Co-ordinators Project" has been devised by the Egyptian Board of Population and Family Planning in collaboration with the department responsible for rural development (Organisation for the Reconstruction and Development of the Egyptian Village).

a multi-disciplinary approach is required[32]. In terms of operational programmes, however, there is still a considerable gap between official statements and the activities that actually get funded.

The problem is partly a technical incapacity to translate policy into action programmes, compounded by the fact that neither in developing countries nor in aid agencies is the administrative structure conducive to the development of genuinely multi-disciplinary approaches. Long-standing habits of sectoral thinking thus tend to be reinforced by bureaucratic structures and vice-versa.

In US AID and the World Bank, for example, responsibility for population activities is organised functionally; in most of the bilaterals, programme responsibility is allocated geographically. In practice, neither arrangement avoids a certain departmentalism in thinking, and thence in actual programme operations. It is precisely to counter such tendencies that the Population Council, for example, has reorganised its structure into new functional groupings; US AID is trying to reorganise its Population Office so as to bring it into closer co-operation with the department dealing with health, nutrition and education; SIDA is trying to build up a multi-disciplinary expertise among its staff, etc.

The World Bank, at the suggestion of the External Advisory Panel which reviewed the Bank's activities in the population field (1976) has opted for the solution of including population "components" in Bank projects in other areas. This could offer a particularly promising way of achieving an effective integrated approach in that the definition of "population component" is very broad (not only family planning, CBD and motivational work, but also such activities as improvement of female literacy, incentives and disincentives, and community involvement). Still more significant is the recommendation that the country concerned *need not necessarily have a national family planning programme.* Indeed, the idea is precisely that population components could open up a dialogue on population with governments which for political or cultural reasons have been unwilling to establish national population programmes.

RESEARCH

Interest in population research has developed markedly since Bucharest. Even countries which have disavowed any national problem of population growth (e.g. Bolivia) are encouraging research into demographic problems. The need for up-to-date and accurate demographic information as a basis for development planning is now widely recognised. Since Bucharest, Bolivia has held its first national census since 1950, and Zaire is planning to do so. Both countries have taken steps to strengthen their national demographic research capacity.

To what extent these developments are a consequence of Bucharest is, of course, impossible to determine. What may, however, be considered a direct response to Bucharest is the changing orientation of population research in those countries which already have population programmes and well-established research capacity.

The most striking change in population research is the greater emphasis on studies relating to fertility motivation, evaluation and action-oriented research. Population projects are increasingly being designed with built-in arrangements for evaluation and some action programmes are themselves designed largely for the purpose of testing out various hypotheses (e.g. Egypt's Integrated Rural

---

32. Cf. the UK White Paper, *More Aid for the Poorest,* Cmnd. No. 6270; the Report of the Commission on Sweden's Future Development Co-operation Policy; the Population Council's Statement on Future Directions, etc.

Development Project). Population research in general has become much closer to both operational activities and to population policy. There is also a growing interest in long-term population planning, using the term "population" to cover not only the demographic size and profile of the country, but also the needs that these imply for infrastructure and social services, and the possibilities of meeting them. In a number of countries (e.g., Egypt, the Philippines, India, Thailand), population research is addressing itself very seriously to the likely shape of things in the year 2000.

Population research in the developing countries is becoming markedly more "national" as experience is being built up (in part due to donor support). Demand for technical assistance in the research field is diminishing, except for certain selected activities, exchanges of experience, and—a continuing need—fellowships for study abroad.

The donors for their part are making deliberate efforts to adapt their research activities in the population field to the changing approaches high-lighted by Bucharest. Where much population research tended to be concentrated on the bio-medical aspects of fertility, there is now increasing attention to the socio-economic aspects also. The Population Council led the way with Mr. Rockefeller's[33] resounding affirmation at Bucharest of the need for the "development approach", although it has retained its long-standing interest in the development of new contraceptive technologies. The Ford Foundation, on the other hand, has decided to shift the focus of its population research on to the broader socio-economic aspects[34].

Virtually all the agencies now funding population research (the foundations, the Population Division of the United Nations, the World Bank, the bilaterals) are increasingly concerned that such research will be policy-relevant and geared to the major gaps in the present state of knowledge. The International Review Group of Social Science Research on Population and Development (IRG) represents a direct response to Bucharest, intended to provide guidance to donors in determining future research priorities. Moreover, with the reduction in the volume of available research funding, population research will probably, of necessity, move nearer to the wishes of the developing countries, i.e. be less home-based and more in accordance with national institutes' research priorities.

Recently, a whole new theme of (interdisciplinary) population research has been opened up by the concept of *"population impact"*. In 1977, the United States Congress mandated that all US development projects must take into account their potential demographic impact and, wherever possible, build motivation for smaller families. Although intended to provide an important new impetus to the "integrated approach" to population, it is far from clear how this provision can effectively be applied in the meaningful way that its authors intended. It would be unfortunate if it were allowed to degenerate eventually into a mere procedural requirement. US AID, together with the Rockefeller Foundation, is undertaking research into this problem.

The "population impact" of future development activities is a particularly complex and subtle matter, for which, so far, there is little practical experience. It is, however, enormously important. In urging developing countries and aid agencies to take an "integrated approach", we are, in fact, expecting them to make just this kind of assessment. Perhaps a useful start might be made to

---

33. Mr. J.D. Rockefeller III: Chairman of the Board of Trustees.
34. This change has been dictated primarily by considerations of finance and comparative advantage, rather than by the views expressed at Bucharest. It may be noted that although the Ford Foundation's budget has been reduced by almost half in the period since Bucharest, population activities have not been reduced correspondingly.

develop a methodology and establish some guidelines by making an examination of the population impact of some *past* development activities. The World Bank and US AID, to mention just two donors, must have a wealth of experience to draw on.

IV. SOME IMPLICATIONS FOR AID

In terms of needs for population assistance and of the actual aid requests that stem from them, the post-Bucharest situation has turned out to be less radically different from that of earlier years than many people had expected. The following paragraphs attempt to sum up briefly the implications for aid of the main features of the present population scene.

First: the period since Bucharest has seen a greater demand for population assistance and, moreover, for activities of the classical pre-Bucharest type than before. Indeed, it would seem that the discussions at Bucharest have awakened new interest among developing countries not only in the basic problem of population growth but also in the traditional forms of population assistance as a means of dealing with it. Thus, only a few months after Bucharest, the UNFPA announced that it had received a larger volume of aid requests than ever before and was accordingly maintaining its seven previously established categories of population assistance[35].

All the countries reviewed here want to continue to receive foreign aid to support their family planning programmes[36], to strengthen their maternal and child health care services and general health infrastructure, to train medical and para-medical personnel in family planning delivery, to carry out demographic surveys, and advise on programme management and evaluation. Even countries that have gone further in the direction of "new approaches" are glad to have large loans from the World Bank to help provide the actual family planning and health services which will be needed to supply the increased demand that it is hoped such approaches will eventually generate[37]. Old-style "population assistance", therefore, is still very much "in", and assistance for family planning in particular. (Reflecting the nature of the requests it has received, the UNFPA has increased the proportion of its total expenditures devoted to "family planning" from just under 40 per cent to slightly over 50 per cent for the period 1976-78.)

Second: the donors have responded to the increase in demand by an *overall increase in the amount of population assistance.* The funds available for population assistance have expanded, partly because the UNFPA has been given an increase in its resources, partly because of the greater volume of World Bank lending for population, and partly because after a period of stagnation[38], US AID funds for population are again rising. In the period 1974-1976, the total funding for population increased approximately 18 per cent.

---

35. These classifications in any case cover a very wide range of population activities: basic population data; population dynamics; population policy; family planning; communication and education; multi-disciplinary activities; programme development.

36. Albeit, in the case of Bolivia, discreetly.

37. As the World Bank has pointed out, even CBD presupposes the existence of a medical referral system of reasonable quality and accessibility—"World Bank Lending Policies and Procedures in the Population Sector", 1977.

38. This was part of a general drop in the volume of US AID's assistance in all sectors reflecting the economic stagnation of that period.

34

The bilateral donors, in particular, in the period since Bucharest seem to have taken new heart. All of them have increased their contributions to the UNFPA, and in addition many, while still desirous of maintaining a low profile[39], are now prepared to make more funds available for bilateral population assistance. Several (e.g. the United Kingdom, Norway and Germany), are frankly disappointed that developing countries still seem to have reservations about bilateral aid for population, and in consequence, have not come forward with a greater demand for the population assistance that they are prepared to provide under their bilateral aid programmes. A number of bilaterals, accordingly, see in some form of joint financing arrangements with either the World Bank or the UNFPA a promising compromise arrangement, whereby they can make an increased bilateral contribution under the umbrella of an international organisation—which would "defuse" any lingering political sensitivities.

Third: a growing sense of "self-reliance" is leading developing countries to insist on national independence in the formulation of population policies. Although this attitude is perhaps not so strong as the declarations of Bucharest might have suggested, it is nonetheless very real[40]. It would seem unlikely that there will occur again situations like that for example in Kenya and Tunisia a decade ago, when a national population programme was established, funded, and, to a large extent, run by foreign aid.

There is a strong feeling that population assistance must be provided according to the country's priorities and not the donors'. This attitude, found in countries whose situation is as diverse as those of the Republic of Korea, India and Brazil, is perhaps partly a fall-out from Bucharest: but there is also a residual resentment that donors in the past have tended to "push" population too hard (even Mrs. Gandhi complained that the donor community was more concerned about India's population problem than the Indian Government). What is certain is that donors' individual idiosyncrasies regarding the priorities, purposes and modalities of their population assistance[41] have been felt as constituting a constraint on coherent population planning, leading sometimes to distortion of national population programmes. (This is felt particularly keenly in the area of research: developing countries are aware that they are often better placed than outside research institutions to study national problems.)

Fourth: the degree of self-reliance shown by developing countries in their attitude to foreign funding of population programmes varies according to the situation of the country. In Mexico, for example, where the national population programme is still new (and where, admittedly, political considerations make the Government a little sensitive about overt foreign aid for population limitation), the National Population Council is concerned that the programme should not get used to over-reliance on aid, on the grounds that foreign funding will not continue indefinitely. Some countries, on the other hand (e.g. Kenya, Tunisia), continue to plan their national population programmes on the assumption of continuing sizeable aid support. Others, that have strong national programmes (e.g. Republic of Korea, Thailand, the Philippines), while not relying on aid

---

39. US AID seems to be the only bilateral donor of population assistance which does not share this concern.

40. The UNFPA's announcement in 1976 of a new programme to help countries establish national population policies appropriate to their needs and to set up minimum population programmes to carry them out, sounds almost anachronistic in the present context: the intention, however, is simply to offer technical advisory services to those who request them.

41. Unrealistic performance requirements, expressed in statistical terms, are frequently a problem.

to finance many regular population activities, are hoping that it will continue to be available for major infrastructure and training programmes and for innovative projects not easily provided for in regular service budgets.

In the area of programme implementation, there is still need for occasional specialist expertise at a high professional level; but this is increasingly a selective requirement and usually short-term. (Resistance to long-term foreign "advisors" in the population field considerably antedated Bucharest.)[42]

One area where self-reliance is seen very clearly is in the diminishing need for imported contraceptives and contraceptive materials, as facilities for local production and packaging are built up. In Egypt, India, the Philippines, Thailand, aid is required to help develop these facilities. This trend, however, has in most countries only recently begun, and there is still (even in the four countries mentioned) a continuing need for aid to provide imported contraceptive supplies.

Fifth: a further interesting development that is becoming apparent in a wide variety of countries is the *growing recognition of the value of foreign aid as a catalyst.* This perception of the role of aid seems to be current notably in countries where population programmes are already fairly well established (e.g. Egypt, Thailand), but where the population authorities would be grateful for additional leverage with parliament, the budget authorities, or other sections of government. It would seem, however, to be equally applicable to countries of weaker government commitment. Foreign aid, particularly large-scale foreign aid provided by an international body (e.g. the World Bank), is sometimes very useful in obliging governments to put up counterpart funds, to respect officially announced programme commitments, or even to make necessary changes in legislation or administrative procedures.

It is tempting to wonder whether the donor community has fully realised the potential it possesses in this regard. Aid, after all, represents only a very small part of the total expenditures on population in a number of developing countries[43]. Perhaps, therefore (without falling into the trap of appearing "neo-colonialist"), the donors could make a more lasting contribution by judicious exercise of this catalytic function to stimulate government action, than by their actual financial input towards the cost of programmes. This is likely to be true in the case of those countries where aid is now beginning to be phased out (Republic of Korea, the Philippines) as the countries move into what US AID calls "the self-sustaining category". It may be equally valuable in the case of countries where programmes are still in the early stages and where aid is contributing to get them well established.

Sixth: faced, somewhat to their surprise, with an increased demand for population assistance, donors have reacted by introducing a *new coherence into their choice of programme countries.* Differing criteria seem to be employed. Some donors give preference to countries most in need of help (UNFPA has formulated a set of criteria which identify 40 priority countries for population assistance); others, to countries where the national population problem is most serious. (US AID has worked out an elaborate rating system with a view to measuring the urgency of countries' claims to population assistance.) Many of the bilaterals (Germany, Norway, Sweden, the United Kingdom) and also the Population Council give priority to the "poorest" countries and those most

---

42. Cf. "Constraints on Population Activities and the Problem of Absorptive Capacity", OECD Development Centre, 1973.

43. The actual proportion, of course, varies widely—from Kenya, where aid currently accounts for 70 per cent of the costs of the national population programme, to India, where it is only 10 per cent.

severely affected by the increase in the price of oil. Both UNFPA and US AID are beginning to phase out of countries deemed to be strong enough to fund their own population programmes in favour of new ones where the economic need is greater.

Cutting across these various criteria, however, is sometimes a simple desire to direct the aid effort to where it is likely to have the most impact. This affects not only the choice of country for population assistance but also the choice of project. Donors naturally tend to prefer activities that are speedy, measurable, and have a reasonable chance of success. In the case of the major population assistance donors, who find that demands tend to outrun funding resources, this preference may sometimes reinforce a tendency to conservatism.

Seventh: only a small proportion of population assistance has so far been devoted to innovative activities. This is due in part to hesitation to commit considerable resources for activities whose return is uncertain and where there is still very little practical experience to draw on.

The general reaction, therefore, is to wait for the programme countries to make the first move. This is notably the attitude of the smaller bilaterals whose self-appointed aid role is to be simply "responsive" to aid requests. But it seems to apply also to those donors who maintain regular dialogues with their counterparts in the developing countries in the context of country programming agreements (e.g. Norway, Sweden) and, to an extent, to the large multilaterals also. Possibly the donor community is over-cautious about the need for non-assertiveness. (The integrated programme for Parasite Control/Nutrition/Family Planning designed by JOICFP did not wait on the countries concerned to *request* such aid.) But perhaps private agencies have a greater latitude than other donors for taking the initiative in introducing new ideas and approaches.

Nevertheless, where the programme countries have taken the lead in introducing innovative activities, the donors have generally shown themselves very flexible in their response. Even some of the agencies generally thought of as conservative are now funding all sorts of unconventional activities. UNFPA, for example, under the broad category of "family planning", is assisting many highly imaginative experiments; and so are a number of other donors, particularly some of the private agencies. Many of these are small-scale activities—but at least the agencies have let themselves be led along some unexpected by-ways.

Eighth: population activities are involving an increasing need for local currency expenditures. These are required for a wide variety of purposes: salary supplements (necessary in particular to induce people to work in rural areas), incentive payments and recurrent costs, particularly of experimental projects. Most agencies are proving very comprehensive in this respect. (The World Bank, for example, under certain conditions, allows for "incremental" recurrent costs to give the borrower time to adjust to future higher expenditure levels; SIDA has agreed to finance the local currency costs of an activity started by another donor agency, etc.) One aspect of local currency financing that is sometimes proving difficult, however, is to determine what is a reasonable time-span. Aid is needed to provide the local currency not only to launch a new experiment, but to ensure that it has adequate time to develop and replicate, even if the government does not pick up the cheque immediately after the end of the initial project period. Donors may recognise this, but are naturally reluctant to envisage an open-ended commitment.

There are few special concessionary arrangements for population assistance; (for example, the aid-tying practices of certain bilateral donors continue to be something of a problem for developing countries, particularly in respect of

37

imports of contraceptive supplies). However, as donors are today increasingly concerned to see that their aid practices are appropriate for "basic needs" activities of all kinds, it can be expected that aid for population activities will benefit from any relaxation of procedures that may be introduced for this purpose.

Ninth: contrary to expectations (or perhaps fears?), *Bucharest has not blurred the distinction between "population activities" and "development activities"* to any considerable extent. Even though some developing countries have formulated new and very comprehensive definitions of their national population policy, which include a whole range of social problems in addition to that of population growth, they do not generally request population funding except for the usually accepted population/family planning elements.

Although the volume of population assistance has increased since Bucharest, the small percentage of total ODA going to population activities (less than 3 per cent) has remained roughly unchanged. Significantly, it continues to be applied very largely, as before, to activities that are considered likely to affect the population factor *directly.* Certainly, there is increasing variety and imagination in the design of such activities. There are also occasional activities which include both population *and* development components, although these are still far from frequent. As yet, however, there seem to have been few attempts to apply population and other development activities in a mutually supportive or "multiplicative" relationship.

Tenth: the message of Bucharest ("population *and* development") *was addressed to the whole of the international community.* The population assistance donors certainly are doing their best to respond. But it is perhaps from the *rest* of development activities that the real leverage on the population factor may come. So far, there has been conspicuously little interest in population problems from other sectors of the international community, whether in international fora or donor agency programmes[44]. The same is often true of the national economic and social programmes of the developing countries—population is not generally a constant preoccupation underlying other sector plans.

A way which offers promise of bridging the dichotomy between population and development is the growing interest in "basic human needs". Although the advocates of basic needs do not often mention their population implications, the principal elements of basic needs and the factors held to be the important determinants of fertility, in fact, coincide. Donors are prepared to support activities likely to have an "impact on population", through their other aid programmes, leaving their "population assistance" to cover for the most part, family planning and the classical population activities.

Assuming that "basic human needs" projects or relevant social development programmes continue to represent an important aid interest, this may be considered a satisfactory arrangement and one that, moreover, enables donors to provide aid for "population problems" almost without meaning to.

---

44. Cf. The UN Conference in Vancouver in 1976 on Human Settlements, or discussions on social development topics in the Development Assistance Committee of the OECD.

ASIA

INDIA
REPUBLIC OF KOREA
PHILIPPINES
THAILAND

Officials in the above Asian countries were interviewed by the author, OECD Development Centre, and Il Hi Kang, World Bank.

INDIA

Total population[1]	613,217,000
Population under age 20[1]	52.5%
Population density per sq. km[1]	187
Rate of growth[1]	2.48%
Crude birth rate (per thousand)[1]	38.7
Crude death rate (per thousand)[1]	13.9
Life expectancy (total)[1]	52.1 years
Per capita national income (1974)[2]	$136
Literacy rate[3]	29%

Sources:
1. UNFPA, *Inventory of Population Projects 1975-76.*
2. U.N., *Statistical Yearbook,* 1976.
3. IBRD, *Comparative Education Indicators,* 1978.

INTRODUCTION

In the vast sub-continent of India, the problems posed by population growth are so overwhelming that they take on a wholly different dimension from those of most other developing countries. The sheer numbers of people, together with the inability of the economy to provide them with even a bare level of subsistence makes the prospect of continuing population increase assume the proportions of potential national disaster. At the same time, the enormous size of the country, its diverse cultural, ethnic and religious traditions, its paucity of communications and variety of climate, geography and economic activity, make nation-wide solutions incomparably difficult to devise and to implement.

India was the first country in the world to set up a national family planning programme. By the time of Bucharest, after two decades of family planning, the fertility rate had already passed its peak[1], but the country was still growing by some 13 million people a year. From 350 million inhabitants in 1953, the year the family planning programme was started, India's population had grown to 593 million by 1974 and, unless the rate of growth were to slow considerably, threatened to reach about 1,000 million by the turn of the century[2].

It accordingly came as something of a surprise to many people at Bucharest that the Indian Government declared that it considered not population, but poverty, to be the key problem. Indeed, the now-famous phrase "Development

1. The 1971-1972 Fertility Survey showed a decline in crude birth rates from 45 to 41 per 1,000 since 1960.
2. By the end of 1977, India's population had already topped 630 million.

41

is the best contraceptive" was first heard in the speech made by the Head of the Indian Delegation to the World Population Conference. With all due allowance for the ideological and political considerations that prevailed at the Conference, the inference seemed to be that the Indian Government had ceased to look to family planning to provide the solution to the desperate problem of India's inexorably increasing population.

Less than two years after Bucharest, it had become apparent that the principal solution that the Government had chosen instead, was not "development", but mass sterilisation of the over-fecund poor. Subsequent events bore out the much-quoted prediction that such a policy would not do much to bring down the birth rate, but might bring down the Government[3]. Across northern India, where local authorities resorted to harsh measures to achieve their sterilisation targets, the resentment caused by that policy created considerable hostility towards fertility limitation by any means, even though entirely voluntary. In the rest of the country, recent programme performance suggests that former levels of voluntary acceptance are being approached, and in some southern States even exceeded.

NATIONAL POPULATION POLICIES

Fear that expansion of population will outstrip the country's possibilities of food production and make any increases in per capita GNP impossible, has been part of Indian official thinking since Independence. Control of population growth has accordingly figured as one of the objectives of each of India's Five-Year Plans, in which targets for population reduction have been set for each State (although they have never been attained).

The strength of the commitment to reduce the birth rate tended to fluctuate until the latter half of the 1960s, when the international aid community began providing active encouragement and massive material support[4]. The aid community made it plain that they considered development to be impossible without cutting the birth rate. Family planning was seen as the indispensable condition. With some aid support, therefore, but primarily through its own resources, India created an extensive family planning infrastructure of clinics and family planning bodies, and made a major investment in related mass communications, training and research.

While it is not possible to assess with any certainty the impact on fertility of this nation-wide build-up of family planning effort, the figures indicate that the beginning of the decline in the birth rate coincided with the period of the major input of population assistance. Family planning, therefore, could reasonably be held to have contributed to India's commencing fertility decline.

However, the vast sub-continent of India cannot be viewed as a single country. The record of the individual States in reducing population growth has been very uneven. This is due, in part, to the varying degree of commitment and the vigour with which they have organised family planning programmes. It also reflects, however, the enormous differences in socio-economic characteristics. The striking variations in fertility patterns shown by the different States are matched by the differences in such factors as the degree of literacy,

---

3. Frank Notestein.
4. Between 1969 and 1975, India received some $95 million in aid for population (DAC figures).

42

education (particularly female education), nutritional standards, infant mortality, morbidity, employment, income distribution, etc.[5]. The varying experience of the different States of India would seem to offer direct evidence of the correlation between fertility decline and the realistic possibilities of aspiring to a better standard of living.

Against this background, therefore, it is quite logical that at Bucharest the Indian Government should have taken a stand on the side of "development". As a practical matter, however, although the Five-Year Plans had included important social objectives (e.g., universal free primary education, a health infrastructure for the rural areas, etc.), changing the economic and social conditions that affect fertility is both long-term and costly. The Indian Government, therefore, continued to put the main emphasis of its population policy on the immediate solutions of population control and family planning.

CHANGES IN POPULATION POLICY SINCE BUCHAREST

India's Fifth Plan hopefully set ambitious targets for population reduction. The crude birth rate was to drop from 35 per 1,000 in 1975 to 25 per 1,000 by 1985, the end of the Sixth Plan Period. On the assumption that the decline in the death rate would continue at the current rate, the growth of the population overall would thus be reduced from 2.4 per cent to 1.4 per cent per year by the middle of the next decade.

To achieve these targets would require that some 50 million eligible couples with three children or more were practising contraception. In 1974-1975, approximately 15 million couples, roughly 15 per cent[6] of the total eligible couples were estimated to be effectively protected. The task, therefore, was undoubtedly beyond what family planning programmes could reasonably be expected to accomplish in a 10-year period.

At the outset, the Government showed some intention of pursuing the development approach. In presenting the Fifth Plan (1975-80), it announced that its objectives were faster economic growth, the eradication of poverty and greater distributive justice. Included was a "Programme of Minimum Needs", which envisaged a package of measures covering health care, improved nutrition and reduction of fertility. Both family planning and sterilisation were to be included as part of the package.

The name "Minimum Needs" Programme might suggest that the Indian Government in 1975 was preparing to base the Fifth Plan on what is now termed a "basic needs strategy", and some of the language employed at the time might lend support to that view ("a frontal assault on the citadels of poverty", etc.). The Plan does, in fact, aim at expanding social programmes in many different

---

5. For instance, the State of Kerala, which boasts a high female literacy rate (54 per cent), low mortality (8 per cent), high per capita expenditure on education and medical services, and a relatively even distribution of income, exhibits one of the lowest State birth rates (26 per cent), while this rate rises as high as 42 per cent for a State such as Uttar Pradesh, where female literacy is only 11 per cent, the mortality rate 20 per cent, and per capita expenditure on education and medical services only one-third of Kerala's. (*Sources:* Population Council, *Country Profile,* May 1976; World Bank: *Economic Situation and Prospects of India,* April 1977; N. Sudhakar Rao, *The Journal of Family Welfare,* December 1976.)

6. Population Council, *Country Profile,* May 1976.

fields, but the population objective was almost at once overtaken by the Government's sudden sense of urgency at what it saw as "a population explosion of crisis dimensions"[7].

About one year after Bucharest, therefore, the Indian Government seems to have arrived at three conclusions regarding India's population problem: first, family planning was not enough ("considerable work has been done in our country in the field of family planning, but clearly only the fringe of the problem has so far been touched")[8]; second, India could not afford to wait for the development approach ("the percolation effect will take too long")[9]; and third, personal human rights would have to give way to the longer-term interests of the nation as a whole ("We must act now to... prevent the doubling of our population in a mere 28 years. We should not, therefore, hesitate to take steps that might be described as drastic. Some personal rights have to be kept in abeyance... for the human right of the nation...")[10].

The reaction provoked by the stepped-up family planning campaign that followed, and in particular, by the Government's attempts to sterilise a large part of the male population, is now international knowledge. The incoming Government, while immediately repudiating the element of coercion and stressing human dignity and the right of the individual to determine the size of his family (thus returning to the principles of the WPPA), nonetheless re-affirmed its intention to press forward vigorously with the family planning programme.

For the first ten months, the Government of Mr. Desai maintained the birth rate targets set for the Fifth and Sixth Plans. However, at the January meeting of the Central Council for Health and Family Welfare, it was recommended that the target of a 30 per thousand birth rate be set back from 1979 to 1983. While abandoning the shrill insistence that characterised the family planning campaigns in 1976 and early 1977, the Government has maintained a firm official commitment to population control as a matter of urgency. It has pledged itself to redress abuses that occurred when the campaign was at its height (it has asked the States to set up "Grievance Committees" and has spoken of financial compensation), but the family planning programme remains a stated priority.

There is, however, a change in the way the programme is now presented. The note of alarm over the overall growth rate has been suppressed and the negative objective of population control has been replaced by the positive one of individual and family welfare. (One of the first acts of the new Government was to change the name of the Health Ministry from "Ministry of Health and Family Planning" to "Health and Family Welfare".) Family Planning is now to be seen as "part of the total concept of positive health"[11], and pursued together with the programmes in other relevant sectors of human welfare. ("At the same time, it (i.e., family planning) must find meaningful integration with other welfare programmes, viz: nutrition, food, clothing, shelter, availability of safe drinking water, education, employment and women's welfare. It will be our endeavour

---

7. Dr. Karan Singh, Union Minister of Health and Family Planning, National Policy Paper, presented 16th April, 1976.

8. *Idem.*

9. Mrs Ghandi's address to the 31st Joint Conference of the Association of Physicians, 22nd January, 1976.

10. *Idem.*

11. "Family Welfare Programme: A Statement of Policy", Ministry of Health and Family Welfare, New Delhi, 29th June, 1977.

to bring about this integration in a greater degree. We expect the States to do the same.")[12]

The "integrated approach" thus described is not new in India (the previous Government was also aware of the relevance of these various aspects of welfare to family size). The indications are that from now on welfare will be given a greater emphasis in terms of Government effort and commitment and that there will be a simultaneous attack both on the immediate problem of high birth rates, and on the longer-term conditions that favour them. But the situation remains one of urgency and the emphasis, accordingly, remains on the direct approach.

STRATEGIES FOR IMPLEMENTING POPULATION POLICY

The present Indian Government has firmly disavowed the element of coercion and stressed the voluntary nature of the whole concept of fertility limitation. With this important distinction, the strategies that it is pursuing for carrying out its policy of slowing down population growth remain very largely those devised by the previous Government.

The main focus of the effort remains family planning, in a context of improved health services.

IMPROVED HEALTH SERVICES

The Government's intention is eventually to establish an integrated rural health service, covering basic health care, MCH and family planning. Recognising that the provision of adequate health coverage for the 80 per cent of the population who live in the rural areas cannot be achieved using traditional health infrastructure and practices, the Government has accepted the necessity of a certain degree of "deprofessionalisation" of medical services.

The plan is to endow the whole country with a 3-tier referral system, which will work up from village level through the primary health centre to the district hospital (fully-equipped). This will involve some additional infrastructure, chiefly at the primary health centre level[13]. The more important need, however, is to make more efficient use of existing facilities, which have generally tended to be badly under-utilised for lack of organisation and appropriate staffing, and to extend their outreach. This is to be achieved through a strengthened network of rural sub-centres, staffed by a large, better-trained force of para-medical personnel. Nurses, nurse-midwives and auxiliary nurse-midwives[14] are to be trained to assume greater professional responsibilities. They are to be supported in some of their work by the traditional village midwives, who are also to receive special training in maternity care.

There will thus be a major need for training (including some new infrastructure for facilities, hostel accommodation, etc.). There will also be a continuing need for effective management, supervision and referral, to ensure that

---

12. *Idem.*

13. Each of India's 381 districts has one fully-equipped hospital and about 16 primary health centres, intended to serve the health needs of an average of 1.5 million people. There are over 5,000 primary health centres (outreach varying from 80,000 to 100,000 people) manned by 2 physicians and other workers, and over 37,000 sub-centres, each run by a nurse-midwife.

14. Matriculation level, with 18 months' special training.

the standards of health services in the rural areas do not, in practice, fall too far behind the desirable norms of basic health care[15].

To raise community awareness of health needs and services, and to provide basic care for the most common ailments, the Government recently launched a Rural Health Scheme involving at least one volunteer worker per village. The intention is to support the work of the paramedical workers by enlisting the help of members of the local community who are to be trained to assume certain health duties. Village health workers (men as well as women) are expected to advise on elementary hygiene, nutrition, education, etc., and to provide simple health care. They will also administer injections, as the Governement develops its programme of immunising children against the most common child diseases[16]. Eventually, it is planned that they would assist in motivation for family planning.

The present Government is following its predecessor's plan of creating a force of "multi-purpose health workers" to combine a certain amount of family planning motivation work, contraceptive distribution and advice, along with other health services. The objective is to have a man-woman team for each 10,000 rural population, but recent recommendations by the Central Council for Health and Family Welfare are to have such a team for every 5,000. This represents a formidable training programme and leads some elements of opinion in India to oppose the multi-purpose approach on the grounds that it may hold up the family planning effort.

FAMILY PLANNING

The Government of Mr. Desai does not contemplate any slackening of the official family planning drive. Within a few weeks of taking office, the State Health Ministers were given a "suggested level of achievement" (the term *target* no longer enjoying official favour) of 10 million family planning acceptors for the year 1977-1978. This was to include fertility limitation by all standard methods: sterilisation, IUD, oral pills, condoms and other mechanical or chemical barriers. It is planned to make all these methods more easily available, particularly in the rural areas.

The Government's preferred method, however, remains the terminal one of sterilisation. Originally taken up on a large-scale in the early 1960s (when it accounted for 60 per cent of all methods used under the national programme), it had a second period of favour ten years later, when it appeared that the IUD, then the principal form of contraception favoured for rural India, was not likely to produce the miracle answer[17]. "Conventional methods", as one State Health Minister expressed it, "are only suitable for a higher level of society. In India, they have very high failure rates: the best means of contraception is thus the terminal one".

That in 1975 and 1976 the Indian Government again decided that sterilisa-

---

15. Moves to "de-professionalise" certain health care functions have the approval of the Indian medical establishment up to a certain point. It recognises that medical education should be less disease-oriented and more community-oriented, and has recommended a slight shortening of the period of medical training. However, it is strongly against any dilution of standards, and takes the view that doctors serving in the rural areas need to be, if anything, more qualified that those working in the cities, where conditions of practice are easier. (Report of the Group on Medical Education and Support Manpower, April 1975.)

16. The "triple vaccine"—against whooping cough, tetanus and diptheria. The Health Ministry is confident that it can be supplied locally at minimum cost, but there remain practical problems of manufacture, storage and distribution.

17. The mass camps organised in some Indian States in 1972 and 1973 resulted in a total of some 3 million male vasectomies before this approach was scaled down to much lower levels.

tion was the most effective solution was no doubt in response to the sheer magnitude of the problem. Despite the highly successful sale of government-subsidised condoms, only one eligible couple in six was covered by some form of contraception[18] and then with varying degrees of reliability. The Government accordingly decided to announce sterilisation targets for each of the States. The target system (passed down from the State Governments to successively lower levels of administration) often led to excessive zeal on the part of those responsible for fulfilling the quotas[19], and the prime targets of the campaign became the rural and urban poor—the most defenceless elements in society.

Although Mrs. Ghandi's Government claimed to have performed 8.1 million sterilisations in the 12 months, April 1976 through March 1977, it never did take the final plunge and make sterilisation compulsory after a certain family size[20]. Mr. Desai's Government, while declaring itself "totally against legislation for compulsory sterilisation either at the central level or by the States", has reiterated the suitability of the "terminal method for those couples who have reached the optimum family size" (left to individual discretion) and will pay monetary compensation (Rs 70) to cover loss of wages and travel expenses to clinics. The operation is performed free of charge and with the simplified and safer methods of tubectomy now available through the new contraceptive technologies of laparascopy and "minilap", female sterilisation is increasingly being sought by women who wish to avoid the burden of additional childbearing.

INCENTIVES

Incentives have been a feature of the Indian family planning programme for over 20 years. They have been widely used in the vasectomy camps and in the promotion of particular methods from time to time. In the intensive sterilisation drive of 1976-1977, although cash incentives played an important part, great pressure was applied through many kinds of disincentives or penalties, which became a prominent feature of the campaigns[21]. Government employees (of the Union and State Governments) and employees of autonomous bodies, e.g. the State Railways, local government and major industries, were expected "to set an example and adopt the small family norm", which meant that chances of promotion and other benefits were linked to smaller families. The pattern of incentives/disincentives, as experience has shown, can very easily shade into coercion. The major difference now is that sterilisation is not necessarily the only method of fertility limitation proposed. (The Government of Mr. Desai has stressed that every family can decide the particular method of contraception that it wishes to use.) The economic pressures to limit family size, however, implicit in the system of incentives and penalties, remain difficult to resist.

In short, the official Indian approach to family planning, despite the removal of the coercion element, and despite recognition of the right of the individual to determine desired family size, remains a tough one—reflecting the scale and difficulty of the problem to which it is addressed.

---

18. Worldwatch Paper 12.

19. The State of Emergency further contributed to abuses by conferring unlimited powers on the bureaucracy.

20. The hesitation may have been caused in part by the growing tide of criticism in the West. The State of Maharashtra had passed a Bill through the State Legislature but it did not receive the President of India's approval, without which the Bill could not take effect.

21. The range of penalties covered was astonishingly broad: the sterilisation operation came to be necessary for jobs, promotions, pensions, housing, education for one's children, ration cards, licences, etc.

The Government is aware of the importance of increasing the demand for family planning services to match the increased supply by building up a greater public awareness of the desirability of smaller families. Not much has yet been done, however, to give effect to this view. Thus, while population education, both in-school and out-of-school, is accordingly part of official population strategy, in practice, population education through the school system has not got very far in India. The Government is urging the States to take up population education more vigorously ("42 per cent of our population is below the age of 15 years. It is this population who will be entering the age of matrimony")[22]. The chief constraint, of course, is the inadequacies of the school system itself.

Diffusion of the family planning message out-of-school, by the use of the mass media, is also to be further encouraged. (The popularity of the cinema in India can be turned to good account here, as can the transistor radio.) The Ministry of Information and Broadcasting is hoping to develop these possibilities further and is urging the States to do the same. The folk media (dances, puppet plays, etc.) are similarly being fostered with the general intention of bringing an understanding of the implications of "family welfare" to village audiences.

Family planning motivational work on the community level, already undertaken to considerable effect in some States by the village Panchayats (leaders) and by voluntary groups of all kinds, is likely to be strengthened in the future by the new emphasis given by Mr. Desai's Government to the decentralisation of administrative and economic activity. This trend, which recalls the desire to return to the simple life and village roots advocated by Mahatma Ghandi nearly half a century ago, may provide a means of effectively spreading the message of smaller families and family welfare. It also may offer the most effective methods of organising, on a basis of local participation and self-help, the provision of the other basic social services that are necessary to convert "family welfare" into a real improvement of living standards.

ACTION TO INFLUENCE THE DETERMINANTS OF FERTILITY

Recognising the correlation between fertility, literacy, infant mortality and early marriage, the Government's population policy includes measures that aim to modify these variables. Legislation was recently introduced which would raise the minimum age of marriage to 18 for women and 21 for men. As a practical matter, it is not clear how this measure is to be enforced. One difficulty is that it pre-supposes an effective system of registration of births and marriages, which does not yet exist in rural India. Further, if young girls are to be deterred from the early marriage that is customary in traditional rural society, they will need to be offered alternative occupations, interests and possibilities of social acceptability and prestige.

The Government is, of course, fully aware of this. Improved educational opportunities for girls are also part of official policy; this can include functional education, as well as formal schooling. To provide these effectively over the whole of rural India implies a tremendous effort in terms of both investment and organisation. With Mr. Desai's call for decentralisation, it is possible that local initiative will assume some of the responsibility for providing practicable alternative vocations for village girls.

---

22. Statement of the Ministry of Health and Family Welfare, 29th June, 1977.

Indian medical research in this field is highly advanced. There are a number of promising developments which it is hoped may lead to major break-throughs before too long. Areas where they could be particularly important are the discovery of a safe, effective and acceptable form of contraception that would be easy to produce and administer, and greater possibilities of reversing sterilisation[23].

MAJOR GOVERNMENT POLICIES
LIKELY TO AFFECT POPULATION INDIRECTLY

The Programme of Minimum Needs set forth in India's Fifth Five-Year Plan was designed "in conjunction with other schemes of growth... to bring about an appreciable impact in the socio-economic status of the people, particularly in the rural areas. This in turn is apt to produce a greater impact on their fertility behaviour"[24]. The Programme accordingly envisages the following:

1. Primary education up to the age of 14;
2. The health, nutrition, MCH and family planning "package";
3. Drinking water in villages;
4. Home-sites for landless labourers;
5. Construction of all-weather rural roads;
6. Expansion of rural electrification;
7. Environmental improvement in slum areas.

The Government recently decided to end the Fifth Plan one year early, in 1977-1978. In any case, to tackle the various problems on all fronts simul-taneously, nation-wide, would clearly be beyond the possibilities of any Government budget, even with generous foreign aid. The strategy is therefore likely to be one of focussing action on selected rural areas, i.e. the least economically-developed States, and in the other States, on their respective backward regions.

There is the further question as to how far these measures of social and environmental improvement can be supported by economic and structural change that will bring about some effective redistribution of income. The Government certainly recognises the necessity for such change ("greater distributive justice" is one of the goals of the Fifth Plan). The major problems, however—notably, how to increase employment and the provision of minimum social security—remain.

Rural development programmes have made a start. It is intended that in the next Five-Year Plan, agriculture will account for 40 per cent of the national budget, as against less than 30 per cent in the present Plan. There is a very strong emphasis on rural development activities of all kinds—co-operatives, easier credit for small farmers and fishermen, technical and financial aid for the most disadvantaged, a minimum agricultural wage, debt relief and consumer and agricultural credit. As the local communities become accustomed to assume a greater degree of initiative (administrative and financial), and mobilise local savings, the benefits of these measures may effectively be extended to increasingly large sectors of India's poorest and over-fertile rural population.

---

23. Provision for reversal of sterilisation is normally made in special circumstances which may arise subsequent to the operation, e.g. such as death of one of the existing children.
24. Population Policy in India. Pamphlet issued by the Ministry of Health and Family Planning.

POLITICAL AND ADMINISTRATIVE STRUCTURE
RELEVANT TO POPULATION ACTIVITIES

A very important move was initiated by the Union Government in 1975 with the idea of neutralising any lingering resistance to the national population programme on the part of individual State Governments. Whereas State representation in the Union Parliament had been based on the size of the State population, representation is to be frozen at the level of the 1971 census until the year 2001. The allocation of central government resources to State budgets is similarly to be based on the 1971 population figures. Further, 8 per cent of these allocations is specifically earmarked against performance in family planning. Each of these policies is being continued by the new Government.

Despite the high degree of commitment of the Indian Government to reduction of population growth and family planning, there is no supra-ministerial body responsible for population policy (i.e. headed by a representative of the Prime Minister's Office or the Planning Commission). There is therefore no structural arrangement for co-ordinating population policy with development policies in other sectors.

Official responsibility for population activities rests with the Ministry of Health and Family Welfare. There is a Central Council for Family Welfare, presided over by the Union Minister of Health, which brings together the Health Ministries of the States, some members of Parliament and representatives of related agencies, including a number from the private sector. It meets once a year and lays down the guidelines for national population policy.

Each State has its own Family Planning Council, presided over by the State Health Minister. Although family planning policy is nationally determined and nationally financed—all the financing for State family planning activities is provided by the Central Government—there is considerable latitude as to the form of implementation—viz. the varying positions taken by different States over compulsory sterilisation.

Within the Union Ministry of Health, there is a Department of Family Welfare headed by a Joint Secretary/Family Welfare Commissioner. This is the body effectively responsible for working out programme strategies in consultation with the States, for administering the national programme and for co-ordination with other services concerned in various population activities (e.g. Education, Social Welfare, Communications, etc.). The administrative structure includes a certain number of special Co-ordination Committees: it is the responsibility of the Family Welfare Commissioner to see that they function effectively.

Although the Health Ministry remains responsible for population policy and for its implementation, the various strategies now included in that policy[25] go way beyond health and family planning. They will involve the active collaboration of a very wide range of Government services and non-governmental bodies, as well as the widest possible co-operation of the nation at large, at all levels, from the States down to the village organisations.

How the co-ordination of all these various bodies will work out is not yet clear. Within each State, as at the national level, responsibility for family planning, health and nutrition measures lies with the Ministry of Health and Family Welfare. But the other activities envisaged in the Minimum Needs programme (required to provide the necessary conditions for the success of the family planning activities) will bring in a host of other ministries and services. The

---

25. Which remains as announced in April 1976 by Dr. Karan Singh, the then Minister, except for the deletion of all references to compulsion.

existing administrative machinery of State and Provincial Governments will have the difficult task of harmonising their respective programmes and activities.

The Government describes its new population policy as "part of a multifaceted strategy for economic development and social emancipation". It does not use the term "integrated approach", although this might seem to be implied. No integration, however, would seem to be envisaged, at the present stage, in respect of organisational structure or administrative machinery to facilitate the implementation of the many inter-related strategies involved.

POPULATION ASSISTANCE

Although in absolute terms, India has received massive external assistance for its population programme, foreign aid has constituted rather less than 10 per cent of the total outlay on population activities. As a consequence, the Indian Authorities today tend to take a somewhat relaxed attitude to the question of the future role of aid for population. There are certain areas where it is felt foreign expertise can be especially useful, and there are many activities where additional budgetary support would be welcome but, on the whole, the prevailing sentiment seems to be that after nearly thirty years of Independence, India should largely take care of its own population programme. It is sometimes added that if aid is to be received, it should be on commercial terms.

This view has sometimes been linked with criticism of the population assistance that India has received in the past. Only a short while ago, Mrs. Ghandi stated publicly that the donor community seemed more concerned about India's population problem than did India itself. Other criticisms have been that donors have their special preferences as to the types of activity to be assisted and that this sometimes distorts Indian priorities, that the inputs into buildings and infrastructure have been excessive, and that aid-financed population projects, being special in both design and inputs, are unsuitable for replication on a larger scale. It is sometimes remarked also that the West has no expertise to offer in family planning programmes run by the State, nor in health technologies and infrastructure appropriate to disadvantaged rural areas.

One area which some Indian officials would like to see receive as much as 10 per cent of all population assistance is research. Foreign contacts and exchanges of experience are sought in respect of research in the biological and medical fields, and for socio-demographic research into population and development strategies. In the field of evaluation, in particular, objective outside experience, combined with Indian knowledge of the local situation, can prove mutually rewarding and constructive.

One question to be resolved is the extent to which population assistance should continue to focus on family planning and associated health activities. At the present time, the needs of India's family planning programme are increasingly for local currency expenditures rather than for imported goods and services. Even if some donors do not agree to provide straight budgetary support (as many Indian officials would like), the provision of local currency for certain specified and approved purposes (e.g. training or salaries) in effect has the result of freeing Government funds for other and non-approved purposes. This "donors' dilemma" presented itself to the Swedish Aid Agency. SIDA used to finance imports of condom supplies from Japan but, as India's own production developed, was persuaded to switch to Indian supplies as a source of "procurement". Finally, SIDA agreed to provide a two-year straight-forward budgetary support to the Ministry of Health.

Donors can get around this dilemma to some extent by applying their aid to other aspects of the health/family planning package and concentrating on the improvement of rural health infrastructure. The Indian Authorities and most donors declare that they recognise that the need is no longer for major infrastructure but to improve the services at the rural primary health centre and sub-centre levels. In practice, this implies a small amount of hardware—for simple infrastructure and equipment (training and service kits)—and a very great deal of money for recurrent operating costs (training of para-medical staff, salaries, supplies, transport, etc.). The simplest way to provide this would be by means of a subsidy to the Health budget. Some donors may be ready to agree to this ("sector support"). Others may feel that it does not offer them sufficient control over how their aid funds are spent. The fact remains, however, that the effectiveness of the Indian family planning programme will depend in very large measure on the efficiency and coverage of the health infrastructure that is to carry it out. Foreign aid can help substantially to accelerate the Government's efforts to provide such an infrastructure where it is most needed.

The nutrition element in the health package also poses considerable problems (one major donor turned down a request put forward under the family planning programme for a special feeding programme for pregnant women and nursing mothers on the grounds that its effect might be to raise fertility). Even aside from such conceptual problems, however, nutrition programmes, as noted earlier, pose various practical difficulties. The principal one is their very high cost[26], which donors are unlikely to be able or willing to keep up for very long. Longer-term solutions need to be carefully explored, and these will involve a simultaneous attack on a number of other problems—local food production, storage and distribution, nutrition education, hygiene, etc. Experience of effective integrated approaches to these various problems in the context of rural development is still fairly new and hesitant. It would seem, therefore, that this is an area where donor agencies and local authorities could well get together to pool their ideas and ingenuity in order to try out novel (and, it is to be hoped, potentially replicable) integrated project approaches.

The Indian Authorities have indicated that they would very much like to see aid applied to the design and implementation of integrated programmes, covering not only nutrition, but including also health and family planning, together with a whole range of rural development activities. The Ministry of Health, in particular, favours a major aid-supported demonstration project along these lines in one particular area. Such a programme (perhaps assisted by several donors?) could also serve as a valuable testing-ground for the administrative and organisational structure that a multi-sectoral approach will require.

Some donor agencies have expressed interest in the possibility of an integrated approach to rural development, though so far in projects on a limited scale only. At the present stage of India's programme, it is in innovatory and experimental activities of this kind that aid can be particularly useful, since Government funds are likely to be already strained in meeting the needs of regular programmes under the Plan, and there will be few official resources available to undertake risk ventures. The difficulty in such ventures will be at the design stage—not so much to avoid "donor bias"—donor agencies and national authorities are alike still groping for solutions—but rather to avoid imposing an "official" bias on an activity that is concerned essentially with popular participation.

The big problem posed for aid donors by India's expanded population policy is that, apart from health (and MCH), family planning and nutrition, the other principal elements in it have not hitherto generally been considered

---

26. The CARE food programme is said to have worked out a $15 a head.

as "population" activities. The provision of educational opportunities for girls, for example, could be an area where very considerable amounts of aid, both financial and human resources, will be urgently needed. The Indian Government now includes this educational programme as part of its "population policy". Will the donors accept this concept and be prepared to include assistance to this programme as part of their "population assistance"?

A number of arguments can be put forward in favour of such extension of the concept of "population assistance". First, foreign assistance for family planning may be less welcome in some Indian circles at the present time than foreign assistance for education. Secondly, as the Indian Authorities well recognise, the family planning programme cannot absorb any major increase in foreign aid. An increase in aid to some other sectors, therefore, would provide better balance for the implementation of the Fifth Plan.

Where an activity has been officially announced by the Government as forming part of its population policy (i.e. female literacy, population education, nutrition, broadcasting for family planning motivation, etc.), donor agencies may possibly be persuaded to take a similarly liberal interpretation of the scope of population assistance. The same question arises, however, in respect of an enormous range of other activities, which, while not specifically mentioned in the National Population Policy, are nonetheless designed to alleviate poverty—the pre-condition of high fertility. Urban renewal, redistribution of income, employment generation, and, of course, the whole complex of activities known as "rural development", in fact, almost any aspect of the Fifth Plan Minimum Needs Programme (which will probably be continued in the Sixth Plan) can be presented as consistent with the Statement of the preceding Minister of Health that the "real enemy is poverty" and as contributing to the eventual reduction of fertility in the medium to long term.

REPUBLIC OF KOREA

Total population (1975)[1]	34,681,000
Population under age 20 (1975)[1]	50.0 %
Population density per sq. km. (1975)[1]	351
Rate of growth (1975)[1]	1.7 %
Crude birth rate per thousand (1975)[2]	24.3
Crude death rate per thousand (1975)[2]	6.6
Life expectancy (1975)[2]	68.0
Per capita national income (1976)[1]	$560
Literacy rate (1970)[3]	91.2 %

Sources:
1. The Bureau of Statistics, Republic of Korea, *Korea Statistical Yearbook*, 1977.
2. Korean Institute for Family Planning, *Major Statistics on Population and Family Planning*, 1978.
3. The Bureau of Statistics, Republic of Korea, *1970 Population and Housing Census Report*, 1971.

INTRODUCTION

The year of Bucharest found the Republic of Korea nearing the end of more than a decade of fertility decline. Long considered a model in matters of population policy, the Republic of Korea started a national population programme in the early 1960s, had received considerable external aid to help in its implementation, and had seen the population growth rate drop by one-third within the space of 10 years. The trend seemed set for continued decrease in fertility, and both the Republic of Korea and its aid donors felt that the problem of population growth was under control.

In the few years immediately following Bucharest, however, the whole situation has changed. Latest demographic trends have shown the earlier optimism to have been unfounded and, at the same time, the principal donors of population assistance to Korea have begun to phase out their activities. A new approach to the problem of population had become an urgent necessity. The new population policies announced by the Government early in 1976 represent a fundamental re-thinking of the nature of the country's population problems and of the strategies for solving them.

NATIONAL POPULATION POLICIES

A national policy designed to slow down population growth began with the Military Government which took over in the Republic of Korea in May 1961, one year after the departure of President Syngman Rhee[1]. It saw such a policy as necessary because of the "increasing rate of growth caused by improving health conditions"[2], which was "detrimental to economic development per capita"[3]. The primary problem, therefore, was seen as one of numbers, resulting in pressure on national resources which a small, already densely-populated country could ill afford.

By the time the Third Plan (1972-76) was prepared, official thinking about population reflected an awareness of the social complexities of the problem. The Third Plan included estimates of the implications of anticipated population growth on the size of the labour force, the school-age population and new housing needs. It assumed that the previously-registered decline in the birth rate would continue, leading to a falling-off in the demand for school places. At the same time, the housing shortage was expected to become "increasingly serious, because of population growth, the dissolution of the traditional large family system and the inflow of rural population to urban and suburban centres".

The Plans have included official targets for fertility reduction. A First Five-Year Plan for Family Planning (1962-66) aimed at a reduction of population growth from 3 per cent per annum to 2.5 per cent by 1966 and to 2.0 per cent by 1971, targets which were, indeed, achieved. A second phase was subsequently announced, aiming at a further lowering to 1.5 per cent by 1976, and to 1.3 per cent by 1981, the end of the Fourth Plan Period.

The 1975 Intercensal survey, however, showed plainly that the new targets were not going to be met[4]. The Economic Planning Board now calculates that even with a strengthened family planning programme, population growth is unlikely to fall below 1.6 per cent by 1981. From now on, the problem of reducing the rate of population growth is going to be much tougher.

The Korean Authorities have a clear understanding of why this should be so. The first reason, and perhaps the most important, is purely demographic: the baby boom which followed the ending of the Korean war will result in an increase in the number of fertile couples by almost 40 per cent between 1970 and 1980. A second factor has proved to be the tenacity of the tradition of son preference that characterises pre-eminently male-oriented Korean society. In the face of this deeply-ingrained prejudice, Government exhortations to limit family size run up against formidable obstacles, particularly among the rural community[5]. Finally, the family planning programme itself has begun to show disturbing trends. The number of acceptors of some form of contraceptive practice is continuing to rise but is being offset by the discontinuance rate among previous acceptors.

---

1. Whose policy had been pro-natalist.
2. First National Development Plan, 1962-66.
3. Second National Development Plan, 1967-71.
4. The 1975 growth rate is given as 1.7 per cent: further, it seems now to be generally recognised that the population figures used as a basis for the Third Five-Year Plan had been under-estimates.
5. According to a study conducted in 1976, 71.9 per cent of parents in rural areas said they must have a son, compared with 49.3 per cent in large cities and 59.9 per cent in other urban areas.
Source: Nam-Hoon Cho, Kyu-sik Lee, Sung Yul Hong and Sung Hee Kim, *Effects of Economic Factors on Fertility Behavior,* Korean Institute for Family Planning, December 1977, p. 117.

The Korean Government sees in this new situation a threat to its whole programme of economic and social development. The present goal is to expand the national product and simultaneously further reduce population growth so as to double per capita national income from its 1976 level (about $700) to $1,500 by 1981[6]. Given the combination of factors militating against rapid population decline at the present time, this will be difficult to attain. The Government has therefore felt it necessary to make an all-out attack on the country's population problems, at the same time seeking new approaches for their solution.

CHANGES IN POPULATION POLICY SINCE BUCHAREST

A striking reformulation of Korean population policy was announced by the Government at the beginning of 1976. Whereas previously, population policy had meant primarily reduction in numbers and, in particular, lowering the birth rate, the new policy not only goes "beyond family planning" but gives to the concept of "population planning" an unusually broad social and environmental dimension.

The philosophy underlying the new approach to population is that in order to achieve balanced economic and social development, three aspects of the country's population must be planned for: its overall numbers; "quality"; and spatial distribution. The new population policy of the Government of Korea accordingly encompasses the following elements:

1. Further reduction of fertility by extending the family planning programme to reach more people;
2. Promotion of population education, in and out of school;
3. Emigration on a planned basis;
4. Raising the status and employment prospects of women;
5. Dispersal of large urban populations.

Population policy thus becomes a much more far-reaching matter than can be dealt with solely by the Ministry of Health and Social Affairs. Most of the principal departments of government are now involved. So, also, are a wide range of bodies outside of government (industry, trade unions, the media, the universities, private associations and religious groups). As the concept of population policy has broadened, the institutional responsibility for population activities has broadened similarly. It has been a deliberate decision of the Korean Government to make the population issue a nation-wide concern and to bring in as many different interests as possible, both within government and outside.

The Government is well aware that this comprehensive approach requires a major effort of co-ordination to ensure that the whole complex of plans and strategies in the different sectors are genuinely integrated. For this purpose, it has set up special machinery, the National Population Policy Deliberation Committee[7], which meets at ministerial level and has the responsibility for formulating and promoting policies covering all the various population objectives of the Government.

The new population policy has evolved as part of the process of consultation and study that has gone into the preparation of the Fourth Five-Year Plan

---

6. These figures were released in the Government's new Plan for the five-year period 1977-81 on 8th December, 1976.

7. Further details are given in the section "Administrative Services and Government Structure Responsible for Population Activities" of this chapter.

(1977-81). Like the World Population Plan of Action agreed at Bucharest, it recognises such issues as the role of women, over-crowded urban settlements and migration as part of a country's population problem—not simply as possible determinants of fertility levels, but as social and human problems in themselves.

The Government has given proof of its political will to deal rigorously with these various problems by creating the necessary structural support for co-ordinated action. During the Fourth Five-Year Plan period, the Government plans to invest a total of around $65.5 million. It hopes that additional finance and technical assistance will be made available from international sources.

PRINCIPAL STRATEGIES
FOR IMPLEMENTING POPULATION POLICIES

The following paragraphs give a brief account of the strategies decided upon by the Government as being most appropriate to realise the five main objectives of the new national population policy, as they were described by Korean officials.

1. EXTENDING THE REACH OF THE FAMILY PLANNING PROGRAMME

The need to bring family planning to a larger public has been recognised for some time, and programmes to this end, in many cases, were started before the new population policy was announced. Three main strategies are being used:

a) making a greater impact on the poorer urban areas;
b) enlisting the co-operation of the private sector;
c) strengthening family planning in the rural areas, by associating it with the community development movement; and
d) strengthening social support policies that encourage smaller families.

a) *Making a greater impact on low-income urban areas*

The Korean Family Planning Programme was somewhat unusual in its early days in that it made the main focus of its efforts the rural areas rather than the cities. The explanation seems to have been that in the towns at that time, much of the demand for contraception was then being met outside of the national programme. This situation "changed abruptly with the rapid urbanisation of recent years and the development of slum areas characterised by high fertility and lack of access to quality contraceptive services"[8]. A programme was accordingly started in 1974 to set up clinic services in low-income urban areas[9]. So far, however, it reaches only a part of the urban poor and it is recognised that there is a need for many more clinics of this kind. The rate at which they will be provided will depend, presumably, on the funds that will be made available for the purpose, once the initial foreign assistance comes to an end.

---

8. Report of the UNFPA Mission to the Government of Korea, 1972.
9. With the help partly of UNFPA, and partly of the Planned Parenthood Federation of Korea (PPFK).

b) *Co-operation with the private sector*

The Korean Family Planning Programme has from the outset worked in co-operation with the private sector (notably the PPFK) to which it entrusted responsibility for certain aspects of the national programme. The arrangement has worked well, and latterly both the Government and the PPFK have been seeking to obtain the participation of various organisations that have not been previously connected with the family planning programme, but conduct other programmes that reach large sections of the public[10].

The industrial sector offers particularly promising possibilities, both for family planning motivation and for distribution of contraceptive supplies. Not only does it include large numbers of people, but it has the great advantage of being able to bring the supplies to the client rather than hope that the client will come to obtain the supplies. The Government has recently launched a project "Family Planning in Industry"[11] (with ILO/UNFPA help), intended to reach about one-quarter of the industrial establishments in the country. It is hoped that the practice will catch on and eventually include most of the country's industrial work force. The initiative looks promising (the Fourth Plan provides for tax benefits for companies operating their own family planning campaigns). Korea introduced industrial health insurance on 1st July 1977: this calls for mandatory participation from all plants having more than 500 workers. It is to be further extended to school teachers and public employees[12]. Under this scheme, all workers and their dependents are entitled to free family planning services.

A big effort is being made to persuade both employers and the unions of the desirability of the scheme and to induce them to provide the facilities and the work-time required[13]. If it develops well, the approach through industry could have a major impact. One interesting aspect is that in addition to providing a convenient source of family planning supplies, the project undertakes motivation work among a particularly sensitive target group—namely, the young, unmarried women who constitute about 80 per cent of the total female work force. Training of motivators will accordingly form an important part of the programme.

Although only the large industrial establishments can run their own clinics, there are a number of private voluntary organisations which can distribute non-clinical contraceptives. The most important of these are the Family Planning Mothers' Clubs, an initiative of the PPFK, which combines family planning work with more general communal activities in practically all of the villages in Korea (although not all are really active). The Mothers' Clubs[14] are non-governmental organisations, run entirely by women, which provide liaison between the Government-employed field workers and the village community. Their contribution is valuable because their membership is small enough to permit personal follow-up

---

10. *Family Planning Through Non-Family Planning Organisations,* PPFK, 1975.

11. The first initiative of this kind in the Republic of Korea came from industry itself—the much admired Sam Yang Tyre Project.

12. This plan was announced by President Park in the Press Conference held on 18th January 1978.

13. The response of employers, predictably, varies considerably. Some seem to be very enthusiastic—even to the extent, in some cases, of trying to insist on sterilisation after two children—others will require more persuasion.

14. The national network of Mothers' Clubs was first established by the PPFK in 1968 to distribute contraceptives and spread the family planning message in the villages. Initially organised in one out of every three or four villages, usually at the initiative of a field worker or the village chief, they now number almost 30,000 clubs with over 750,000 members. They are vertically linked through county-level and provincial-level federations.

of each individual's contraception history and record. Up to the present time, they have been able to issue oral pills free, thanks to generous supplies provided to the Korean Government through foreign aid[15]. These stocks will shortly be used up, and in future it will be necessary to make a small charge to the client.

c) *Association of family planning with the Community Development Movement*

The association of family planning with community development (known in Korea as the "New Village Movement") is a new decision. Designed to strengthen family planning in the rural areas, the new policy envisages a comprehensive family health service, with semi-skilled personnel, at village level and (eventually) an established referral system to hospital services.

In principle, the general health care at village level is to be oriented more to environmental hygiene than curative medicine, but this may take time, as most medical training has not hitherto been oriented along those lines. The New Village Movement is generally considered a very effective "self-help" endeavour (on a voluntary basis) for the revitalisation of rural life. It has not, however, previously included family planning among its activities. To do so now will require a new type of "multi-purpose" village worker, trained to provide family planning services together with other more general activities. Some concern is already being voiced in family planning circles in Korea, lest the family planning side of the work be held up while the new type of worker is still being trained. Most people agree, however, that integrating family planning with general village development could provide a great stimulus to family planning practice in the countryside, where there are still too many villages which are doctorless and too few field workers to reach all areas[16].

The need to train more multi-purpose health workers remains a constant theme of Government planning. Para-medical health workers at various levels are likely to be required in increasing numbers as the programme simultaneously extends in the many different directions envisaged. The main problem, however, is less that of training than of incentives, qualified personnel generally preferring to work anywhere than in the countryside. The Government has made a start on this problem by adopting a policy of salary differentials for doctors serving in the countryside. To extend the policy to the various levels of para-medical workers also, would impose a heavy budgetary burden. SIDA at one time proposed an aid-financed salary supplement for rural medical workers, but both sides eventually decided that it was not feasible.

These practical problems will not be easy of solution. Nevertheless, the strategy of linking family planning with the community development movement is particularly interesting as being one of the few cases where an "integrated" *programme* approach is envisaged. The whole philosophy of the new population policy of the Korean Government is, of course, predicated upon an "integrated" approach—in the sense that it links population problems to a more equitable social development of the country. The integrated approach has now also begun to be reflected in some of the proposals for *implementing* the policy. For example, in August 1977, the Government combined the Family Planning Mothers' Clubs with the New Village Women's Clubs. Although this step is expected to contribute to an integrated approach to comprehensive community development,

15. Primarily SIDA and US AID.
16. PPFK estimates that the establishment of contraceptive supply points through non-medical personnel for easy accessibility can raise the level of family planning practice by as much as 60 per cent.

a considerable amount of time and effort will be necessary for training, supervising and co-ordinating the clubs.

d) *Strengthening social support policies that encourage smaller families*

Since 1974 the Government has enacted a number of measures to encourage people to have smaller families and to adopt family planning methods, especially sterilisation. To combat the preference for sons, a principal cause of large families, it was made possible for daughters as well as sons to inherit their parents' property. To discourage large families still further, income tax reliefs were limited to two children only.

Incentives and disincentives to encourage family planning include tax reliefs for companies furnishing contraceptive services to employees, preference in the allocation of public housing for acceptors of sterilisation with fewer than two children, and to encourage sterilisation, compensation for loss of earnings for low-income acceptors. Additional measures of this type are under consideration.

2. POPULATION EDUCATION

a) *In-school*

The Republic of Korea, like many other countries at the present time, is exploring the possibilities opening up through population education. Population education presupposes that awareness of the implications of population growth—on the personal, the family and the social levels—can be conveyed through lessons in geography, history, science, mathematics, etc.

A start is being made[17] to prepare curricula for this purpose suitable for elementary, middle and high school levels, teachers are being trained in its use, and the results are being carefully tested at every stage. Nothing has yet been done in respect of education for the very young, but the Government would like to start working on material for kindergarten teaching also, if outside experience were available to assist. At the other end of the scale, the universities have begun to run a few courses on particular aspects of the population problem (e.g., Population and Women's Status in the Future, Population and Society, etc.).

A plan to extend population education to the educational system of the whole country began in 1977. In order to implement this plan, the Korean Education Development Institute (KEDI) is presently conducting a series of training courses for selected teachers of elementary, middle and high school levels. Actual education is planned to start in high schools in 1978, in middle schools in 1979, and in elementary schools in 1980. The Government has given ample budgetary support, but is hoping for a continuation of foreign aid (population education is one of the few areas where Korean officials indicated that they would like expert advice from resident consultants). At present, it looks unlikely that the current foreign aid contribution will be extended beyond the preparatory stage for which it was intended[18]. In practice, however, the preparatory stage is likely to be a long-continuing process and a very costly one, and although there will be need for foreign expertise, the bulk of the costs will be for recurrent expenditures (text-books, teacher-training, etc.). Some officials are already worried that foreign aid will not be available to assist the follow-through.

---

17. The Ministry of Education has entrusted the task to the Korean Educational Development Institute—a project assisted by UNFPA and the Rockefeller Foundation.
18. Only UNFPA assistance for the "pre-service" training for prospective teachers is to last through 1980.

b) *Out-of-school*

Population education out-of-school—part of what is now termed "Information, Education and Communication" (IEC)—is not, of course, new. Activities seeking to "reach into the minds of selected audiences for the purpose of achieving awareness, acceptance and adoption of effective family planning measures"[19] have been going on for years in many different contexts, using a variety of media, methods and approaches. As part of its comprehensive attack on the population problem, the Government would like to see these activities strengthened.

IEC activities include family planning motivation among selected groups and institutions, some of them on an almost person-to-person basis (e.g., the Village Mothers' Clubs). They include also public campaigns addressed to a much larger audience, usually to put across a more general message (e.g., the two-child family norm, the idea that girls are as desirable as offspring as boys, etc.), and making use of the mass media. In both types of activity, the appeal is primarily to the young—the parents of tomorrow, or young couples whose families have not yet reached the desired size. This is in contrast to the earlier days of the National Family Planning Programme, when IEC was mainly directed towards women over 35 or those who already had five children or more. Special efforts are accordingly being made to reach the young wherever they are likely to be grouped in large numbers (the Army, the Homeland Reserve Force, teachers' training institutions, and, as already noted, the factories).

There are now a variety of private initiatives designed to promulgate family planning and the small family message. (The family-size message has shifted since 1970 from the original "Have a proper number of children and bring them up well", to "Daughter or son: stop at two and bring them up well".) The boldest of these initiatives was undoubtedly the campaign organised by the Korean Federation of Housewives' Clubs, which, in preparation for Bucharest, sought to make 1974 "No Pregnancy Year" in Korea[20]. The results in terms of births averted may not have been all that significant—but it performed a useful function by creating greater awareness of family planning among widely different sections of the population. It is interesting also as a response to the World Population Conference on a popular rather than a government level.

3. PLANNED EMIGRATION

Emigration from the Republic of Korea has been proceeding on a small scale for many years. The new population policy seeks to organise this flow as an additional means of keeping the national population down to an economically-acceptable size.

Whereas emigration has hitherto been mostly that of individuals, the Government is hoping to make country-to-country agreements to regulate the flow. Present plans envisage the emigration of 0.18 per cent of the population each year[21], some of which will be permanent and some on a contractual basis. It is

---

19. PPFK, *op. cit.* PPFK is responsible for much IEC work on behalf of the Government (the message is likely to be better received if the government-inspiration is not too plainly apparent). The Korean Institute for Research in the Behavioural Sciences has played a part in research and development for population education out-of-school on an experimental basis.
20. Assisted by a grant from the Asia Foundation. With a second grant from the same source, the ladies went on to declare 1975 the "Year of More Male Contraception". They have also been influential in persuading the Government to withdraw income tax concessions after the third child.
21. Working Group for Population Planning, Economic Planning Board, *The Fourth Five-Year Economic Development Plan: Population, Employment and Manpower Development Plan (1977-1981)*, December 1976, p. 23.

expected that the flow will not only include the highly-educated and skilled emigrants, as in the past, but the less-skilled also, and it is proposed to arrange special training for the latter to meet the needs of the receiving countries. The chief destinations of Korean emigrants have hitherto been the United States, Canada and the South American countries. Now it is hoped that the Middle East oil countries may open up new possibilities.

The Korean Authorities do not fear that encouraging emigration may lead to a serious brain-drain. They feel that their highly-educated nation can absorb the loss. Also, they have demonstrated (through the experience of the Korean Development Institute) that when it is possible to offer sufficiently interesting professional responsibilities and sufficiently attractive financial prospects (contributed in large part by outside finance), a brain-drain—however long it may last and at whatever level—does not have to be irreversible.

4. RAISING THE STATUS OF WOMEN

That Korean women have remained singularly disadvantaged socially, economically and legally, despite the country's otherwise remarkably modern visage is a much-discussed feature of present-day Korean society. The Government has decided to tackle this issue as part of its new population policy—partly as a means of combatting the traditional son-preference, but also because of the new concern with social justice in official thinking. ("Inequality is a problem in itself".)

The immediate field of attack is the legal aspect—specifically, the complex of "Family Laws" which discriminates heavily against women in matters of inheritance, property, divorce, education of children and even the transmission of the family name. Due in part to the efforts of a nascent movement of organised solidarity among a small educated feminist elite, in 1977 the Korean National Assembly revised these laws so as to give women more equal treatment.

On the economic front, the position is more difficult, as the Government recognises, since the prejudices are more psychological than legal or institutional. Educating the employers—and often the workers—is the first requirement.

5. DISPERSAL OF LARGE URBAN POPULATIONS

Spatial redistribution is no new idea in Korea, but it is given a new priority at the present time, as is attested by the designation of a First Minister Without Portfolio for this responsibility.

The chief need for redistribution arises in respect of the capital city Seoul, the main centre of government, trade, industry and culture[22]. It is thought that dispersion of some of these activities would tend to reduce inequalities between regions, ease urban congestion in Seoul, and possibly help to reduce fertility by expanding the area of "modernising" influences.

How best to do this has yet to be worked out. The first task must be the dispersal of economic activity and this must be followed by good quality social facilities, and particularly good schools—a priority for Korea's education-oriented society. The Government is aware of the complexity of the problems involved and is keen to learn from the experiences of new towns, industrial estates and regional development projects in other countries. A start has already been made. In 1977, the Government announced its intention to construct the new provisional administrative capital in a less densely populated area and is offering inducements to industries, schools, etc., to establish themselves in rural areas.

---

22. Seoul accounts for 60 per cent of total college enrolment in the Republic of Korea.

GOVERNMENT POLICIES AFFECTING POPULATION INDIRECTLY

In the Republic of Korea, many government programmes in a number of different sectors, which might have an indirect effect on population, are themselves part of the national population policy. In addition, some other activities proposed under the Fourth Plan will have some indirect impact on population, albeit less significantly than those included in the comprehensive package of measures envisaged in the Government's present population policy. Most of these other activities are attempts to give practical effect to the new concern with social welfare and greater equality.

While the first three Plans were concerned primarily with economic growth, the Fourth emphasizes social welfare[23]. As part of this policy, therefore, the Government is introducing health insurance, welfare benefits, fiscal reforms, special hospital care and food programmes for the needy, and other measures calculated to bring about a more equitable distribution of income and greater social justice. (Improving the status of women can be considered also in this light.) The exact programmes, in most cases, have already been formulated[24].

THE ADMINISTRATION OF POPULATION ACTIVITIES

At the beginning of 1976, the Government announced the creation of a new body to formulate population policy in the different sectors of the economy and to co-ordinate it at the highest level. The National Population Policy Deliberation Committee (NPPDC) is chaired by the Deputy Prime Minister in charge of the Economic Planning Board, and its Deputy Chairman is the Minister of Public Health and Social Affairs. Its members include the heads of most of the major sector ministries and other officials of Government[25].

The creation of the new Committee and the publicity attending its first meeting may be considered as an indication of the new importance that the Government now attributes to population problems. Most of the separate elements of the Government's "new population policy" had been started before NPPDC was created. What is new is partly the determination to make them effective and, even more significantly, the idea that they should be treated as a single multi-faceted effort. The creation of the Deliberation Committee is intended to give the notion of "integrated approach" the necessary structural support.

The creation of co-ordinating machinery, even at the very highest level, does not, of course, necessarily ensure that the principle of an integrated approach will be effectively translated into genuine co-ordinated policies and programmes (ministers tend to have other pre-occupations, find it difficult to attend meetings, etc.). In the Korean case, however, co-ordination will be reinforced by means of a Working Group (chaired by the Deputy Minister of the Economic Planning

---

23. Which, thanks to the economic progress of past years, the Government now feels it can afford.

24. For example, the Government provided free medical services to a total of 4.5 million welfare recipients and low-income people in 1977.

25. a) Ministers of: Public Health and Social Affairs, Home Affairs, Finance, Education, Justice, Construction, Culture and Public Information, and the First and Second Ministers Without Portfolio;

b) Mayor of Seoul City, First Economic Secretary to the President, and Director of the General Office of Administrative Co-ordination of the Prime Minister; and

c) Selected experts.

Board) set up to provide regular and institutional liaison between planning experts and the nation's policy-makers. The first task of this Group is to study the implications of various elements of the population policy and make recommendations to the NPPDC. The Korean Development Institute[26] serves as Secretariat to the NPPDC and its Working Group. Plans and programmes approved by the NPPDC have been incorporated in the Fourth Plan. It is envisaged, however, that this process of study, consultation and recommendation will be a continuing feature of government, to permit continuous readjustment of the Plan.

Responsibility for implementing the various elements of the national population policy is split up among the various Departments concerned, with the Economic Planning Board having overall financial responsibility. There are thus, in effect, two influences making for a real co-ordination of population policy and action under the present structure: at the level of policy formulation through the specially-created NPPDC, and as part of the normal functioning of the administration through the Economic Planning Board, which has the final word on all programmes because of its budgetary role.

POPULATION ASSISTANCE

The Republic of Korea has received considerable aid from the donor community since the start of the National Family Planning Programme[27]. The flow of population assistance, however, has been greatly reduced during the past year or so and it looks as though in the future South Korea will figure as a minor recipient only[28].

At the moment, it is too early to see how the situation will develop when the major donors have completed their scheduled phasing-out[29]. It will be tempting for the Government to seek alternative sources of aid (as they successfully did for the supplies of oral pills). Another possibility would be to accept population assistance in the form of loans instead of, as previously, on grant terms. (US AID is now providing all its assistance to the Republic of Korea in the form of soft loans.)[30]

It is just possible, however, that the very nature of the Republic of Korea's new comprehensive population policy will provide, to some extent at least, its own solution. Donors of aid who feel that it no longer needs "population assistance" as in the past, might still agree to provide aid for projects to relieve urban congestion, to train potential emigrants, improve the rural health infrastructure— all of which are now elements of the national population policy.

---

26. Which receives assistance for the purpose from UNFPA.

27. According to an *unofficial* source, approximately $ 20 million were donated by a variety of foreign agencies from 1962 through to 1977.

28. The explanation would seem to be in part the very vigour of the Korean Programme, which makes donors feel that scarce assistance funds should rather be applied to needier and less advanced recipients. The strength of the national economy is another factor reinforcing this view.

29. UNFPA's $ 6 million assistance to South Korea ends 1977: it is not yet clear what degree of help may be forthcoming thereafter. US AID had announced that it would phase out completely in 1976 (although there will be some population assistance from other US sources); SIDA, which had earlier provided the entire supply of oral pills, had already ceased to do so in 1973, and US AID was persuaded to replace them as source of supply for a further two years.

30. US AID has currently a $ 5 million loan at 3 per cent to develop low-cost health services.

For the first ten years of the National Population Programme, the main focus of assistance effort was fertility reduction—both the donor community and the host country thought of population programmes primarily in these terms. The aid projects started or agreed within the past year or so, however, indicate a broadening of approach, and an interest in innovative programmes (e.g., family planning in industry, population education). Nonetheless, the Government still hopes to receive a certain amount of assistance for straight family planning activities (e.g., laparoscopic equipment for female sterilisation and training in its use). The approaching end of the present US AID-supported programme will not end the need for such assistance.

The Republic of Korea has no hesitation about continuing to seek foreign aid for its population programmes. When it feels there are gaps in national experience, foreign advisers are still desired (in some cases, even on a resident basis, e.g., in the field of population education), and fellowships for study abroad, still more so.

In the field of research, the interest is more qualified. Korean research institutions sometimes say that they would be pleased to consider institution-to-institution co-operation. There seems, however, to be considerable apprehension that the foreign institution will try to impose its own research priorities, while those of the host institution fail to get financing. This seems to have been a not uncommon experience in the past.

The main concern of the Korean Authorities at the present time regarding population assistance is that the donors will withdraw their support from the innovatory-type projects that they have helped launch, before the projects are sufficiently established to continue on their own momentum (e.g., low-income area urban clinics, family planning in industry). The concern is understandable, but the prime requirement for the continuance of such activities is budgetary support for current operating expenses—not normally considered a function of foreign aid in the case of a country with a healthy economy. The use of foreign aid funds for these purposes requires that the donors' procedures are flexible, and do not involve cumbersome reporting and accounting procedures which can hold up the flow of funds. On the other hand, continuing foreign support can be a means of developing a promising initiative and extending it to other parts of the country more quickly than the Government can afford to do. The problem is one of opportunity-cost for the donors in the use of scarce aid resources.

PHILIPPINES

Total population[1]	44,437,000
Population under age 20[1]	56.3 %
Population density per sq. km[1]	148
Rate of growth[1]	3.01 %
Crude birth rate (per thousand)[1]	41.2
Crude death rate (per thousand)[1]	9.1
Life expectancy (total)[1]	60.7 years
Per capita national income (1975)[2]	$325
Literacy rate[3]	87 %

Sources:
1. UNFPA, *Inventory of Population Projects 1975-76.*
2. U.N., *Statistical Yearbook,* 1976.
3. IBRD, *Comparative Education Indicators,* 1978.

INTRODUCTION

At the time of Bucharest, the Philippines had barely three years experience of official population policies and of Government-sponsored programmes to implement them. Family planning activities had been operating in the Philippines under private auspices since the mid-1960s, but although President Marcos had signed the U.N. Declaration on Population in 1967[1], practically no official support was provided for these private initiatives. By 1970, however, the pressures implied for the country's future economic and social development by a rate of population growth that was currently among the highest in the world (over 3 per cent), and which threatened to double the population of the country in only 23 years, could no longer be ignored. The Government of this Catholic Asian country was obliged to adopt family planning as a national population policy.

In the event, the major constraint to the effectiveness of the Government's programme has been less the attitude of the Church than that of the people. By culture and tradition, the Filipinos would seem to be markedly pre-disposed to large families and pronatalist attitudes. Despite the sharp reduction in mortality rates, and the visibly increased infant survival rates, completed family size in the Philippines is still one of the highest in the world (average 6 children in 1970)[2]. Given this situation, it was inevitable that the Philippine Authorities,

---

1. "... The population problem must be recognised as a principal element in long-range national planning, if governments are to achieve their economic goals and fulfill the aspirations of the people."
2. National Demographic Survey, 1973.

quite independently of Bucharest, would come to recognise that family planning services alone were not enough and that some "wider" approach to the problem was required.

NATIONAL POPULATION POLICIES

Since 1970 the Philippine Government has pursued an official policy of slowing down the country's rate of population growth. The previous year, President Marcos had set up a Commission on Population (known as "POP-COM") to study the problems posed by the rapid increase of the population and to propose measures to deal with it. The Commission accordingly recommended that "the Government should actively intervene in reducing population growth through establishing family planning programmes, through legal and administrative measures that bring about a balance between family size and social and economic goals, and through population education on the adverse effects of unlimited population growth on family life and national welfare". The President responded by empowering the Commission to direct and co-ordinate population activities as an integral part of overall development strategy. In Fiscal Year 1971-1972, the Government appropriated funds for population activities for the first time. Until then, family planning programmes in the Philippines had been largely supported by foreign aid.

The Philippine Authorities describe the national Population Programme as being based on four broad principles: non-coercion, integration, multi-agency participation, and cooperation with the private sector. Thus, for example, although the Government has made strenuous efforts to change attitudes in favour of smaller family size, it has made a point of leaving the individual couple to decide how many children it considers appropriate.

The Commission on Population declared at the outset that it saw the population problem as "multi-dimensional and multi-faceted in nature", requiring simultaneous efforts in four areas: "provision of clinical services; training, information, education and communication; and research and development"[3]. In all four areas, a wide variety of non-governmental organisations are involved, as well as the Government itself. POPCOM has the task of co-ordinating their various activities, a mandate that is far from easy, not only because of the number of bodies involved but because they tend to have very different approaches.

The National Family Planning Programme set itself the goal of bringing down the population growth rate from something over 3 per cent per year in 1970 to 2.5 per cent by mid-1977. The Population Institute of the University of the Philippines estimates that during the period 1970-1975, the annual growth rate averaged 2.8 per cent, having declined to about 2.6 per cent by the beginning of 1975[4]. In 1976, a National Acceptor Survey estimated that contraceptive use had risen from 12 per cent of MWRA[5] in 1970 to 25 per cent in 1976 (programme methods: 32 per cent all methods). The current target is to reduce the population growth rate by an average of 1 per cent per year.

The actual delivery of family planning services under the national Programme is split between the Department of Health and a wide range of private bodies. The latter are likely to continue to play an important role in the

---

3. The Four-Year Development Plan 1974-1977, Chapter 16, "Family Planning".
4. Based on preliminary 1975 census figures.
5. Married Women of Reproductive Age.

Programme for some years to come. However, now that the Government is beginning to exercise an increasingly active role itself, some re-allocation of tasks is taking place. On the service delivery side, the Government is seeking to assume the main responsibility for the rural areas, leaving the private organisations to provide most of the services needed in the towns. The Family Planning Organisation of the Philippines (FPOP)[6] has accordingly passed some of its clinics over to the Department of Health. By the end of 1977, family planning was being dispensed by 2000 Government health facilities against 500 private family planning clinics, plus the family planning facilities provided by industrial establishments.

The private sector is also very important in training programmes of various kinds and in the promotion of a wide range of innovative activities in the population field, where the flexibility of private bodies is an advantage[7].

The financial commitment of the Philippine Government to population activities has increased since the Programme began. This is partly a natural consequence of the growing momentum of the national Programme, but partly also to compensate for the declining contribution of foreign aid. In 1974, the Philippines received a larger volume of population assistance than any other developing country. Much of this is now being phased out. This means that a considerable increase will be needed in the Government's contribution to population programmes over the next few years, simply in order to maintain them at their current level of activity. The Government has stated its intention to provide the necessary budgetary support on an annually increasing basis, as the aid input diminishes. In 1975-1976, of the total spent on population activities in the Philippines from all sources (Government, private funds and aid), the Government contributed 55 per cent.

DEVELOPMENTS IN POPULATION POLICY SINCE BUCHAREST

In considering developments in population policy in the Philippines since Bucharest, it is probably more accurate to speak of policies than a single policy. There are, in fact, at least three separate strands of policy discernible in the population programmes that are taking place in the Philippines at the present time.

The first is the straight family planning approach—that adopted by a number of private bodies before the Government entered the field, and still continuing. The second is the health approach. The Department of Health sees family planning as part of a general health concern—notably as one means of helping reduce the high rate of infant mortality (particularly in the rural areas). The third may be broadly termed the "development" approach and is gaining increasing favour with the Commission on Population.

In the period since Bucharest, POPCOM has been experimenting with various ways in which population activities can be linked with other aspects of development at the local level. Their approach is based on the belief:

a) that people are more likely to be drawn to accept family planning if it is offered in association with the satisfaction of other needs of

---

6. An affiliate of the IPPF.
7. For example, in 1976 the Family Planning Organisation of the Philippines organised a seminar on abortion, a subject which would have been impossible for an official body to handle.

more immediate urgency (e.g. drinking water, roads, fertilisers, agricultural credit, etc.);

    b)   that effective family planning motivation depends on a rising standard of living;

    c)   that the initiative and responsibility for determining what the local needs are (including family planning) and for taking steps to meet them should rest with the local authorities.

The various initiatives whereby POPCOM is trying to link population and development are therefore associated with a policy of progressive *decentralisation* of population activities.

PRINCIPAL STRATEGIES
FOR IMPLEMENTING POPULATION PROGRAMMES

The principal population strategies which have come to the fore in the Philippines in the period since Bucharest clearly reflect the diversity of approaches noted above, as well as the unusually wide range of bodies, public and private, that are participating in population work. The strategies may briefly be described as follows:

1. Bringing population into development by using local government structures ;
2. Improving service facilities in the rural areas;
3. Intensification of IEC activities;
4. Legal measures and incentives to encourage smaller families;
5. Active involvement of industry, banking, etc. in the promotion of family planning;
6. Greater emphasis on sterilisation.

1. POPULATION AND DEVELOPMENT

In 1975, the Commission on Population made the first move to intensify population work in the rural areas by means of assigning a special population staff to the local government authorities at the various levels and giving responsibility for their work to the local government authorities concerned.

The first attempts to implement this approach was through six pilot projects ("Total Integrated Development Approach"). A second scheme was worked out a year later with US support. It similarly seeks to achieve an effective increase in family planning practice in the rural areas[8], partly by active motivation efforts and improved family planning supply and delivery, and partly by linking population work to the existing community structures and their various local activities at the village level ("baranguay committees"), and similarly at the city and province levels.

The principal agents of the programme are some 3,000 specially trained[9] "Full-Time Outreach Workers" (FTOWs). They are chosen from the local village community and each serves a clientele of about 2,000 married couples of reproductive age, equivalent to roughly 16,000 people). One of their principal

---

    8.   Together with other Philippine population efforts, the target of the Family Planning Outreach Project is to raise the percentage of couples practising family planning from the present approximately 24 per cent to 35 per cent by the end of the project period (1980).

    9.   Three weeks training.

tasks is family planning motivation. On the supply side, they are serviced by abundant "barangay (village) supply points" at which volunteer workers distribute free oral pills and condoms to their neighbours and maintain simple records. (The supplies are provided by US AID.) It is significant, however, that these FTOWs are not purely family planning workers but have a range of other activities covering health, nutrition, education, agricultural extension, etc.— according to the interests of the particular local community and their personal expertise and background. They are, therefore, multi-purpose workers, but their prime responsibility is their population work.

A similar association of family planning with other local development concerns is to be effected at a higher administrative level by the introduction of City and Provincial Population Officers into the relevant local government structures. These Officers, like the FTOWs, are to be *local government employees,* and it is the local government authority concerned that has the responsibility for supervising their work. Thus it is the local government authorities that are now being made responsible for the implementation of the National Family Planning Outreach Project.

2. IMPROVING FAMILY PLANNING SERVICE FACILITIES IN THE RURAL AREAS

Of the eligible women still to be reached by family planning services, over 70 per cent are rural. They are a more difficult target group than an urban population, partly because of cultural factors and partly because of the physical distances from the nearest family planning services. (When it is remembered that the Philippines consists of over seven thousand separate islands, it becomes obvious that some of the rural areas are very remote indeed.)

The Department of Health, which includes family planning as part of the health service (health infrastructure and personnel are considered as "multi-purpose"), is currently engaged in a programme to strengthen the rural health services. Assisted by a major loan from the World Bank, the programme envisages some increase in the number of higher-level health facilities, but the major emphasis is on making better use of existing facilities and supplementing them by the creation of many more health centres at the village level. It is accordingly planned to more than double the number of village health centres (from 1,500 to 3,500 by 1980), and to increase their effective coverage by means of mobile health vans. An intensive programme of training and re-training of nurses and midwives is under way. The objective is to have 9,000 village health centres staffed by qualified midwives by 1980 (in recognition of the practical difficulties of getting qualified doctors to serve in the rural areas). The midwives will have been trained to do IUD insertion and to prescribe oral pills.

3. GREATER IEC EFFORT

Both the Government and the voluntary organisations doing family planning work recognise the particular need for family planning motivation in the Philippines, given the traditional desire for large families. (The first efforts at population education in the Philippines go back to 1970, with foreign aid provided under Colombo Plan auspices.)

The Commission on Population, in collaboration with the Department of Education and Culture, has developed an intensive programme of population education in schools which is intended for inclusion in the school curriculum throughout the country. Work is currently underway on curriculum development and teacher training[10], with the support of the UNFPA, the Pathfinder Fund and the East-West Center. The government is devoting very considerable attention to the programme, which covers health education, nutrition, home economics, etc., starting at kindergarten level and proceeding up the school, until, for adolescents, "population education" takes the form of straight sex education.

Information and communication activities in order to promote population education out-of-school in the Philippines cover a wide range of media, methods and types of programme. They also cover a variety of participating institutions, governmental (e.g. the National Media Production Centre, the University of the Philippines, the Department of Social Welfare) and private (including commercial enterprises).

In 1975, the Population Centre Foundation[11] launched a commercial contraceptive distribution project[12] in Greater Manila, accompanied by a massive promotional campaign in the press. (The opposition of certain Catholic groups in open debates in the press and on television provided valuable additional publicity.)

The Filippino public, by virtue of their literacy and ownership of radio and television sets, would seem particularly suitable for the mass-media approach. Some people, however, are of the view that the impact of these methods is too generalised and diffuse, and that person-to-person communication is still the most effective method of family planning persuasion.

4. LEGAL MEASURES AND INCENTIVES TO ENCOURAGE SMALLER FAMILIES

Considerable publicity was given to a new ruling by the Philippine Government in the latter part of 1976 that marriage licenses can only be issued after prior instruction in family planning and responsible parenthood. More quietly perhaps, legal measures are increasingly being used to provide incentives for smaller families (resettlement housing schemes, maternity leave benefits which stop at the fourth child, income tax exemptions, etc.).

The Government has not to date tried to get across any "ideal" family size, but has hoped that couples would decide that four or fewer was sufficient. It is however, now considering officially advocating three children as the ideal family norm and the figure may be reduced to two in the future. The adoption of such norms would, of course, be voluntary.

5. PARTICIPATION OF INDUSTRY, BANKING, ETC. IN FAMILY PLANNING PROMOTION

The National Family Planning Programme in the Philippines enjoys close collaboration from the industrial sector and from the Department of Labour. Employers of more than 200 persons are required to provide family planning information and services. The obligations on the employer are now considerable —to train clinic personnel, to provide time off for clinic attendance, lectures, etc., and to include family planning in existing health and educational programmes. (Visiting teams from the Department of Labour are to inspect for compliance.)

---

10. Starting in the school year 1975-1976, all educational institutions whose faculty members received population education training from the Department of Education and Culture were authorised to offer an under-graduate course in population education.
11. A semi-official body established by the First Lady, Mrs. Imelda Romualdo-Marcos, in 1972.
12. Commercial channels can now be used to dispense contraceptives previously restricted to pharmacies and drug stores. A medical prescription is no longer needed for contraceptive pills.

The intention (supported by UNFPA) is to bring family planning to all organised workers, not only in industry, but in agricultural industries, mining, the plantations, etc. With the collaboration of the FPOP, seminars are organised to encourage the management to set up the necessary services. Where these arrangements are already operating, the contraceptives are supplied free by POPCOM. The intention is to pass on this obligation eventually to the enterprises themselves.

The Department of Labour has given further striking proof of its support for family planning by a requirement that all collective bargaining agreements must now include a provision for family planning services to be made available for all workers covered by the agreement.

The banks are also being mobilised to support the Government's family planning programme by asking them to give preference to loan requests from people with small families. It is hoped that this practice will prove a particularly valuable incentive to family planning among rural communities.

6. GREATER EMPHASIS ON STERILISATION

It has for some time been apparent to the Philippine Authorities that the earlier concentration on acceptance rates was giving misleading impressions as to the real coverage and effectiveness of the programme. In particular, drop-out rates were disturbingly high and there seemed to be a growing shift towards the less effective methods of contraceptive protection. (Although the Philippine Government has prided itself on its "cafeteria approach"[13], the availability of all kinds of contraceptive methods is not all advantage.)

The present emphasis is therefore on continuance rather than acceptance, and on sterilisation as the permanent form of contraceptive protection. The first sterilisation drive started in 1973 under the auspices of the voluntary organisations[14]. In 1976, social security benefits were extended to cover sterilisation.

ACTIVITIES AFFECTING POPULATION INDIRECTLY

At the macro-level, Philippine planning, while keenly aware of the effects of population on development, has not so far seemed to reflect particular concern with the effects of development on population[15]. However, some slight moves in this direction have recently been made. The current Development Plan, for example, explicity states the close inter-relationship between population, nutrition and health.

The Government is presently promoting nutrition programmes among the specially vulnerable groups (infants, young children and nursing mothers) and these may be expected to have an important influence on fertility, even if they were not undertaken with this particular purpose as the prime objective. The programmes include nutrition education, the development of cheaper weaning foods and the promotion of vegetable cultivation to remedy vitamin and mineral

---

13. Everything except abortion.
14. One of which is a non-Catholic Church Group, the Iglesia ni Cristo, which not only preached family planning from the pulpit but also organised mobile sterilisation camps, with aid from the Family Planning International Assistance of America (FPIA).
15. This may change in the next Plan. The ILO is currently undertaking a planning exercise on behalf of the Philippine Government (the Bachue Model) which attempts to demonstrate the likely outcome in terms of population growth and the satisfaction of basic needs of different hypotheses regarding economic development and social policies.

deficiences. In addition, the First Lady has her own programme "Project Compassion", which links nutrition, family planning, the green revolution and the environment. (Support at this level is one of the most effective methods for creating a national awareness of the inter-relationship between these three factors and of the necessity to tackle them by an integrated approach[16].) A similar movement, headed by the President himself, is directed at the nation's youth.

Although few development programmes have been designed specifically for their likely effects on population growth, it can be expected that any measures which succeed in raising the standard of living of the very poor will eventually accelerate the decline in fertility. Philippine society shows wide disparities between rich and poor. The rapid growth of the population has aggravated the situation by increasing the numbers of landless labourers and homeless squatters. A start has been made with agrarian reforms, credit for poor farmers, the development of cottage industries, etc., to mitigate these problems. But it is unemployment that looms as the most serious threat, and firm proposals for employment creation are still modest in scope[17]. The generation of employment is, however, one of the principal objectives of short, medium and long-term national development plans.

An important objective of current Philippine planning is the dispersion of industry so as to lessen the importance of Metropolitan Manila, with its almost five million people, by creating new poles of industrial development in other parts of the country. At present, however, problems of the geographical distribution of the population are not considered as part of the national "population policy".

STRUCTURES FOR IMPLEMENTING FAMILY PLANNING POLICIES

A particular feature of population activities in the Philippines is the very large number of organisations involved. Some 40 organisations, governmental and private, participate in the national family planning programme. For example, the body responsible for community development—the Presidential Arm for Community Development (PACD)—was already including family planning motivation among its appointed tasks, and working in co-operation with the Family Planning Organisation of the Philippines before 1971. This body, which shortly after became the Department of Local Government and Community Development, has continued to be associated with family planning in the local areas and is closely involved in the National Family Planning Outreach Project.

Responsibility for co-ordinating the family planning activities of these many different bodies is the task of the Population Commission of the Philippines. Placed directly under the Office of the President, its mandate is to formulate national population policy, approve and co-ordinate project proposals and report annually to the President on the progress achieved. Harmonisation of population policies with national development plans in other sectors is the task not of POPCOM but of the National Economic Development Authority (NEDA).

POPCOM was also given responsibility for specific population activities (clinic services, training, IEC, research and evaluation). While this did not, of

---

16. "Family Development Councils" mobilising local government and community effort, aim to improve nutrition for over 400,000 pre-school age children, improve food output, ensure clean water and proper waste disposal, and double the rate of family planning acceptances from the present estimate of 15 per cent of eligible women.

17. World Bank: *The Philippines Priorities and Prospects for Development*, Basic Economic Report, May 1976.

itself, confer an operational role, it brought it much nearer to actual operational responsibility than might be expected of a policy-making and co-ordinating body.

Latterly, two trends are discernible in POPCOM's policies. One, as noted above, is a move to decentralise responsibility for carrying out and supervising its population programmes. The second seems to be a desire to play a more direct operational role, rather than to continue as policy-maker and co-ordinator for a host of other bodies. The National Family Planning Outreach Project may be seen as an expression of this trend.

ASSISTANCE FOR POPULATION ACTIVITIES

Both the form and the substance of the foreign aid provided by the Philippines for population activities has begun to change in the period since Bucharest. The Philippine Authorities and the donor agencies have been reviewing their respective policies and programmes with a view to bringing them closer into line with the realities of the present situation. Thus POPCOM, NEDA, and the Population Center Foundation have reappraised their priorities for population assistance. On the donor side, US AID and UNFPA have carried out a similar re-appraisal[18].

PRIORITIES FOR POPULATION ASSISTANCE

POPCOM has identified its priorities as: innovative activities; training of personnel for outreach activities; community-based distribution; sterilisation, and training of nurses and midwives in IUD insertion.

Within these areas, there is need for fellowships, research assistance (both financial and conceptual) and for advice on designing evaluation. Foreign personnel are no longer required, except for short and highly specialised missions. Strengthening of infrastructure should take the form of training and equipment rather than construction. As foreign aid will no longer supply condoms, it is hoped that it will help to establish local production.

It is hoped also that aid will be forthcoming to cover salaries and incentives for the personnel working on experimental population activities. The need for aid to cover staff costs ("good people can only be attracted through good salaries") poses a problem for many donors who may be willing to assist innovative activities but are often not prepared to follow through much beyond the pilot stage, on the grounds that operating costs should be progressively assumed by the national authorities concerned.

ATTITUDES TO PAST POPULATION ASSISTANCE

The Philippine Authorities commented that some of the population assistance they have received in the past has been "tied" as regards foreign personnel[19], and the source and even the type of contraceptive supplies[20]. The tying of aid for the purchase of contraceptive supplies has in fact largely determined the pattern of methods now in use.

---

18. US AID preceded their re-appraisal by an evaluation survey of their population programme in the Philippines: UNFPA, at the time of the Development Centre mission, was considering something of the same.

19. Some donors used to require the services of their own experts as part of the aid package.

20. Condoms from Japan are claimed to be both cheaper and more suitable than those provided under other commodity assistance.

Donors have also sometimes set rigid and unrealistic quantitative performance targets[21], and the attempt to reach such targets is liable to distort the project. This implies a real dilemma for the donors, as population assistance becomes more development-oriented and quantification of impact consequently becomes very much more difficult.

A further criticism is that some donors have assisted particular agencies directly without passing through the official Philippine bodies responsible for co-ordination of population policy (POPCOM) or external aid (NEDA). This situation, although greatly improved, still causes some concern, particularly in respect of the private agencies. The problem of co-ordination, however, is more a general one of aid administration than specific to population assistance. What is more serious is that some Philippine officials still have the feeling that it is the donors' priorities rather than those of the Government that prevail.

Even if the donor agencies do not transgress by by-passing the appropriate Philippine co-ordinating bodies, their idiosyncracies of funding criteria or policy preferences sometimes make for difficulties. For example, US AID at one time was concerned almost exclusively with family planning (it was said that projects in other sectors had to be made to look like family planning in order to quailfy for US aid). Sometimes a major donor has later reversed its declared policy (as US AID did over commodity assistance). Such shifts tend to complicate the task of forward programming.

CHANGING TRENDS IN POPULATION ASSISTANCE

The "political climate" as regards population assistance is recognised both by donors and the Philippine Authorities to have changed distinctly since the start of the Programme in 1971. The changes are recent (beginning about 1975) and reflect a new desire for "self-reliance" in population programmes (expressed as such by President Marcos), and a greatly increased interest in innovative approaches.

The nature of population assistance to the Philippines has thus largely moved away from its two initial emphases, which were institution-building and straight family planning. The former was earlier a particular favourite of the major population assistance donors[22], and the Philippine institutions which they have assisted now feel themselves well fitted to assume responsibility for the formulation both of national population policy and of the specific programmes necessary to implement it. While family planning is still, of course, the core of any population activity, it is increasingly being associated with innovative approaches or means of delivery (the Outreach Project, family planning in industry, etc.).

An important reason for the changing nature of population assistance to the Philippines at the present time is simply the shrinking of available aid funds. This of itself imposes a degree of selectivity that was not necessary in the earlier era of ample aid resources. It has led US AID to abandon straight budgetary assistance to family planning in favour of a specific project approach. The projects themselves still focus on family planning services rather than on more complex issues of social change, etc. Nonetheless, by agreeing to pick up the service delivery component of the National Family Planning Outreach Project, US AID is de facto contributing to the Philippines' most innovative population approaches[23]. Further, US AID, feeling that the Philippines is now well beyond

---

21. For example, a target decline in age-specific fertility rates over a given period.
22. POPCOM was financed by US AID and the UNFPA: the Population Center Foundation by US AID, the Rockefeller Foundation, UNFPA, the Pathfinder Fund, etc.
23. US-based universities, funded by AID, will no doubt continue to provide grant aid as in the past.

the point of take-off, is considering providing population assistance in the future on a loan rather than the traditional grant basis.

The Philippine Authorities see a particular importance in the continuation of foreign aid for population, over and above the value of the actual assistance received. In the Philippines, there is no lack of new ideas and initiative, but there is danger that such initiatives may flag if they do not get continuing national support. Foreign aid for an activity obliges the Government to put up the counterpart to the foreign input. It thus not only ensures continuation of the particular activity, but taking the programme as a whole, accelerates the effective process of its implementation. The Government, however, realises that external aid for population will eventually be phased out, and it has been providing a steadily increasing proportion of the total expenditures for population activities.

THAILAND

Total population[1]	42,093,000
Population under age 20[1]	56.8 %
Population density per sq. km.[1]	82
Rate of growth[1]	3.23 %
Crude birth rate (per thousand)[1]	41.6
Crude death rate (per thousand)[1]	9.3
Life expectancy (total)[1]	60.3 years
Per capita national income (1975)[2]	$318
Literacy rate[3]	82 %

Sources:
1. UNFPA, *Inventory of Population Projects 1975-76.*
2. U.N., *Statistical Yearbook, 1976.*
3. IBRD, *Comparative Education Indicators, 1978.*

INTRODUCTION

Thailand did not make an official entry into the field of population planning until relatively late. Although there had been some experimental family planning programmes on a limited scale, the Government did not give official support to or embark on a national programme until 1970. Nevertheless, by the time of the Bucharest Conference, Thailand was already being hailed as one of family planning's success stories.

The progress achieved has been remarkable. The national programme recruited almost 2.5 million acceptors in its first five years and trained almost 20,000 medical and paramedical personnel. The population growth rate has dropped steadily from its peak of over 3 per cent per year in 1970 to 2.5 per cent in 1976. Acceptance of family planning has increased markedly, a wide variety of contraceptive measures are available, and there is increasing demand for sterilisation.

The Thai National Family Planning Programme has several sources of strength. The integration of family planning with the health services has worked well—within the limits of the health service: outside these limits (where health service coverage is not adequate) the Ministry of Public Health (MOPH) has taken an increasingly liberal view of outside initiatives to provide family planning services. The Thai population has proved particularly receptive to family planning: the Buddhist religion is in general favourable to it (although against abortion) and the only group averse to both is the Moslem minority in the South. The Programme has been generously assisted by foreign aid: between the start

77

of the Programme and 1975, some 80 per cent of total expenditures on family planning were aid-financed, and the donor community is well pleased with the results.

The prospects for continued population decline look promising. However, as the country enters the fourth Five-Year Plan Period (FY 1977-81), the foreign aid funds available to Thailand for population activities are being sharply reduced at the very time that the scope of these activities is being considerably broadened. Unless new sources of population assistance become available, the Government will be faced with making difficult choices between expanding the badly-needed health structure and family planning delivery systems and developing some of the newer, less traditional approaches which seem to be offering promising results.

NATIONAL POPULATION POLICIES

The official decision to adopt a national population policy was taken after careful study of the likely implications, both social and economic, of a continuation of the country's high rate of population growth[1]. Economists demonstrated that the availability of arable land would be unable to keep pace with the growth of the labour force[2], that the increasing demand for food would reduce the available export surplus, and that the country would not be able to provide the school and health facilities required by ever-growing numbers of children. To these predictions had to be added other more immediate preoccupations. The disproportionate growth of the capital city and its industrial environs was bringing problems of slums, unemployment and delinquency, with its recognised potential for social unrest. In Thailand, therefore, as in many other countries of Asia, the problem posed by population growth versus resources led inevitably to family planning.

The Government accordingly accepted the necessity of slowing down the country's high rate of population growth as a pre-condition of continued economic and social development and accepted a recommendation of the National Economic and Social Development Board (NESDB) that a reduction of the population growth rate of over 3 per cent to 2.5 per cent per year be made one of the objectives of the third Five-Year Plan (FY 1972-76). Funds for family planning were included in the Plan budget, and the National Family Planning Programme was formulated and incorporated in the functions of the Ministry of Health.

In Thailand, the Government has taken the unusual step of writing population policy into the Constitution[3]. The language is significant: "Thailand will have a population policy consistent with its economic and social development, its resources and security". There is thus no permanent commitment to the goal of population *reduction*—nor to a purely quantitative interpretation of population policy, whether in the one direction or the other. Population policy must be a function of the nation's needs at any given time.

There is no doubt, however, about the Government's genuine concern about its population problem. The population policy is designed to achieve a further

---

1. In the mid-1950s, it was still the official policy of Thailand to *increase* the national population—for military and manpower reasons. A World Bank mission in 1958 recommended that the Government study the adverse implications of this trend on future economic growth. Three National Population Seminars were accordingly held between 1963 and 1968, leading in March 1970 to the Government's decision to support voluntary family planning.

2. It is estimated that the land reform scheme will use up all available land by the end of the century.

3. In 1974, following the military coup d'etat of the previous year.

decline in fertility during the Fourth Five-Year Plan (FY 1977-81). A new target of 2.1 per cent annual growth rate by 1981 has been set and backed up by substantially increased budgetary allocations. Six times as much money is allocated than under the Third Plan—a total for the whole period of 485 million bahts (approximately $26 million). In addition, the Government has received an IDA credit of $33.1 million for a family planning project which, with foreign grants, give the programme a total of 885 million bahts (approximately $47 million). This represents 0.2 per cent of the National Budget. In comparison, the proposed public health expenditure will be only three times as great as under the Third Plan—but will amount to 18,905 million bahts (approximately $1 billion) or 9.4 per cent of the total.

The Government is also giving increasing attention to the necessity to improve social conditions and to the problems caused by urban growth. An increasing awareness of the "quality" and distributive aspects of population is a feature of the normal evolution of economic and social planning, and the Thai Government already announced at Bucharest that this was its approach. However, at present, the Thai Government still makes a distinction between these concerns and the quantitative approach pursued by the National Family Planning Programme.

Thai population policy, which was still in the early stages of formulation at the time of Bucharest, has evolved since in response to experience in Thailand, but the main thrust has remained unchanged. Thai planning officials have, from the outset, recognised the inter-relationships between population and the other economic and social factors that affect the life of the nation, and the population policy of the Third Plan was predicated on them. In preparing the Fourth Plan, they have attempted to put these calculations into quantitative form. Many officials consider that in so doing, they are in fact "going beyond Bucharest".

PRINCIPAL POPULATION STRATEGIES

The various strategies adopted in Thailand for the implementation of the National Family Planning Programme have shown an unusual readiness to combine the innovative with the traditional. As the Programme has evolved, approaches have evolved also and the innovative aspects are becoming of increasing interest and importance.

At present, the Thai Government is directing its action in the population field in accordance with the following broad strategies:

1. Concentration on the rural areas by means of:
   a) extension of health infrastructure and services;
   b) greater use of auxiliary health personnel.
2. Decentralisation of family planning activities by means of:
   a) encouraging community action at the village level;
   b) increased participation of the private sector.
3. Integration of family planning with other economic and social activities.
4. Increased motivational effort through population information, communication and education.
5. Greater attention to continuation rates and contraceptive technology.

1. CONCENTRATION ON THE RURAL AREAS

Inevitably, family planning has made less progress in the countryside than in the towns. (The proportion of eligible married women practising contraception is given as 22 per cent average in the countryside as against 48 per cent in Bangkok and 41 per cent in provincial towns)[4]. The principal constraint, it is generally agreed, is the lack of facilities rather than lack of motivation[5]. Accordingly, a major effort is planned to increase the means of family planning delivery in rural areas.

a) *Extension of public health infrastructure and services*

The hard core of Thai strategy to implement the National Family Planning Programme will remain for the time being the traditional one of extending and strengthening the public health infrastructure. The Programme has from the outset been administered by the MOPH and incorporated in the MCH services. This has the advantage of economy—in that it was not necessary to set up a separate service—and in general has worked well. But the very limited geographical coverage of the public health infrastructure in the rural areas has denied the Family Planning Programme an adequate delivery outreach.

An ambitious five-year health development programme has been prepared (with WHO advice) to create new infrastructure, rationalise the use of already existing facilities, improve equipment, supplies, etc. The MCH services are to get special attention (more maternity wards, more village midwifery centres). A major training programme goes with it, involving in all 14 different categories of health workers from doctor down to village volunteer. The main focus, however, will be to build up auxiliary health capacity.

But this is clearly a long-term task. Large as the MOPH resources seem in comparison with those for Family Planning, they will still only amount to less than 10 per cent of the total budget while Education takes 20 per cent or more. Even with foreign aid to accelerate the implementation of the Plan, there will for some time to come be a continued shortage of family planning service facilities in the countryside within the national health system. Hence the continued need for alternative strategies in order to by-pass them.

b) *Greater use of auxiliary health personnel*

Thailand was one of the pioneers in the use of non-medical personnel for family planning services. The National Family Planning Programme from the outset began by recruiting two types of auxiliary personnel: "Family Planning Workers" (high-school graduates) to assist the clinics with record-keeping and some medical aspects; and "Home Visitors" to undertake family planning motivation at village level. In 1975 nurse-midwives were authorised to do IUD insertions. Now auxiliary nurse-midwives are also to be permitted to do this and a large-scale training programme is being mounted, backed by improved logistical support (supplies, vehicles[6], etc.), with the aim of making IUDs available in some 2,000 rural clinics by 1979.

---

4. Thailand: Annual Statistical Report for 1975.
5. It is estimated that while the Thai urban population (15 per cent) are well served by public, private and commercial sources of contraceptives, only 35-40 per cent of the rural population, which is largely dependent on the public health network, is covered. *Population Dynamics Quarterly*, Spring 1976.
6. Important for mobile sterilisation teams and to improve the mobility of the village midwife.

2. DECENTRALISATION OF FAMILY PLANNING ACTIVITIES

The Thai Government is increasingly taking the view that the administration cannot itself effectively carry out all the social strategies of the Development Plan. As one Thai official expressed it, "400,000 civil servants are not enough as change agents". It is accordingly turning to local communities and the private sector for help in carrying out its social development programmes.

a) *Encouraging community action at the village level*

The plan is to develop a community responsibility for family planning by building up a corps of health and family planning workers at grass-roots level. Over 22,000 village volunteers are to be selected, trained and supervised by the MOPH to diagnose and treat simple endemic diseases, recruit family planning acceptors and distribute contraceptive pills in areas beyond the reach of health centre personnel[7]. It is a bold programme, and not without numerous practical difficulties since record-keeping and supervision will put a strain on health centre staff. Nevertheless, community action in the health field has considerable appeal, partly as a practical expression of "self-help", direct action, etc., and partly as a means of expanding services at low cost. Donors have reacted enthusiastically and a number are already contributing to different aspects of the programme[8].

b) *Increased participation of the private sector*

The National Family Planning Programme in Thailand has had private participation from the outset through the activities of the Planned Parenthood Association of Thailand (PPAT), which was set up at the same time as the official Programme (1970). PPAT is largely independent of Government financing and has the advantage of being able to operate with more flexibility than the Government in organising experimental approaches and in enlisting the participation of private sector groups (e.g. industry, youth, housewives, etc.). The Government is increasingly looking upon the PPAT for the training of family planning workers in the private sector and for information activities.

The Government is also encouraging the private sector to help in delivering contraceptive supplies, particularly in the more difficult areas. The system of community-based distribution (CBD), which started independently of the Government (with IPPF financing), is becoming an important component of the National Family Planning Programme.

"Since family planning receives less than one per cent of the national budget, a commercial-based action is an obvious solution." This sentiment expressed by the organiser of Thailand's Community-Based Family Planning Services (CBFPS)[9], is endorsed by the MOPH and increasingly by the donor community also.

One advantage of CBFPS is its very wide range of outlets. The Government allows CBFPS to arrange distribution of pills as well as condoms through village stores, local schools, etc. as well as pharmacies—even when this is not in strict accordance with the law. In this way family planning supplies can be made available even in remote rural areas. CBFPS activities only covered about one-tenth of Thailand's 550 districts, but it was estimated that by mid-1976 one-quarter of the Government figure of pill acceptors—approximately 400,000—

---

7. They will receive one month's training and be expected to devote 10 per cent of their time to health and family planning activities.

8. UNFPA, IDRC (who have collaborated in the project design), US AID (who have provided the contraceptive supplies).

9. Mr. Mechai Viravaidya, Project Director, Community-Based Family Planning Service.

would be reached by these means[10]. The Government is preparing to finance the extension of these activities in two major target areas—the slum districts of Bangkok and the high-density, high-fertility North-East Region (where operations are complicated by the long-continuing state of insurgency). Both US AID and IPPF are supporting these efforts.

The varied and informal approaches taken by CBD (even though they sometimes tend to by-pass regulations) are being watched with interest by the Thai Authorities: first, because they promote increased community participation and the association of family planning with other social and economic development activities; and secondly, because as contraceptive supplies cease to be provided through foreign aid, the commercial aspect of CBFPS has obvious attractions. In 1977, the national budget paid for half the supplies used under the Programme. At present there is a small charge for contraceptives in the Ministry of Public Health clinics. It is the aim of the CBFPS Programme, however, that the small sum charged to the user, together with the profits of sundry commercial under-takings, will eventually be sufficient to "make family planning pay"[11].

3. INTEGRATION OF FAMILY PLANNING WITH OTHER SECTOR ACTIVITIES

As the Thai National Family Planning Programme has evolved, it has come to use a number of other ministries and government services in addition to the MOPH as vehicles for the provision of family planning supplies and information —some as seemingly unlikely as the Border Police and Army, for example, members of which have been trained by MOPH and PPAT and are now distributing contraceptive pills and doing motivational work.

An example of the increasing interest in integrating family planning with other social and economic development activities is provided by the Land Settlement Programmes under the Ministry of the Interior. The gradual evolution of these programmes well reflects the changes that have taken place in development approaches over the past two decades. The Land Settlement Schemes were started in the 1940s with the object of preventing the drift to the cities and were primarily economic activities. Social programmes (education, health) were added in the 1960s. Since the creation of the National Family Planning Programme, a family planning element has been included also, together with school nutrition programmes.

Although the Land Settlement Projects touch barely one per cent of the total population (80,000 families, say 400,000 people), they present an excellent example of the multi-sectoral approach. The co-ordination of the different government services concerned takes place both at central and local level, and the private sector (PPAT) is also actively involved. Some foreign aid donors (UN/ESCAP, Germany, US AID) are now showing interest in both the design and the financing of this integrated approach to rural development and population. Others, whose aid has hitherto been purely development-oriented, may learn from it to broaden their own approach[12].

Another example of the innovative and integrated approach is the joint parasite control/family planning/nutrition project sponsored by the Japanese (JOICFP)[13] currently running in Thailand and four other Asian countries. It

10. Continuation of use and follow-up may be another story, to which CBFPS organisers are now beginning to give some attention.
11. Slogan used by Dr. Pai, pioneer promoter of family planning clinics in Bombay.
12. Hitherto, aid inputs into Land Settlement for purely economic development include the Asian Development Bank—rubber plantations; US AID—silk culture; World Bank—development of the North East.
13. Japanese Organisation for International Co-operation in Family Planning.

shares the same assumptions as CBD activities, namely that one effective "way in" to increased family planning acceptance is to offer family planning together with other benefits which appear of more immediate local priority. It may be noted that the project is the brain-child of the donor agency rather than a response to a specific national request, which, however, has proved no obstacle to its ready acceptance.

4. INCREASED MOTIVATIONAL EFFORT THROUGH POPULATION INFORMATION, COMMUNICATION AND EDUCATION

The Thai Authorities are of the opinion that the population growth target under the Fourth Plan (2.1 per cent per year by 1981) will be more difficult to achieve than the earlier one, in that the majority of couples already desiring some form of contraception are now covered[14]. In any case, a target of three million new acceptors in five years will clearly need to be backed by a highly effective IEC campaign.

A "master plan" for this purpose is now being carried out (with the assistance of UNFPA). The plan will provide teaching aids, information materials and communications support for the host of village volunteers and part-time health workers who are to be co-opted to do family planning motivation. It will also enable existing activities in this field to be systematised and expanded. It is hoped it will strengthen the collaboration of other sectors of Government with the Family Planning Programme.

The mass media have not been used very extensively as yet for family planning information, partly because of the expense of buying time on radio and television. However, with the increasing number of transistor radios in use in rural areas, the Government is interested in expanding this medium of publicising the family planning message and has obtained foreign aid (UNFPA) for building up programme material, special staff, etc[15].

Population education through the school system is also part of the Thai Government's population strategy. Courses are envisaged covering the whole complex of issues that go to make up what is now fashionably labelled the "quality of life"—i.e. environment, pollution, hygiene, nutrition, etc., as well as population problems. A special Committee within the Ministry of Education has been set up to plan its development. Preparation of curricula, text-books, teacher training, etc. has been proceeding for several years with the assistance of the UNFPA, the Rockfeller Foundation and other donors. The Government has not so far, however, made more than a small budgetary commitment to carry on the work into the regular operational stage[16]. Although there is continued need for research and experiment, exchange of experience, etc., the major requirement now is for operational costs (salaries, teacher-training, text-books, etc.), items which donor agencies generally consider the country's own responsibility.

Population education out of school in Thailand is very much an activity of the private sector, which organises a wide variety of vocational training schemes, student volunteer service schemes, housewives' groups[17], courses for out-of-school youth, etc. On many of these (and on the few that are given as part of the Government's adult education programme) it is possible to include an element of family planning—generally through PPAT.

---

14. Some foreign observers are so optimistic about the Thai programme that they feel the target could have been set at 1.5 per cent annual growth by 1981.

15. UNFPA will pay salaries, with the Government taking over on a phased basis.

16. There was no budgetary allowance for population education in the Third Plan, and only a small one ($ 350,000) in the Fourth.

17. The Korean Family Planning Mothers' Clubs are much admired as a model.

Family planning education in industrial enterprises is also being encouraged, as a useful way of informing large numbers of young people in the towns. The experience to date is considered very encouraging.

5. Greater Attention to Continuation Rates and Contraceptive Methods

Whereas the main focus of the National Family Planning Programme to date has been on number of acceptances, it is recognised that greater attention needs to be paid now to continuation rates and, as a function of this, to choice of methods likely to give more permanent protection than the pill and the condom.

It is envisaged that the pill will remain the core of the Programme (60 per cent of the 600,000 new acceptors planned for 1977)[18], partly because of the popularity of this form of contraception, partly because it is suitable for CBD. However, the Government is currently promoting various alternative methods. One is the use of injectables (Depo-Provera—supplied by Belgium). Another is sterilisation, for which the experience so far suggests there is substantial demand (especially vasectomy) and which, if the specialist training programmes are effective, does not need necessarily to be hospital-based. The aid donors UNFPA and US AID have greatly assisted this programme by, in effect, making incentive payments to the Government (either matching the cost on a dollar to dollar basis or paying the whole cost over and above a certain number).

Abortion is not part of the official Programme as it is against the law, except in special cases. Although some Thai opinion would wish to see the legislation changed, the matter is delicate as the Buddhist religion forbids abortion.

PROGRAMMES AFFECTING POPULATION INDIRECTLY

Half-way through the Third Plan period (1974), the Government introduced an impressive number of new laws and programmes designed to reduce inequalities of income, create greater social justice and improve the "quality of life" for the poorer sections of the community. The vigour with which these programmes has been carried out is, inevitably, a function of available resources and relative priorities. In concept, however, they represent a concerted attempt to deal with the problem of minimum needs.

The programmes include, for example, a plan to create new economic growth poles so as to divert migration away from Bangkok, and a housing programme to construct 20,000 new housing units a year for low-income families. There are also a number of measures to redistribute the tax burden and to promote social expenditures likely to benefit the lower income groups.

A series of measures for the benefit of rural communities include plans to reform agricultural institutions, raise rural incomes, provide six years of compulsory schooling in all rural areas, and ensure better nutrition for school-age children by a programme which includes provision of nutritionally-enriched meals, some nutrition education (for the mothers) and the production of high-protein foods.

---

18. The national acceptor targets are set by the Ministry of Public Health on a province to province basis.

Finally, in its efforts to improve the conditions of life in the rural areas, the Government follows the policy, noted above in connection with delivery of health and family planning services, of promoting local initiative and responsibility. An interesting example of this is the "Tambon" project[19], which would transfer considerable tax revenues directly into the hands of the village councils, who thus become responsible for the planning and carrying out of local development activities. The central Government will still have to provide the basic infrastructure, and it will take some time to work out how the respective areas of responsibility are to be divided. It nonetheless is a promising experiment of central government planning to promote development initiative on the periphery.

The Thai officials who have been talking in terms of the inter-relationship between population and development since before Bucharest, are well aware of the relevance of these various activities to the success of the Family Planning Programme. In some of them, the MOPH (or the PPAT) is actively participating. In others, their potential contribution to the goals of the Programme is indirect and long-term.

THE ADMINISTRATION OF THE POPULATION PROGRAMME

The Thai Government, once convinced of the necessity for a national population policy, took two significant steps which demonstrated the high priority it accorded to the problem. One, as mentioned earlier, was to write the need for population policy into the Constitution. The second was to create a National Population Commission at Cabinet level to ensure integration of population policy with economic and social development policies.

The ministerial-level National Population Commission in fact has never been operative, but the purposes it was intended to serve are now being discharged by a working-level body set up in 1974 by the National Economic and Social Development Board (NESDB), the national planning authority. This body, the NESDB Executive Sub-Committee on Population Policy and Planning, is chaired by the Secretary-General of the NESBD[20], with members drawn from a wide range of Government departments and from the NESDB. It meets regularly, NESDB providing the Secretariat. The Sub-Committee is responsible for formulating national population policy (including fixing targets)[21], determining the resources and measures necessary for implementation (including foreign aid) and evaluating its progress. It acts, in effect, as expert adviser to the Cabinet on population matters. Although the Cabinet is not bound by its advice (notably in matters relating to the population share of the national "cake"), the Executive Sub-Committee does effectively ensure, by means of a regular flow of information, that the nation's chief decision-making body is kept aware of the population issue and of how activities planned in other sectors may affect it.

Co-ordination between the NESDB, the Ministry of Public Health and other Government services (Education, Interior, National Statistical Office, etc.) is facilitated by regular contacts between the key officials concerned. The Thai

---

19. A Tambon is a grouping of 8-10 villages, numbering about 6,000 people.
20. Vice-Chairman is the Director of the Institute of Population Studies at Chulalongkorn University, Thailand's senior authority on population matters and who by his ex-officio seat on most special Government Committees relating to population and social matters, provides an invaluable coordinating link with other social sectors.
21. The mandate is officially described as "To develop the overall frame of population policy in order to cover the *quantitative, qualitative* and *distributive* aspects of population".

Authorities find this more effective than more formal arrangements for co-ordination, although they admit that there is still room for improvement (e.g. greater involvement of the universities in data collection, research and evaluation).

The co-ordination between population and other services that is being achieved in Thailand at central Government level is now beginning to be tried at the peripheral level also. Two initiatives in particular—the integrated approach to education, nutrition and family planning which is being worked out in the context of the Land Settlement Programmes, and the "Tambon" projects—indicate a new trend towards inter-sectoral co-ordination at the local level—where the action actually takes place.

POPULATION ASSISTANCE

The Thai Government realistically accepts that foreign aid for its population programme cannot go on for ever, and is preparing to take over a progressively increasing share of the programme's local costs. The question now is whether it will do so promptly enough to prevent some operations from slowing down or even foundering altogether.

At a time when donor resources are shrinking, Thailand tends to be rated as of a lower priority for population assistance than other more obviously necessitous countries. (Some Thai officials comment ruefully that they are being "penalised for their good management".) In principle, the Thai Government recognises that at this stage of the development of the population programme, aid should be applied to filling the gaps in Thailand's own experience, competence or resources: the problem lies in the definition of such gaps. In the field of population education for example: the donors are willing to assist in the preparatory and creative stages, in training, experiment and evaluation. But if the need is for payment of salaries or other general operating costs, will they be prepared to make up the deficiencies in the Government budget allocation? A similar problem arose when UNFPA[22] was unable to continue its support of the vasectomy programme and the programme came to a halt. Fortunately, different donors have different criteria and while UNFPA has preferred to concentrate its new pro-grammes in Thailand on more innovative activities, US AID has decided to finance the back-log of vasectomy demand, leaving the Government to deal with the regular demand.

There is general agreement among both the Thai Authorities and the aid community that needs have changed as the programme has evolved. Although, presumably, there will be continued need to import hardware and equipment (a foreign exchange problem) for the expansion of health infrastructure, there will be diminishing demand for contraceptive supplies as Thailand follows other countries in organising its own production. The principal types of aid input now sought might broadly be described as "intellectual"—to strengthen research capacity, to collaborate in formulation and design of projects, and to evaluate results. There is thus considerable interest in senior overseas fellowships, in local training at various levels, and in high-level specialist advisers. Thailand, while having little need of foreign personnel for current programmes, is very open to what outside experience may contribute to the more innovative approaches to population problems.

---

22. The Programme was so successful that the funds allocated for 1976 were spent in 1975.

In the health field, the Thai Government would like to see aid applied to training of para-medical personnel, to research and to the evaluation of different programmes and approaches. There is a new interest in improving statistics and collection of basic data in all fields relevant to demographic and social trends, and there is continuing need for aid in the still new and developing fields of population information and education.

The best proof of the extent to which the Thai approach to population assistance has broadened is the keen interest in obtaining outside experience to help develop the "community" approach to population activities. The Thai Authorities admit that although they "know what they want to do, they do not know how to do it". Thus help and advice is eagerly sought at all stages—for social research, for feasibility studies, for training, for the design of integrated projects, for programmes to fit community development activities into the context of regional development plans, for project management and for evaluation. In what is still a very largely untried area, they feel that progress is likely to be best achieved by a multi-disciplinary, multi-national co-operation.

Some donors have already shown interest in these broader approaches, and as "population assistance" to Thailand of the classical kind diminishes, may well consider some aspects of community development as promising alternatives.

In respect of future aid, the Thai Authorities would like to see improvements in two areas. The first is the simplification of what they consider burdensome and time-consuming procedures of the multilateral agencies. The second is in respect of aid co-ordination. This is particularly a problem in the field of research. There is sometimes duplication or overlap among the research activities of the various institutions and universities concerned with population and social development problems. It is not quite clear to what extent this is a problem at the donor end or at the Thai end, but since it seems to be a cause of considerable concern, the donors could perhaps assist Thailand to establish some more effective means of co-ordinating the foreign contributions to its own research efforts.

MIDDLE EAST

EGYPT
TUNISIA

Officials in the above countries were interviewed by the author and Julien Condé, OECD Development Centre.

EGYPT

Total population[1]	38,228,180
Population under age 20[2]	51.2 %
Population density per sq. km.[2]	37
Rate of growth[3]	2.57 %
Crude birth rate (per thousand)[3]	38
Crude death rate (per thousand)[3]	11.7
Life expectancy (total)[2]	54.9 years
Per capita national income (1973)[4]	$ 245
Literacy rate[1]	43.5 %

Sources:
1. Central Agency for Public Mobilization and Statistics (1977), Preliminary results of the 1976 census.
2. UNFPA, *Inventory of Population Projects 1975-76.*
3. Central Agency for Public Mobilization and Statistics (1977), *Statistical Yearbook.*
4. U.N., *Statistical Yearbook,* 1976.

INTRODUCTION

Egypt, a country where pressure of population on available resources of cultivable land and urban accommodation seems to be almost visibly on the point of explosion, has had a National Family Planning Programme since 1966. Between the mid-1960s and the early 1970s, the crude birth rate dropped from its high of 42 per 1,000 to 34 per 1,000, in accordance with the target set by the Programme. Since about 1972, however, the number of family planning acceptances began to flatten, and the period following the halting of the Middle East War in 1973 saw the beginning of a new baby boom. The population of Egypt is still increasing by 1 million persons a year.

To the Egyptian officials responsible for population policy, the message of these figures seemed to be that the direct family planning approach would not, of itself, bring about the major and continuing decline in fertility necessary to bring the country's population growth into balance with its development possibilities. The goal should be the improvement of social and economic conditions for the masses of the very poor, so that the people themselves would *want* to limit the size of their families. Only then would family planning programmes be really effective.

In 1973, therefore, one year before Bucharest, Egypt had already embarked on the second phase of its population policy, which it now based squarely on the "development approach". Looking back at the events leading up to the Conference, notably the preparatory Conference, held in Cairo in 1973[1], and the

1. Symposium on Population and Development, June 1973.

active participation of Egyptian population planners in the drafting of the final World Population Plan of Action, it seems reasonable to suggest that the resounding assertion of the indivisibility of population *and* development made at Bucharest may well itself have owed something to the population policies that were already being formulated in Egypt.

NATIONAL POPULATION POLICIES

It might perhaps have been expected that in Egypt, a country where only 3.5 per cent of the total land area is suitable for cultivation, where over 99 per cent of the inhabitants are crowded together in the fertile strip of the Nile Valley and the Delta, and where the rest of the land surface is mostly inhospitable desert, the need to limit population growth would long have been recognised as an urgent political imperative. In the first half of the twentieth century, the population doubled from 10 million inhabitants to 20 million, and the 1960 census recorded a further leap to 26 million. The generally prevailing attitude, however, seems to have been that a large population was a valuable national asset. It was not until the early 1960s that the Egyptian Authorities felt constrained to take official action to try to contain an almost literal "population explosion".

The turning-point came with the evaluation of the implementation of the Five-Year Plan 1960-1965, and the discovery that it was falling some 30 per cent behind target. In 1965, a Presidential decree made provision of family planning services an official responsibility of the Egyptian Government. This was not a dramatic change of attitude on the part of the Government. The Egyptian Family Planning Association[2], which had been doing family planning work since 1953, had enjoyed official recognition and sponsorship by the Ministry of Social Affairs, and President Nasser had made the first official announcement of the need to adopt a national family planning programme in the National Charter of May 1962. Now, however, an official infrastructure was created to carry out a national family planning programme. A Supreme Council for Family Planning was created and the Ministry of Health allocated funds to provide family planning services as part of the health function.

But already by 1972, as noted above, the very dynamics of the situation seemed to indicate that the problem could not be solved in this way. It would not perhaps be true to say that the Egyptian Authorities as a body underwent instant conversion to the "socio-economic approach". Nevertheless, those elements, at least, within the Government who were responsible for the formulation of population policy became convinced that such an approach offered the only effective means of dealing with Egypt's population growth and the problems related to it. Specifically, the Family Planning Board (the body set up to be technical advisor to the Supreme Council for Family Planning), in 1973, shifted from the traditional family planning approach, which had been the first phase of the national population policy, to a new and more comprehensive approach that sought to deal with the problem of high fertility by attacking the causes that were tending to perpetuate it.

This second phase of Egyptian population policy was founded on the assumption that as long as it remained economically advantageous, as well as culturally desirable, for the poor to have large numbers of children, family planning

---

2. Originally the Egyptian Society for Population Studies.

programmes would be unlikely to have much appeal. Population policy should, therefore, aim at bringing about the socio-economic conditions that would effectively make family planning a meaningful option.

Having stated the philosophy, the new socio-economic approach to fertility reduction went one stage further and selected nine variables that seemed most relevant for the dual purpose of improving the conditions of life and reducing fertility. Specifically, these were identified as: raising the socio-economic standards of the family ; education, and in particular, functional education and education related to employment; women's employment; mechanisation of agriculture; industrialisation, particularly in rural areas; reduction of infant mortality; improved social security; information and communication; and improvement of social services, in particular family planning. The statement stresses that the nine factors are not listed in order of priority but must be developed simultaneously: it also stresses the critical importance of family planning.

A population policy that includes such objectives as these is, by definition, taking a long-term perspective. In this, it differs from a population policy which aims at reducing fertility by means of family planning, where the time-span for anticipated results is normally fairly short (one or two Plan periods, for example). Predictably, the opinion is sometimes expressed in Egypt that the long-term perspective does not face the urgency of the problems caused by Egypt's galloping population growth. To which the answer is returned that the experience of the first phase of the national population policy (1966-72) suggests that a family planning programme alone may prove to be just as slow in achieving the desired results. The obvious conclusion therefore is that the two policies are complementary and should be pursued simultaneously.

CHANGES IN POPULATION POLICIES SINCE BUCHAREST

The Government's commitment to the national population policy in its second phase was included in its overall "strategy for a new civilisation", which was put to the nation after the 1973 war and approved by referendum. Recently (in 1975), the policy has been further refined in a third phase, which, its authors claim, is not a shift of policy, but simply a reformulation responding to the inherent logic of the 1973 development approach.

In this third and latest formulation, population policy has moved from concern with fertility reduction to a broader concern with "population problems". These are defined as having three facets. In addition to the obvious one of growth rate and size, they include also geographical distribution (including migration), and what are called "characteristics" or "conditions", which cover such features as age structure, level of education, occupation, and the status of women. Population policy now extends to these three aspects of the population problem and aims to address them simultaneously. As thus formulated, it will be seen that current Egyptian population policy has gone one stage further than being predicated on the inter-relationship of population and development. Population policy and development policy have, in fact, coalesced. It is perhaps relevant to note that this approach is not restricted to the population specialists at the Family Planning Board[3]. Thus, for example, the chief of the Census Agency (Central Agency for Public Mobilisation and Statistics) said in an interview in

---

3. Now re-designated, together with a newly-invigorated Supreme Council, under the title "Population and Family Planning". The Board is now entitled the Board for Population and Family Planning (BPFP).

May 1977, that he believed birth control programmes would not be successful until the literacy rate had greatly improved[4]. President Sadat, addressing the National Assembly early in 1977, defined the national population policy in the following terms:

"1. Reduction of the population, which includes reduction of natural increase and mortality rates.

2. Population re-distribution according to a new population distribution map. This includes also discouraging rural migration to large urban centres, the design of physical development plans at governorate levels, the reconstruction of Egyptian villages and rural development, as well as the laying down of an integrated plan of development, where all concerned local and central institutions would share the responsibility in providing for general cleanliness, a factor which has implications from the health, tourist and social aspects."

He added that new census data would no doubt give important insights into "changes in population conditions", and that the "efforts of the whole population" should be geared to the achievement of new targets for population growth—specifically a decline from the present rate of 2.3 per cent per annum to 1.6 per cent by 1985.

While the prime goals of Egyptian population policy are reduction of fertility and checking urban growth, the approach presently adopted by the Egyptian Authorities responsible for population policy (the Board for Population and Family Planning) might well be considered as the ultimate embodiment of the "spirit of Bucharest". Let every service of Government (and this includes the family planning services) get on with its appointed job and do it efficiently, so runs the argument, and it will automatically be helping to deal with the population problem in its diverse aspects. Each sector's plans will cover some part of these problems. By addressing such questions as what kind of education should be provided for women, what forms of investment are needed for redistribution of the population, what will prevent urban drift, etc., each department of Government is helping to deal with "population problems".

In practice, of course (and as the Supreme Council and its Board well appreciate), political and financial constraints will inevitably tend to interfere to some extent with the actual working out of this harmonious scheme of things. A great many national problems in Egypt are recognised as having high priority at the present time, and some will undoubtedly prove to be of greater urgency than others. Ministers recognise the problems of population growth, of land shortage, of over-crowding, of urban blight, and of infant mortality. But other problems, such as productivity, the emphasis on consumption rather than investment expenditure, foreign indebtedness, etc., are also clamouring for attention[5].

At the present time, it has realistically to be recognised that shortage both of resources and of management skills, represents a major constraint on the speedy implementation of a population policy that covers action in so many different areas. The Family Planning Board, however, can already lay claim to two notable achievements. The first is that the various sector Ministries have, for the most part, now accepted the idea of the "population aspect" of their respective areas of responsibility. The second is that official planning is already concerned with the likely implications of the population problem in the long-

---

4. The illiteracy rate among women is shown by the census of 1966 as over 70 per cent.

5. Some senior Egyptian officials maintain that the population problem must be dealt with in the context of all the other economic expectations, including peace in the Middle East.

term. The Government is keenly aware of the problems that present population growth is inevitably storing up for the future, not only in economic terms, but also in terms of social, spatial and psychological problems[6]. Planning how to meet the needs of Egypt's population in the year 2000 is one of the tasks to which Government planners are already seriously beginning to address themselves[7].

STRATEGIES FOR IMPLEMENTING POPULATION POLICIES

Given the extremely comprehensive nature of Egypt's national population policy in its present phase, it follows that the strategies employed are equally wide-ranging. Broadly speaking, these fall into two groups, corresponding to the two main strands of the population policy.

The first group consists of strategies intended to improve family planning facilities and to motivate more people to make use of them. The second may be described as strategies designed to raise the standard of living of the people in general so as to create the conditions that will eventually lead to a reduction in desired family size. It would be interesting to have some idea as to the respective degree of effort that goes into each of these two separate and parallel population strategies. Since the second one, however, may be interpreted as including virtually any effort to raise the country's overall level of development and bring about a more equitable distribution of the benefits, it clearly is not meaningful to compare the respective inputs in quantitative terms.

The following paragraphs present a brief account of some of the principal activities currently undertaken under each of the two broad strategies.

IMPROVING FAMILY PLANNING SERVICES

Eighty per cent of the 3,500 or so family planning services in Egypt are delivered through the regular hospital and clinic services of the Ministry of Health. The clinics of the Family Planning Association[8], and various private bodies provide the rest. Egypt is unusual in that a high proportion of family planning outlets are situated in rural areas: the ratio as between units in urban and rural areas is 36 to 64, corresponding almost exactly to the population distribution of the country (some 60 per cent of the Egyptian population is rural). Egypt is also unusual in the extent of its health service coverage, which comes very close to the World Health Organisation's norms.

The problem in Egypt, as the Authorities well recognise, is not the health service infrastructure, but the low level of performance prevailing in much of it. In respect of family planning services, this problem is compounded by the fact that in Egypt, as elsewhere, the medical personnel operating the health services

---

6. Projections made in 1976 showed that even allowing for a decrease in the rate of population growth from 2.5 to 2.0 per cent per annum, and a total emigration of 1½ million people, the population of Egypt would still almost double (present level 34 million) by the end of the century.

7. At the time of the Development Centre mission in May 1977, a seminar on "Population Prospects up to the Year 2000", sponsored by the Egyptian Academy of Science was being held in Alexandria. It was attended by seven Ministers of State.

8. The historical explanation of the split of responsibility between the Ministries of Health and Social Affairs for running family planning activities is that when the Government first entered the field in 1966, its funds were inadequate to provide family planning services for the whole nation. It was accordingly very pleased to let the Family Planning Association, which had its own sources of funds (IPPF), continue to run its own clinics, under the sponsorship of the Ministry of Social Affairs.

often tend not to give family planning a high priority, particularly in the rural areas where it is most needed[9].

Earlier plans to expand the health service network have been superseded recently in favour of a concentrated effort to make the existing infrastructure (both general health and family planning) work better. This endeavour is being supported by foreign aid, notably by the World Bank[10], US AID and UNICEF, each donor contributing to a special aspect of the task. Thus, US AID is concerned primarily with up-grading the health infrastructure in rural areas, the World Bank's aid is oriented more specifically to family planning services, and UNICEF is concerned particularly with activities intended to reduce child mortality.

In Egypt, unlike many developing countries, up-grading the health and family planning services in the rural areas does not imply recourse to para-medical personnel. There are doctors in abundance (the University of Cairo alone has 8,000 medical students and other universities are not far behind), and the legal obligation to spend two years in service in a rural area after graduation ensures that even allowing for the large numbers that emigrate, there is no shortage of doctors in the countryside. The problem is that their presence does not assure the countryside the desired level of service, partly because young doctors tend to consider rural service as a period of penance, but more particularly because their training is not suitable[11]. Training in family planning is especially lacking and intensive courses to remedy this deficiency are recognised as an urgent need. US AID and the American University of Cairo have made a start, but the need is to give family planning an adequate place in the medical curriculum throughout the country, so that young doctors will be seriously interested in this aspect of health practice.

Improving family planning services is not, of course, limited to clinical services. A number of measures are being experimented with to make contraceptives more effectively available to those who want them, and, hopefully, to attract a certain latent demand[12]. These include house-to-house distribution (the distributors being paid a small salary by US AID), a more efficient national distribution system to ensure continuity and consistency of supplies, and introducing a greater variety of contraceptives[13] in the hope of compensating for the disappointing results of more conventional methods.

INFORMATION AND EDUCATION

Together with the problem of improving the service goes that of expanding the demand for it. Acceptance rates overall are currently low, although estimates differ widely. US AID estimates that, on average, only about 7 per cent of the target population are practising contraception, of which 12-14 per cent are in

---

9. Their task is further complicated by factors such as the erratic supply of contraceptives, continuous changes in family planning incentives, etc.

10. The World Bank project to up-grade the rural health and referral services, which initially included a large component for buildings, vehicles, equipment, etc., now reflects the change in Government policy. The planned follow-up project will put greater emphasis on supplies, training, service, delivery, etc.

11. The fact that the medical courses are so over-crowded in itself diminishes the quality of the training provided.

12. Contraceptives (oral pills and condoms) can be sold by over 2,500 pharmacies all over the country, although the supply sometimes tends to be erratic. In addition, condoms are sold by coffee and barber shops, grocery stores and street stands.

13. The National Family Planning Programme has relied mainly on pills. Neither sterilisation nor abortion are officially accepted methods in Egypt, although in practice there is considerable use of both.

the city, and 3-4 per cent in rural areas[14]. The Population and Family Planning Board estimates the acceptance rates among eligible women at 12-14 per cent.

The Government recognises that the main problem is to reach the people who have the big families. It has deliberately opted against a strategy of incentives and disincentives on the grounds that it would be the children who suffered. The intention, therefore, is to try and reach people through population information and education, in the hope of persuading them that it is in their own interest to have fewer children and to space their births.

Although use is made of the mass media, informational campaigns to promote the idea of family planning have to proceed with some discretion in Egypt in order not to antagonise religious opinion. Much low-key information and communication activities at village level are, therefore, undertaken in collaboration with local religious leaders (often using sophisticated audio-visual equipment supplied by aid funds). They are supported by considerable research and evaluation effort, some of which is action-oriented, and some designed to obtain a better understanding of the attitudes of different groups of the population to demographic and social problems.

At the school level, population education in Egypt has already made significant progress. By 1975, the text books were ready and "population" was officially introduced as a subject into the school curriculum throughout the country. The teaching staff, however, are not yet used to it, and the effort is now on teacher training, in order for population education to be genuinely absorbed into the curriculum as part of regular teaching practice. There is also a simultaneous attempt to introduce population as a topic at university level (with UNFPA help). It is generally considered a significant achievement that at Al Azhar University, the most venerable Moslem seat of learning in the Middle East, a number of faculties are now doing research on demographic problems.

RAISING THE STANDARDS OF RURAL LIFE

The prime strategy, however, for eventually extending public acceptance of family planning is through raising the conditions of life, and particularly life in rural areas. At the present time, the Authorities well recognise that the number of children in an Egyptian rural family is high (average 8 births, of which fewer than 5 survive through early childhood) because children, especially sons, are a valuable economic asset[15]. Accordingly, rural development to change this situation has come to be recognised in Egypt as a necessary underpinning of the national population policy.

The Government's plans for rural development were set out in 1971 with the announcement of a Programme for the "Reconstruction and Development of the Egyptian Village"[16] and the creation of a new Department (ORDEV)[17] for the purpose. The development approach to population problems, as President Sadat's speech to the National Assembly explicitly states, now includes this purpose as one of the objectives of the national population policy. Under the auspices of the Board for Population and Family Planning, two interesting

---

14. A national fertility survey conducted in 1974/75 found that an average of 27 % of married women (15-49) were practising some form of contraception (41 per cent in urban areas and 16 per cent in rural areas).

15. Mobilisation for the army, emigration and urban drift have caused the price of agricultural labour to rise three-fold over the past few years. Child labour is accordingly badly needed for cotton-picking, pest control and tending animals.

16. "Village" in Egypt is a sizeable administrative unit, comprising not just one village community, but maybe as many as 10 or 11, with a total population of 20,000.

17. "Organisation for the Reconstruction and Development of the Egyptian Village".

initiatives have recently been started which are intended to sharpen the on-going rural development programme and thereby accelerate the process of change.

INTEGRATED RURAL DEVELOPMENT

The first project, known as the Integrated Rural Development Project, is essentially a piece of action-oriented research. A four-to-five year activity that is just getting under way (in 1977), the idea is to bring to bear central government research, planning and management expertise to act as a catalyst in order to mobilise local mechanisms for internal change. The purpose is the regeneration of the Egyptian village, through community action, but with judicious help from the centre.

A pilot group of 8 villages has been selected in the Delta region and the village council will be assisted to define its own development needs, resources, aspirations and population problems. The first step has been a comprehensive socio-economic survey (undertaken by the Population and Family Planning Board). Once the needs have been defined and the community's own plans for meeting them established, government resources will be provided to help realise them. The final stage will be evaluation to assess the population impact, identify the most significant elements for feed-back to other areas (e.g., the optimum mix of activities[18], the process of "social engineering", by which they can most effectively be implemented, etc.). This exercise in accelerated and specially nurtured social development is being undertaken in one area on a pilot basis. It already involves a very considerable research input and in due course will require substantial priority for government resources to implement the development plans decided upon. Although the Board is hoping to persuade some of Egypt's universities to undertake similar research in other villages, there are obvious problems in replicating this experience on a national scale. Nevertheless, it should yield valuable lessons, both on the dynamics of local development and on its effect on population.

CO-ORDINATORS' PROJECT

The second initiative whereby the Population and Family Planning Board is trying to tackle the problems of population at the community level is the so-called "Co-ordinators' Project". This is an attempt to establish a working mechanism whereby population considerations will be linked to the other pre-occupations of Government at the three levels of administration. The Supreme Council for Population and Family Planning[19] itself represents an attempt to co-ordinate population with economic and social development planning at the central government level. The idea now is to create a formal structure of co-ordination at the regional (Governorate) and local (Village) levels also.

The immediate focus of the Co-ordinators' Project is on the Village level, although it is designed to extend also to urban districts. A specially-created and trained staff of "co-ordinators" will be placed in the local "Village" administration to constitute a bridge between considerations of "population" (in all its facets) and the general development considerations that are the normal subjects of local government concern. At the same time, since the latter involve a large number of different government departments and services, the co-ordinators will be required also to provide a link between the programmes and activities of the

---

18. The emphasis would seem to be on social development, i.e., education, communication, water, etc.
19. See section on "Administrative Structure" below.

different services involved by seeing that all of them pay due regard to the "population dimension".

The co-ordinators will work through the existing local government structure. They will be responsible to the Village Councils and will be chosen from civil servants native to the area where they are to serve. They will be of medium rank, are to be very rigorously selected and intensively trained[20].

The Project is proceeding in collaboration with ORDEV. It was planned to staff 150 villages with specially-trained "co-ordinators" by the end of 1977 and a further 100 the following year. It is still not clear, however, how these somewhat low-key civil servants are, in practice, going to tie in with the existing local government structures, and still less, how they are to co-ordinate all local development activities in the interests of their potential impact on population. It they succeed, it will constitute a wholly new approach to population problems.

The approach has been described by one foreign observer as an attempt "to create a revolution by the Establishment". Revolution? Possibly. What is significant about this attempt, however, is that it is the *population* service of the Establishment that is initiating it. The more conventional approaches to population (family planning, IEC, etc.) are, as noted earlier, being pursued simultaneously, as parallel activities. The body responsible for formulating the country's population policy, however (the Board for Population and Family Planning), in its search for solutions to Egypt's population problems, is now concentrating its main hopes on indirect approaches intended to change the environmental framework.

PROGRAMMES AFFECTING POPULATION INDIRECTLY

In view of the breadth of the Government's stated population policy, it could reasonably be argued that all the development programmes currently being pursued by the Egyptian Government are not only likely to affect the population factor indirectly, but are recognised as such. At the time of writing[21], the Socio-Economic Development Plan for the period 1978-1982 had still not been finalised. It therefore was not possible to know the relative priorities that would be given to the various social and economic programmes, nor how it was proposed to implement the nine objectives recognised in the National Population Policy as those most relevant to the condition of the population in the future.

Discussion with senior Egyptian officials seems to suggest, however, that in Government thinking, the emphasis is currently on three main lines of approach: the creation of new centres of population and economic activity; improving the physical environment of the Egyptian village; and improving the general level of efficiency, both in administration and the private sector.

Plans to relieve the pressure of population on the Delta and Nile strip and to create new settlements in the desert area are now well advanced, thanks to the irrigation possibilities provided by the Aswan Dam. In the south, some four million feddans[22] of land which can be irrigated with underground water from Lake Nasser have been located for agricultural reclamation.

In the north, the Government has already embarked on a plan to create new cities based not on agriculture, but on industrial and commercial activity

---

20. A special training course, covering eight weeks in very wide ranging subjects is in preparation.
21. June 1977.
22. 1 feddan equals approximately 1 acre or 4,200 square metres.

(tourism, new industries, oil) and which, it is hoped, will absorb some five million people. The plan is long-term (20 years), but the infrastructure, in the shape of roads, canals, telecommunications systems, is being constructed now. Significantly, the Government Authorities concerned (and not just the Population and Family Planning Board) are intending that active family planning programmes should accompany these plans at all stages.

The concept of the regeneration of the Egyptian village seems to underlie most of the current thinking in Government circles about the future development of the country. There is a certain "mystique" attached to it ("we must start with the regeneration of the individual"). There is also realism: ("the Government cannot assume the whole task itself; its responsibility is to do the preparatory work—the planning and the provision of the infrastructure"). There is also interest in getting outside advice ("foreign aid could perhaps help us find the model(s) which the villages would be recommended to adopt"). The two projects of the Population and Family Planning Board designed to activate village-level initiative, which have been described above, are a part of this philosophy.

The philosophy, of course, includes also specific action programmes in the various sectors concerned. Much of the emphasis in these would seem to be on improved hygiene (both environmental and health services) and on better nutrition. These are activities which traditionally are supported by foreign aid (e.g. UNICEF's programmes of immunisation, MCH clinics, etc., and CARE's $12 million feeding programme for family planning acceptors, infants and small children). These are also activities which frequently are aided as part of "population" assistance, thus bringing together both the classical and the "wide" approaches to population programmes.

The third need, for better management, was officially recognised by President Sadat in his address to the nation of 1st May, 1977. His call—one bound to be welcome anywhere—was for "an end to red tape". It corresponds, however, to a practical reality felt throughout all sectors of the nation's life—a spirit of dynamism must be restored and the structure must be such as to encourage and not impede it.

The relevance of this to population programmes is direct enough. The poor performance of the health services has already been noted. The family planning services are unlikely to do much better. Indeed, it would be unreasonable to expect that a family planning service will function at a level of efficiency superior to that of the other services of the country concerned. Raising the level of efficiency in the nation's services (and economic activities) as a whole, will assuredly have an effect on population by enabling the effort and resources invested in population programmes (both direct and indirect) to give a greater return.

ADMINISTRATIVE STRUCTURE

By the Presidential decree of 1966, establishing a Supreme Council for Family Planning, Egypt was creating a supra-ministerial body for population, such as was later to be recommended by the World Population Plan of Action. The Council, headed by the Minister of Social Affairs, and more recently by the Prime Minister, is one of the Standing Committees of the Council of Ministers, and its membership includes the Ministers in charge of all the relevant sectors of Government (including the Minister of Planning). In 1974, the Council underwent some modification and changed its name to the Supreme Council for *Population* and Family Planning, thus attesting to the Government's new and broader approach to population problems.

Since ministerial-level bodies, in practice, tend to suffer from the conflicting claims on the attention of Ministers, the Council was endowed with an Executive Board, to be responsible for population matters at an effective working level. Although, in the early days, the Board undertook some operational activities in respect of the family planning programme (training, motivation work, distribution of pills, etc.), the Board has never, in fact, had any legal responsibility for executing programmes, and the word "executive" has since been dropped from its title (Population and Family Planning Board).

The Board has, however, been effective not only in formulating the national population policy on behalf of the Government, but also, a significant achievement, in convincing other sectors of Government of the dimensions of the population problem and of its relevance to their respective areas of responsibility. This would seem to be due partly to the reputation and seriousness of the Board itself and partly to a structure of co-ordination which it has been successful in organising. In each of the concerned Ministries, a senior Under-Secretary is designated as responsible for co-ordination, and these meet together periodically with the Board. These co-ordinating meetings were held regularly for some years and then dropped. They were re-activated in 1976 when they met six times, under the chairmanship of the Senior Under-Secretary of Planning.

In theory, similar co-ordinating bodies exists also at the level of the Governorate. In practice, however, this has not proved a workable reality, and the Board's present "Co-ordinators' Project" represents a new attempt to organise co-ordination arrangements at the Governorate and community levels.

The Board is the national planning body for population matters. As part of this responsibility, it has an active research function. It also has overall responsibility for IEC activities including training (although this is increasingly being passed to the Ministries of Information and Education).

Most of the service responsibilities under the family planning programme are exercised by the Ministries of Health and Social Welfare, who between them operate most of the family planning outlets (the latter Ministry, it will be recalled, has administrative responsibility for the clinics run by the Family Planning Association)[23].

The split of responsibility between the two Departments does not seem, in practice, to pose any special problem[24]. More important, perhaps, is the split between the planning responsibility of the Board and the executive responsibility of these two Ministries, which, as described above, has led *de facto* to the emergence of two parallel approaches to population problems in Egypt.

ASSISTANCE FOR POPULATION ACTIVITIES

International assistance provided to Egypt for population has until now been applied for the most part to activities of the traditional type. That is to say, it has made substantial contributions to the improvement of the health infrastructure, to improved mother and child health, to the supply of contraceptives, to bio-medical research and training, other forms of research and training, IEC activities, and demographic and census surveys, etc. In addition, aid funds have provided general budgetary support to the Population and Family Planning Board

---

23. The Minister of Social Affairs is Chairman of the Board of Directors of the Family Planning Association.
24. The Family Planning Association clinics use Ministry of Health doctors part-time.

(including salary supplements) and to the Egyptian Family Planning Association (UNFPA and IPPF respectively)[25].

The Board of Population and Family Planning recognises the necessity to adapt to different donors' aid policies and criteria. To the extent possible, however, it prefers its aid relations to be limited to a small number of donor agencies, so as to narrow the range of differing aid requirements and establish known bases for a continuing aid collaboration.

Certainly, the Board has out-paced the donors in respect of novel and innovative approaches. This is only to be expected, partly because the country itself will always be best placed to explore possible new solutions appropriate to its particular circumstances, and partly because donors' financial commitments to on-going activities tend to limit the flexibility and speed with which they can consider new ones. (Donors' reactions to "integrated projects" is a case in point. For example, a new project for land reclamation, to be financed by a bilateral aid donor, was not originally designed to include a family planning element: it was the Board, not the donor, who urged its inclusion.)

The present, almost open-ended, approach to population of the Egyptian Board for Population and Family Planning undoubtedly presents the donor community with a dilemma. The Board's attitude is that anything the donors do that will accelerate economic and social development will be a contribution towards solving population problems, and it is irrelevant whether donors label their support "population assistance" or not. The donors, for their part, are unaccustomed to population policy including such a broad spectrum of social activities, and are still hesitant as to how to react. Thus, for example, UNFPA, which has been requested to support the implementation of the Board's new population policy, has indicated that it would, in principle, consider contributing to the Integrated Rural Development Project, but is waiting to examine the details of the equipment required before making a definite commitment. Similarly, US AID has not yet made a decision on a request by Egypt[26] for assistance to support local manufacture of contraceptive supplies. Pending such decisions, which imply a reorientation of assistance policy, it is convenient to continue with conventional programmes and to supply contraceptives, etc., as in the past.

Nevertheless, the chief donors of population assistance to Egypt have already demonstrated their willingness to participate, albeit at first tentatively (one is almost tempted to say "gingerly"), in the new approaches being worked out by the Population and Family Planning Board. Thus US AID, pending decision on a new long-term (5 year) strategy of population assistance to Egypt, is actively searching for novel approaches and pilot projects that it can support. (Among these activities may be noted a village-level community development project[27] to be carried out in association with the American University of Cairo, examining the possibility of using agricultural co-operatives for various social welfare activities, and strengthening the family planning department of the Ministry of Health.)

Similarly, UNFPA is sponsoring a number of small pilot projects as a basis for action-oriented research, such as providing industrial employment for women

---

25. US AID assistance, for political reasons, was for some time provided only indirectly through intermediaries (primarily IPPF, but also through various U.S. foundations and universities). Direct aid to Egypt has now been resumed. Since it comes technically under the heading of "Support Assistance", rather than Title X funds, there is a potential for greater flexibility in its use.

26. Together with a number of other countries: situation at the time of the Development Centre mission.

27. It will differ somewhat in conception from the Board's Integrated Development Project in being based primarily not on economic but on social development (i.e. education, social security, etc.).

in a particular area, in order to check the effect on fertility, providing contraceptives for industrial workers and studying their attitudes towards fertility and family size.

UNFPA has made a 5-year agreement to provide Egypt with approximately $2 million of aid a year. Some of this is already being applied in support of "innovative approaches", partly through its budgetary support to the Board, and partly because it can be used to finance local currency expenditures (operating costs, salary supplements, etc.) that are an important part of the Board's experimental projects. Nearly $1 million in 1977 is to be used to provide hormones as the basis of Egyptian production of contraceptive pills. This aid will extend over at least three years, with a slightly decreasing input each year[28].

In considering donors' reactions to Egypt's "wide approach" to population, however, it is important to remember the duality of the Government's population strategy. There is still a major need for conventional family planning programmes and there is little chance of its being satisfied with the necessary speed and efficiency unless aid continues to provide financial support. Thus, the World Bank is assisting a second population project in Egypt to strengthen the rural health infrastructure and enable it to provide post-partum family planning. The project is important also indirectly, in that the Bank's support for infrastructure obliges the Egyptian Government (in this instance the Ministry of Health) to provide the equipment to go with the infrastructure, and thus make a bigger contribution from the Government budget than it otherwise might have done. Similarly, US AID is considering picking up some of the work until now supported by UNICEF in the fields of mother and child health and infant mortality.

Both the urgency of Egypt's population problems and the breadth of the strategies envisaged offer donors the opportunity to decide their own preferred "mix" of conventional and innovative aid programmes by way of solution.

---

28. For the various project activities supported by UNFPA, Egyptian Government institutions have taken over the role of executing agency previously performed by U.N. Specialised Agencies.

TUNISIA

Total population[1]	5,747,000
Population under age 20[1]	56.0 %
Population density per sq. km.[1]	35
Rate of growth[1]	2.65 %
Crude birth rate (per thousand)[2]	35.0
Crude death rate (per thousand)[2]	8.5
Life expectancy (total)[1]	56.6 years
Per capita national income (1977)[2]	$ 800
Literacy rate[3]	55 %

Sources:
1. UNFPA, *Inventory of Population Projects 1975-76.*
2. Tunisian National Statistical Institute.
3. IBRD, *Comparative Education Indicators,* 1978.

INTRODUCTION

Since the early 1960s, the Government of Tunisia has seen the rapid increase of the population as a grave national problem: population growth was threatening to outstrip the possibilities of economic growth. As President Bourguiba said: "Nous risquons d'être engloutis par la vague provoquée par l'explosion démographique" ("We are in danger of being swallowed up by the tidal wave caused by the population explosion"). An official family planning programme was accordingly launched as far back as 1963, with the strong support of the President himself[1].

As stated in the Four-Year Plan (1973-76), the goals of Tunisia's social policy are full employment, equality of income distribution and improvement in the quality of life. The Plan puts control of population growth, together with job creation and a better adapted educational system, as the trinity of measures indispensable to the "creation of a better and more equitable society".

Since the mid-1960s, the birth rate has declined from 43.8 per 1,000 to 35.4 per 1,000 in the mid-1970s. This is still not considered low enough to solve the problem of population growth and, in particular, the problem of finding employment as more young people enter the labour market each year. However,

1. "En instituant le 'Planning familial', notre principal souci a été d'assurer l'équilibre entre l'augmentation de la population et l'accroissement du revenu national. Pour qu'elles aient le même rythme de croissance, il était nécessaire de *planifier la natalité* en même temps que la production." ("Our chief object in introducing family planning is to maintain a balance between the growth of population and that of national income. If they are to grow at the same rate, we must plan births as well as production.") - President Bourguiba, 1966.

the favourable economic conjuncture of the immediate post-Bucharest period allowed the Government to feel that the problem, although important, was not critical[2].

Since Bucharest, the Government has maintained its policy of population limitation, although it has shifted the approach from family planning and population control to "family welfare". Bucharest has provided a useful ideological justification: " ...la conciliation de l'idée de la régulation des naissances avec le 'droit' proclamé par la Conférence de Bucarest... à l'épanouissement familial" ("...harmonising the idea of regulation of births with the "right" proclaimed at Bucharest... to the fullest development and welfare of the family"). The concept of "family welfare" (covering health, social welfare and family planning) in fact neatly brings together the State's concern with overall population size and the concern of parents for their children.

POPULATION POLICY

Before Bucharest, the planning of population growth to within economically-acceptable limits was already part of the national development policy and written into the Four-Year Plans. But the Government's main preoccupation with the population problem was governed by its implications for employment. The Plans envisaged, therefore, "vigorous measures to limit births" in order to reduce the number of new job-seekers entering the market in the future.

This objective was written into the Plan in terms of a minimum target of births to be averted. Because of the high proportion of women at the most fertile age, natural fertility would tend to offset the results of family planning programmes. The Development Plan accordingly separated births to be averted through direct family planning (300,000 over the decade) from those to be averted by legislation to discourage births (progressive reduction of children's allowances and liberalised abortion). Within these two overall targets, sub-targets were set for each region.

Since Bucharest, the Government has been emphasizing the social importance of population limitation in terms of increasing family welfare. The family planning "message" is now expressed in terms of the health of the mother, the financial burden for the father, and the higher standards of education and nutrition enjoyed by small families.

It is difficult to judge to what extent this shift of emphasis away from "family planning" to "family welfare" marks a change of policy, or whether it is simply a change of *approach*, i.e. a change of packaging rather than policy. Tunisian officials themselves give differing interpretations, depending for the most part on the nature of the responsibilities that their respective departments are called upon to carry out. What is certain is that everyone in Tunisia who is concerned with "family welfare" in any of its aspects would agree that limitation of births should be one of its *results*.

Despite the Tunisian Government's clear recognition of the importance of the need to contain population growth, the budgetary resources allocated to family planning activities have been distinctly modest. (In 1974, the allocation for family planning from the national budget amounted to the equivalent of $0.47 per capita, i.e. 0.2 per cent of the total budget[3] compared with 7.6 per cent for health.)

---

2. Tunisian officials were taking the line that "our population situation fortunately is not dramatic—it is not like that of some countries of Asia".
3. World Bank, *Report on Resource Allocations to Family Planning, 1967-75.*

PRINCIPAL STRATEGIES
FOR ATTACKING THE POPULATION PROBLEM

Within the concept of "family welfare", the Government's strategies for tackling the problem of population growth fall mostly in the category of the direct approach. The principal lines of attack are two-fold: population education, and improved public health services, including family planning facilities. These have been accompanied by a number of legislative measures designed to facilitate contraceptive practice and abortion.

1. POPULATION EDUCATION

The keynote of population education in Tunisia is, advisedly, discreet pervasiveness rather than massive publicity ("pas de matraquage"). Leading Government figures refer to family planning in their public speeches with remarkable frequency (the Minister of Health does so at least once every week), and take pains to reassure the public that the practice of family planning is not only condoned by Islamic law but positively encouraged by the Prophet (in the interests of relieving the family and the individual from the grosser burdens of material cares). On the other hand, there is very little "advertising". Tunisian towns are rarely adorned with campaign posters urging family planning, small families, etc., and although radio and television are sometimes used for short "family welfare" type family planning messages, there is as yet no Western-style mass media campaigning[4].

Since 1974, a concerted attempt has been made to use the industrial structure as a channel for population education. The National Company of Tunisian Railways already had their own family planning services, and by now some form of population education and family planning services are provided in most of the major State enterprises as part of industrial medical services. A beginning is also being made in private industry, small firms being grouped together for the purpose. In this way population education can reach male workers as well as women.

Population education receives valuable support through the powerful National Union of Tunisian Women. Their contribution is particularly important in respect of women who have no paid employment and who would not otherwise be easily accessible to "modernising" influences outside the home.

The Tunisian Government is enthusiastic about the possibilities opened up by population education ("creating a revolution in attitudes"[5]) at all levels and is gradually introducing it throughout the school system. Beginning with a number of secondary schools on a pilot basis with, at the same time, special training for teachers, the idea is to get the "population" message across to students, not as an 'extra' subject in the curriculum but by infusing it into the regular course subjects. The project includes some foreign assistance but it is essentially national in its inspiration and development of the subject matter. It is the intention to extend this approach to primary education, as soon as staff resources make it practicable. (Secondary school staff already familiar with this approach will be mainly responsible for training the primary school teachers.)

---

4. At the time of the Development Centre visit to Tunisia, one aid donor was trying to interest the Tunisian Authorities in an advertising campaign to promote the sale of contraceptives.

5. Description given by the enthusiastic Director of the Programme.

2. IMPROVED PUBLIC HEALTH AND FAMILY PLANNING SERVICES

The second part of the Government's population strategy is the more traditional and the more costly. It reflects the close structural association between the body responsible for population (Office National du Planning Familial et de la Population) and the Ministry of Health. Despite occasionally elaborate attempts to dissociate the idea of family planning from "illness" in the popular imagination, it is essentially a medical service approach.

The programme envisages the construction of health centres, maternal and child health care clinics and maternity hospitals at an accelerated rate with a view to effectively covering the whole of the country. Training and re-training facilities form part of the plans. Also included, in the hope of providing (and maintaining) better services in the rural areas, is housing accommodation for rural midwives. Rural health services are presently a recognised weak spot in the nation's health infrastructure, and the emphasis of the expansion programme is on the building up of facilities in the rural areas.

The capital costs in terms of construction of buildings are considerable. So are the attendant operating costs, which include a constantly-growing demand for vehicles (for visiting health workers and midwives), as well as for staffing at both senior and para-medical levels.

The training and provision of vehicles could well prove in time to be one of the most valuable parts of the programme. It is significant that present plans envisage re-training of midwives and other para-medical personnel. If, as is intended, their activities really broaden out to include family planning services, nutrition education, child care, and health prevention as well as cure, they can carry the "family welfare" approach to the client, rather than create a service and wait for the client to come to it.

3. NEW LEGISLATIVE APPROACHES AND INCENTIVES

Parallel with the efforts to improve and expand the official family planning programme, the Government is also seeking to facilitate individual access to fertility control methods. Thus, abortion previously authorised on "social grounds" only has been made available to anyone who wishes and, according to the statistics, is becoming increasingly popular.

Another new approach now makes it possible to buy contraceptive supplies at the local pharmacy, at only a minimal cost (with a heavy Government subsidy) and upon presentation of a once-only doctor's prescription. The fact that this measure has been carried into law suggests that medical opinion in Tunisia is not an insuperable obstacle to a certain de-professionalising of family planning services.

Tunisia is also developing financial incentives to encourage a small family norm: for example, family allowances now cease after the fourth child. (The fact that *four* children is considered a reasonable family size may perhaps be taken as a sign of the Government's generally relaxed approach to the problem of population growth; or it may attest to a realistic sense of what is likely to be acceptable in the context of current mores and traditions.)

PROGRAMMES AFFECTING POPULATION INDIRECTLY

The policies pursued by the Tunisian Government under the Fourth Development Plan which would seem of most immediate interest for their potential effect on population are in the following areas: employment, and associated with it, migration; rural development; and income redistribution. All these are part of the attempt to raise the quality of life, as stated in the Plan. Education has not been included here, despite its recognised relationship with fertility levels, because the Tunisian emphasis on education is so well established. (Our concern here is primarily with development strategies that appear to offer *new* possibilities for tackling the problem of population growth.)

Under the present Four-Year Plan (and according to all accounts, also under the Fifth), the creation of new employment possibilities is a primary planning goal. The problem of unemployment, and particularly that of young people, has suddenly become much aggravated in that emigration possibilities, which hitherto provided a comfortable safety valve for Tunisia's unemployed, have drastically shrunk with the recession in the host countries of Northern Europe[6]. New openings have therefore to be found at home, and the Government is actively pursuing programmes of "création et consolidation d'emplois" (new labour-creating investments and re-training).

Government planning is assuming that in due course emigration in substantial numbers will eventually cease, which means, of course, not only an addition to the effective population, but to the population of the country as a whole. From the population point of view, therefore, it is urgently necessary to create jobs for the labour force that will thus be increasing even faster than the already rapid rate of natural growth. At the same time, it is particularly important that the new job and training programmes be backed up by intensive and consistent family planning education and services.

The programme of rural development is still in the experimental stages (40 million dinars under the present Plan, rising to possibly 100 million under the Fifth Plan). Both amounts are modest in relation to the magnitude of the task.

The policy is designed to improve conditions of life in the rural areas in order to arrest the drift away from the land (there is actually a shortage of agricultural labour in Tunisia). It is a genuinely "integrated" approach, comprising the intensification of agricultural production in the newly-irrigated areas, creation of new farming activities in under-utilised areas, training of young men and women (with particular attention to providing some better possibilities of living to those at the lowest levels of education and economic situation) and, a very important aspect, using these various activities as incentives to re-grouping the highly dispersed populations of certain regions of the country into new village communities. Such measures, by raising the standard of living of the rural poor, are likely also to eventually reduce fertility. The National Office of Family Planning and Population now collaborates closely with the Ministry of Agriculture in training field workers to take family planning into the rural areas.

Redistribution of income, the third policy, is being attempted by a number of means—family allowances, the introduction of a minimum industrial wage (the same for women as for men) and also of a minimum agricultural wage, and tax exemption for the lower paid workers. All these measures, by helping to raise the level of the poorest sectors of the population, are, as the Bucharest Conference pointed out, helping to solve "the problem of population".

---

6. The situation has since been further compounded by the return—for political reasons—of thousands of Tunisian workers from Libya.

ADMINISTRATIVE STRUCTURE

The Tunisian Government structure has for some time included a special body concerned with population matters. In 1973, it was up-graded from its original status of "Institut" (National Institute of Family Planning and Mother and Child Health) to that of "Office" (National Office of Family Planning and Population). The new body, now separated from the MCH function, has far broader responsibilities. It is still, however, ultimately dependent on the Ministry of Health and uses the Ministry's organisation and staff to carry out its field activities.

The function of the Office is broadly that of translating the Government's population policies into actual project activities. The policies are formally handed down through the "Supreme Council for Population", which is presided over by the Prime Minister, and on which are represented all relevant Ministries and national organisations. The Head of the Office (Président Directeur Général) is Secretary of the Council: the Vice President is the Minister of Public Health.

Councils of a similar composition to the Supreme Court of Population are held in each of the regions, presided over by the Governor. The annual meeting of these Regional Councils enables the Office to get local opinion on the programmes that it is proposing to carry out in the area. The central Government at the present time seems to expect the regional Government to be very "population-conscious". (Not only does each "Gouvernorat" have its family planning targets, but the central Government awards annual prizes for the three most successful programmes of family planning, including sterilisations. In practice, however, the extent of the concern in the regions for the promotion of family planning activities tends to vary with the interest of the individual Governor.)

The Office is responsible for drawing up the population programmes (the three fields of activity are educational and promotional, medical and research). It has a small head-quarters staff and budget for this purpose but no field staff and no budget for field operations. For project purposes, the Office operates through the most appropriate government department, or in some cases, with non-governmental bodies (e.g. Trade Unions, the National Union of Tunisian Women). Thus the school population education programme is carried out by means of a specially created Committee within the Ministry of Education; family planning clinics are constructed and staffed by the Ministry of Public Health; family planning and welfare workers are provided through the Ministry of Social Affairs, and the family welfare message on radio and television is put across through the Ministry of Information. The service concerned provides not only the personnel but the financing required for the activity.

In theory, the role of the Office in the implementation of the policies formulated by the Supreme Council for Population, would seem to facilitate an integrated approach to population, whereby the Office would effectively co-ordinate the activities of the various sector Ministries which are relevant to population. In practice, however, the Office still concentrates on the link between family planning and health programmes (both included in the term "family welfare"), and on population education activities. This is partly, no doubt, because of the structural relationship between the Office and the Ministry of Public Health, and partly perhaps because of the close working relationship between the Président Directeur Général of the Office and the Health Minister.

Although it would be true to say that there is good co-ordination between the different services involved in family planning, this is not widely true in areas outside the health service. As a result of its primarily health service orientation, the Office is not often involved in "indirect" population activities. It feels that it is not its function to sponsor programmes in other sectors that may have an "indirect" effect on fertility, nor does it actively seek to encourage other sector Ministries to undertake them. The necessity for a genuinely integrated approach to all aspects of improving social welfare, including family planning, is recognised in principle (cf. President Bourguiba in 1975: "La meilleure prime d'incitation à la contraception... est la lutte contre la malnutrition et le sous-emploi") ("The best incentive to contraception... is the struggle against malnutrition and unemployment.") But in practice, population is not necessarily always the priority consideration. For example, current official employment policies are deliberately discouraging new employment possibilities for women, on the grounds that recent new industrial investment has tended to create jobs for women rather than for men. In this instance, concern for the traditional equilibrium of the family has been put before that of creating paid employment for women as a disincentive to fertility.

POPULATION ASSISTANCE

The Tunisian Authorities admit that their population programme would have had great difficulty in getting off the ground had it not been for external assistance. In particular, aid made a major contribution to the construction of family planning clinics and health centres and to the training of personnel. It would appear that the expansion and operation of the national Family Planning Programme is predicated upon the continuance of such assistance. The population education programme also needs foreign assistance for audio-visual materials and equipment.

Some donors are becoming much more flexible in the terms and nature of their assistance to population activities. Aid is now used to finance the operating costs of the family planning programme in local currency, as well as to finance construction costs. One new programme is experimental door-to-door distribution of contraceptives.

One point on which the Tunisian Administration seems to be unanimous is that the population programmes no longer need foreign assistance in the form of expert personnel. There now exist, thanks in part to aid-financed training programmes, sufficient numbers of qualified personnel at both senior medical and para-medical levels to staff the expanded family planning/public health services. It is claimed moreover, that there will shortly be so much over-concentration of the medical profession in the cities that the problem of getting doctors to practice in the countryside will be taken care of by sheer force of professional competition.

The present picture suggests that by far the greatest share of foreign assistance available for population activities will continue to be channelled into family planning and other "direct" population programmes (i.e. population education, family welfare, etc.). This is largely because the Office, which is interested primarily in this sort of programme, is regarded by many aid donors as the only valid channel for population assistance. Any donors, therefore, who are interested in supporting also some indirect approaches to population, will need to seek out some other Government body sufficiently interested in the population problem to assume responsibility for such an activity.

It is likely that the indirect approach to population assistance will not commend itself to those donors who require prospects of a satisfactory return on their programmes in cost-benefit terms. On the other hand, it may well be possible to interest some donors who prefer not to get involved in direct population programmes but are concerned about population and favour the "wide" approach, i.e. alternative "ways in" to problems of population. Some of the indirect strategies of the Tunisian Government could usefully benefit from outside assistance to accelerate and broaden the actions proposed. For instance, the interesting initiatives in the field of rural development (although some of these are somewhat in the nature of "micro-projects") could, if expanded, offer possible alternative approaches to direct population assistance.

These activities have an additional advantage for aid donors in that the department of the Tunisian Government responsible for them is the Ministry of Planning. Since the Ministry is, by its mandate, responsible for taking an overall view of development needs and strategies in the different sectors, it could also constitute an appropriate point of contact for donors interested in contributing to integrated approaches to the population problem.

The Tunisian Authorities are just beginning to be interested in "integrated" approaches to population. Aid could be useful to encourage these approaches and to help design specific integrated population projects.

LATIN AMERICA

BOLIVIA
BRAZIL
MEXICO

Officials in the above countries were interviewed by Dr. Angela Molnos, consultant.

BOLIVIA

Total population[1]	4,647,836
Population under age 20[1]	52.17 %
Population density per sq. km.[1]	4.23
Rate of growth[1]	2.10 %
Crude birth rate (per thousand)[1]	43.72
Crude death rate (per thousand)[1]	17.96
Life expectancy (total)[1]	46.75 years
Per capita national income (1974)[2]	$ 299
Literacy rate[3]	41 %

Sources:
1. Plan Social Operativo, 1978.
2. U.N., *Statistical Yearbook*, 1976.
3. 1976-1980 Five Year Plan.

INTRODUCTION

The Bolivian Government had no declared population policy at the time of Bucharest, nor has it adopted one since. With a total population of barely 5½ million people and an average population density of barely 5 persons per square kilometer, most Bolivians feel that their country is under-populated and needs more people for its development and defense. Where a national "population problem" is recognised at all, it is in the form of the economic problem resulting from an unbalanced geographical distribution and loss of valuable labour force through emigration.

At the same time, Bolivia is characterised by a high rate of fertility, very high infant mortality, and a high rate of sickness among both mothers and children. The Bolivian Government periodically manifests concern about these problems. However, the very strong anti-family planning stance of the Church and of certain political groups in Bolivia has so far prevented the Government from any consistent attempt to offer family planning services as part of public health care. One such attempt was made between 1964 and 1969, but the Government was forced to withdraw under pressure. A second initiative, attempted since the Bucharest Conference, has met the same fate.

At the present time, therefore, developments in the field of population since Bucharest have been, if anything, a set-back. The experience to date seems to show a series of small advances on the part of the Government, followed by retreats. The Bucharest Conference, although it aroused considerable interest and discussion, does not seem to have broken this pattern.

Although the Government of Bolivia has no official population policy, the country's circumstances make for a pro-natalist outlook.

Bolivia is very conscious of its situation as a small land-locked country, surrounded by richer and more powerful neighbours (to whom, in the 19th century, it had lost two-thirds of its territory). Although it no longer fears external aggression, Bolivia still sees the danger of further de facto losses of territory, through encroachment of foreign settlers. On both political and military grounds, most Bolivians would like to see the national population increase in size.

For the Bolivian Authorities, there are two aspects of the country's population characteristics that cause serious concern. The first is the uneven geographical distribution. Bolivia's rich tropical lowlands in the east and north-east, the areas of greatest economic potential, are markedly under-populated, while the bulk of the population is crowded into the High Sierras (the Antiplano), an inhospitable region of very limited absorptive capacity. As a consequence, Bolivia sees its best lands attracting foreign settlers from across the borders, while Bolivians in other parts of the country are being forced to emigrate in large numbers for lack of job opportunities at home.

Emigration is thus the second disturbing aspect. It embraces skills at all levels: professionals, skilled workers and agricultural labourers[1]. The country, in fact, is caught in a vicious circle of people leaving because of lack of jobs, while at the same time the economy suffers from a shortage of qualified workers.

Those people who do not emigrate, but who can no longer subsist on the land, tend inevitably to drift to the cities. The resultant problem of "los marginales", the non-educated, jobless and homeless in the capital city of La Paz, in particular, is growing steadily more disturbing. Significantly, at the two Latin American Regional Meetings on Population in San José (April 1974) and Mexico City (March 1975), Bolivia made no reference to fertility, despite the fact that its birth rate is one of the highest in the region. It did, however, state that it felt that its urban concentration was too high.

Economic and political considerations apart, Bolivia's high rate of fertility is itself a cause for concern in that it is accompanied by very high rates of infant mortality and a high rate of sickness among both mothers and children. Demographic data for Bolivia are not very firm: the estimates for fertility rate range from 43.7 per 1,000 to 47.0 per 1,000, and for infant mortality, the estimates again vary widely, some going as high as 157 per 1,000[2]. What is clear, however, despite the variations in the figures, is that they indicate a social and health problem of disturbing magnitude.

It seems clear also that the Government would like to be able to do something about it. In 1968, it took the first tentative steps to explore the possibility of introducing some family planning services as part of the public health function. A "Department of Family Protection" was set up within the Ministry of Health

---

1. Some professionals emigrate immediately after graduating, without even attempting to look for employment in Bolivia. Even among the peasants who seasonally migrate to Argentina under temporary harvesting contracts, a substantial number remain outside Bolivia for good.

2. For example: United Nations figures, for the period 1970-1975, estimate the average rate of population growth at between 2.48 per cent and 2.69 per cent; the annual birth rate at between 43.7 and 43.9 per 1,000; the death rate at 17 or 18 per 1,000; and the rate of natural increase at 2.5 or 2.6 per cent. The Population Council gives slightly higher estimates: birth rate 47 per 1,000; death rate 18 per 1,000; and annual rate of growth 2.9 per cent. IBRD estimates the birth rate at 43.7 per 1,000; rate of growth at 2.6 per cent; and infant mortality rate (1970 estimate) at 154 per 1,000.

to be responsible for studying and co-ordinating proposals for child care and family planning. At the same time, a Mixed Commission on Demography and Family Planning was established to sponsor research into population problems. Neither of these were yet action programmes, but they were the first signs of official concern in this area.

The prevailing political atmosphere in Bolivia prevented these small beginnings from developing further. Not only is family planning anathema to the Church, but, as in many countries of Latin America, any idea of "population policy" is thought to be synonymous with "population control". This brings in not only the Church, which the Government is very reluctant to defy, but also the young leftists, ever ready to label any family planning initiative as "biological imperialism", "genocide", etc., and the work of outside "imperialist" donor agencies[3].

The Government accordingly made no further effort to pursue these first initiatives and it was not until 1974, the year of Bucharest, that PROFAM, a national affiliate of the IPPF, was established in Bolivia.

Still without declaring any national population policy, the Government of Bolivia was proceeding modestly to provide some family planning services to its poorer citizens as part of maternal and child health care, when the results of the 1976 census became known. The first nation-wide census to have been held since 1950, the fact of its being organised at all was generally considered (by the international community) as a great step forward. As it turned out, it has provided ammunition for the pro-natalists' cause, as its results showed the actual population of Bolivia to be below the estimated figure. As a consequence, the opponents of population programmes have been able to present any attempt to limit fertility as a reduction in the size of the national population and hence a threat to national security. The Government has bowed to the renewed strength of this pro-natalist wind. While not itself pro-natalist, it has stopped for the time being any further attempts to offer the means of fertility limitation.

Population policies have thus again been brought to the fore-front of the political scene in Bolivia. At the present moment, the situation is much more restrictive than two years ago when (thanks to lobbying by PROFAM among Bolivian women's leaders), the right of women to family planning services was included in the official Bolivian statement at the International Women's Year Conference.

DEVELOPMENTS SINCE BUCHAREST

The World Population Conference at Bucharest, with the intensive preparation that preceded it in all parts of the world, and the subsequent Latin American Consultative Conference in Mexico, undoubtedly stimulated considerable awareness and interest in Bolivian educated classes regarding the whole population issue. In the months following the Conference, a public controversy ensued as to the position the Government should take.

The Church promptly launched a fierce anti-birth control campaign. In a pastoral letter, it condemmed as "modern genocide" and international domination,

---

3. It appears that between 1960 and 1968, clandestine sterilisations were performed in rural areas without explaining to the women what the operation meant and its irreversible nature. Although those presumed responsible were banned from Bolivia nearly ten years ago, the issue is still used and makes headlines. An example is a speech reported in the Mexican newspaper El Día as recently as 19th October 1976 (La Esterilización de Indígenas, Plan para Desaparecer al Pueblo Boliviano).

the foreign aid that had been given to family planning activities in Bolivia. The Government replied that it was supporting programmes of "responsible parenthood", but disclaimed any intention of seeking "birth control" in the sense of regulation of fertility. The Church eased tensions to a degree by giving its approval to the Government's limited position. At this point, the Church even went so far as to recognise, with the Government, that education for "responsible parenthood" should include sex education. With this qualified approval, the Government began to provide some family planning services as part of a programme to reduce infant and maternal mortality.

The Government used PROFAM (incorporated in April 1974) to help get the programme started. Working under the aegis of the Department for the Protection of the Family, within the Ministry of Health, PROFAM ran the Government's clinics as well at its own. There were five PROFAM clinics in La Paz and one belonging to the Ministry; a PROFAM clinic in Santa Cruz and a Ministry post-partum clinic in Cochabamba. PROFAM assisted the Ministry in providing training in family planning in La Paz for physicians, nurses and other para-medical personnel. It was also assigned responsibility for processing national family planning service statistics and carrying out family planning information and education activities.

In January 1976, the Government launched a Five-Year Comprehensive Programme of Maternal and Child Health Care, with the assistance of UNFPA. (The UNFPA contribution to the Programme was to be approximately $1.5 million; that of the Bolivian Government $9 million.) The Programme was to cover cancer detection, treatment of venereal diseases and infertility, and extend progressively to pre- and post-natal care, family planning, birth delivery, child care and nutrition.

But this initiative was short-lived. Because of internal political pressures, the Government has had to sacrifice its family planning activities sponsored in this way. In fact, it has been forced to stop all official and private family planning activities. In August 1977, the corporate charter of PROFAM was declared invalid, the co-operation between PROFAM and the Ministry of Health ceased and the family planning clinics run by PROFAM and/or the Ministry of Health closed down. There are therefore no official population programmes in operation in Bolivia at the present time.

PROFAM, up to the reversal of Government policy, had gained support for family planning among certain sectors of the population through its information and education activities. Some of the labour unions, for example, have been offering family planning services within their health coverage for families of workers. (It is not known how long these activities will continue.)

OTHER POPULATION-RELATED ACTIVITIES

Sex Education

Sex education has been accepted by the Church in Bolivia as part of education for family welfare, but on the understanding that it does not extend either to the societal implications of population trends or to knowledge about modern methods of contraception. The Bolivian Association for Sex Education (ABES) works in collaboration with the Ministry of Education and Culture, the Ministry of Health and, interestingly, the Education Department of the Catholic Church. The objective is to provide sex education in schools with a view to inculcating the idea of responsible parenthood, partly among groups who will themselves have a "diffusion role" (teachers and parents) and partly among school children through inclusion of sex education in the public school curriculum. In 1975, the activities of ABES were included in the National Plan of Education and received some funding from US AID.

Research

The Bolivian Government encouraged demographic research through a number of bodies, leading up to the national census. One of the objectives of the various field tests and sample surveys undertaken in the preceding years was to provide training for personnel to conduct and analyse the results of the nation-wide census. The most important body involved in demographic research is the National Family Centre (CENAFA), a semi-autonomous, non-profit making organisation created in 1968. Its objectives include, in addition to research and training in the field of population and human reproduction, a certain amount of technical assistance and dissemination of information. CENAFA was instrumental in improving the family planning climate in Bolivia until the creation of PROFAM, when its importance in the informational aspect of family planning work began to decline.

The census itself, assisted by funding from UNFPA, was initiated in 1974 and enumerated in the latter half of 1976. Before this, the precise demographic situation of the country was not known. The first Five-Year Development Plan 1976-1980 was prepared by the Ministry of Planning and Co-ordination without the benefit of the census results. Although introduced as representing "an important step in the process towards the full and integrated realisation of the Bolivian man" and intended "to define a development strategy for the country", the Plan does not make any reference to population as a possible factor in that strategy.

There is also a Centre for Social Science Research in Bolivia (CIS)[4]. Although not a specialised population body, it has a special interest in the population field and carries out some experimental projects as part of its research activities.

PROGRAMMES AFFECTING POPULATION INDIRECTLY

One aspect of the country's population characteristics with which the Government of Bolivia is directly concerned is its unbalanced geographical distribution. The people of the Highlands, mostly Aymara and Quechua Indians (representing 40 per cent of the population) live in conditions of very great deprivation and the notion of resettling them on the Plains has long held a romantic appeal[5]. Although the Government has a general policy of integrated development, designed to incorporate these communities more closely into the mainstream of the national life and raise their living standards, it does not have the resources for the ambitious master plan that would be needed to carry out this policy on a national level.

Meanwhile, various "integrated programmes" are taking place under different auspices, mostly limited in scale. One such is the Food and Nutrition Programme

---

4. Supported by US AID and the Population Council.
5. Several attempts over the years have been made by the Bolivian Authorities and the international community to improve the standard of living of the Indian communities, generally with little lasting effect.

in the countryside around La Paz, using Mothers' Clubs as its nuclei. A Government programme, started with FAO help, its original purpose was to provide subsidized foodstuffs for rural communities unable to support themselves. In 1972, education, health and socio-economic activities were added. The programme is now based on a principle of self-help: each Mothers' Club is autonomous, its success depending on the members' skills at originating and carrying out projects (some, by 1976, had become self-supporting community businesses). The Government has promised to improve health facilities in those villages where the Mothers' Clubs are strong. As and when family planning services become acceptable again in the context of MCH and general health care, these "Clubs" could offer a useful way of bringing family planning information and supplies to rural communities.

FOREIGN AID

In all fields of development, with the exception of population activities, Bolivia welcomes foreign aid, and the aid community, hopeful of the sustained political and monetary stability of the country since the present Government took over in 1971, has been glad to provide it[6]. There has been no lack of offers of assistance—even for family planning.

Up to 1977, the Government had accepted aid for a number of population projects. The largest single contributor has been UNFPA which helped to finance the census and had begun to contribute towards the Government's MCH programme: it is now considering how to allocate the amount which the Government is unable to spend on family planning (for instance, whether there are some population activities which are acceptable in the present political climate). Other donors have included the IPPF, the Population Council and the Pathfinder Fund. Bilateral aid has come from US AID. Most of this assistance has gone to support private or semi-private Bolivian institutions.

As direct aid for population activities is no longer acceptable (since August 1977), the only way at present in which the aid community can help Bolivia alleviate her population problems is by the indirect approach. By focussing on uncontroversial but obviously useful measures that affect people's daily lives (improving the health services, particularly in the rural areas, expanding primary education, etc.), aid can help create conditions conducive to eventual decline in infant mortality and fertility rates. Some interesting initiatives ("micro-projects") are currently underway at the community level.

---

6. Bolivia's per capita national income places her outside the category of "Least-Developed".

BRAZIL

Total population (1977)[1]	112,830,000
Population under age 20 (1977)[1]	52.2 %
Population density per sq. km. (1975)[1]	12.5 %
Rate of growth (1975)[1]	2.7 %
Crude birth rate (per thousand) (1978)[1]	33.0
Crude death rate (per thousand) (1976)[1]	10.0
Life expectancy (total) (1971)[1]	61 years
Per capita national income (1973)[2]	$ 729
Literacy rate (1970)[3]	65.9 %

Sources:
1. Brazilian Government figures.
2. U.N., Statistical Yearbook, 1976.
3. IBRD, Comparative Education Indicators, 1978.

INTRODUCTION

Brazil, with a population of over 110 million, the fifth largest country in the world, potentially one of the richest and most powerful, has traditionally been strongly pro-natalist. Many Brazilians still feel that far from the population outstripping the country's resources, the missing factor for Brazil's fulfillment is people. They point to the self-evident need for more people in the sparsely-inhabited provinces of the north and west, if these are to develop. This view has been backed by the powerful Roman Catholic Church, which shows no signs of softening its hostility to family planning. It was therefore expected that Brazil would stand by her populist policies at Bucharest. The Government's volte face surprised everyone.

The Brazilian Government declared at Bucharest that it recognised the right of every couple to plan their family and the obligation of the State to provide the necessary information and means. Given the Federal structure of the Brazilian Government, the initiative is left to the individual States and municipalities to introduce family planning programmes if they so wish. The interest of the Brazilian experience since Bucharest is the extent to which the States have acted on the broad authorisation for family planning implied in the Federal Government's statement in 1974.

Brazil's official policies remained pro-natalist right up to the eve of the Bucharest Conference. As late as the meeting of the U.N. Population Commission in 1973, the Brazilian Government was publicly proclaiming its resistance to the idea of limiting population growth[1].

Until the 1950s, Brazil was a predominantly agricultural country, where a large labour force (unskilled and semi-skilled) was the basic need. Since then, a period of rapid industrialisation and economic development had brought in its train, among the other inevitable problems, a new class of urban poor, clustering round the industrial centres, deprived, overcrowded, badly educated and often unemployed. In response, a greater concern for social welfare and social justice, as well as economic growth, has gradually developed among educated Brazilians.

Brazilian economists are aware of the significance of the demographic factor in the planning process and of the need to provide means of fertility limitation to poor families. By the time of Bucharest, these views had gathered sufficient popular support and political weight for the Government to change its official approach and support voluntary family planning[2].

The Government's population policy, as expressed at Bucharest, is support for the basic human right of the individual to determine the size of his family and have the knowledge and means to do so effectively. It is written into the Second Development Plan (1975-76): "The orientation of Brazilian demographic policy is that of respecting each couple's freedom in deciding the desired number of children, once the information is made available which permits full examination of the question. The option is free, without any pressure towards either increasing or reducing fertility"[3].

At the same time, the Government of Brazil now overtly recognises the need to maintain an overall balance between economic development and population growth. The Second Development Plan includes a clear statement of the economic and social problems posed by unrestricted population growth: "It is obvious that given a certain GNP growth rate, the greater the population growth rate, the slower will be the average increase of per capita income; and given a certain investment rate, the greater the allocation of resources for social needs, derived from the population growth (especially in a country with a predominantly young population like Brazil), the less resources will be available for investment in economic infrastructure and in the capacity increase of the directly productive sectors." In effect, Brazil, almost a continent in itself, requires several different regional population policies according to the economic needs of the particular areas of the country.

---

1. In what was probably the last public pro-natalist statement on behalf of the Brazilian Government, the Brazilian Ambassador to the UN, in October 1973, made a vehement attack on the draft World Population Plan. He maintained that his Government repudiated the conclusions of "The Club of Rome's" report "Limits to Growth", because it believed, to the contrary, that all resources, including non-renewable ones, were virtually infinite, that States need power, and that one element of power is a large population. He even suggested that the word "action" should be taken out of the draft Plan.

2. The official opposition even looks on the issue as a potential vote-getter and plans to include family planning in its political platform.

3. This emphasis on the freedom of the couple to make their own decision is important since in Portuguese "planejamento familiar" (family planning) can be misunderstood. The word "planejamento" is understood as something planned by the State. In fact, this is far from the Government's policy, which is clearly based on the human rights principle and on the voluntary approach to family planning.

Since the Bucharest Conference, the Government has given its new approach to population minimum publicity inside Brazil. No targets have been set either for population growth or reduction and no family norms publicised. In fact, there are still many Brazilians, even in positions of authority, who know nothing about the Government's stand at Bucharest or its new population policy.

Since Bucharest, implementation of the new official policy has proceeded slowly. Where family planning is offered as a public service, it is linked with health services, in the interest primarily not of lowering fertility rates, but of reducing high infant mortality and improving the health of mothers.

At first, the Government simply gave overall authorisation for the individual States to set up their own programmes: one State had already done so in 1971, four others have since followed suit. The State of Rio de Janiero wrote into its 1975 Constitution the promise that as part of its public health measures, "the State will pay special attention... to family planning and eugenic awareness within the family". But in Sao Paulo, an attempt to implement a family planning programme was defeated. However, the activities of the (private) Family Planning Association (BEMFAM)[4] have been increasing steadily and some of the States implement their family planning programmes with its co-operation.

In July 1977, the Federal Government finally committed itself to more direct, but still very limited initiatives after a decision by the Social Development Council that the Government should supply family planning information and services through the Ministry of Health's Maternal and Child Health Programme. In fact, the family planning element in the programme is still very small. The Social Development Council is under the chairmanship of the President of the Republic, so the Government is committed at the highest level. Even so, the decision was presented by the Minister of Health as a minor element in the campaign to promote mother and child health. It was intended in no way to stop population growth and indeed, might have the opposite effect, since it would ensure the survival of more healthy children.

This evolution is part of the Government's growing concern for social development. Having now achieved remarkable economic growth without accompanying social development, it is no longer expected in Brazil that health and social problems will solve themselves automatically through the "trickle-down" effect of economic growth. It is now recognised that many social problems (malnutrition, infant and maternal mortality, morbidity, abandonment of children —all of which are increasing even in the most prosperous areas like Sao Paulo) are linked to population. The Government is just beginning to tackle social problems directly by initiating policies and large-scale programmes concerning migration, urbanisation, regional disparities, education, health, nutrition and social security. It may be that dealing with these problems may eventually lead to a more active support for the closely-related problem of population growth also.

GOVERNMENT STRATEGIES

Implementation of the Government's population policy is only just beginning. The principal means are described briefly below:

DEVELOPMENT OF THE HEALTH SERVICE

The Federal Ministry of Health announced a programme of MCH care in 1974, but its role being normative and not executive, it defined the policy

---

4. Sociedade Civil de Bem-Estar Familiar do Brazil—an affiliate of the IPPF.

and objectives and left to the States the responsibility for running their own health services. Following the 1977 decision of the Social Development Council, the Federal Ministry of Health is now giving high priority to the establishment of an MCH programme in all the States.

At present, the programme includes family planning only for women classed as high-risk pregnancies, who will be offered free contraceptives. When announcing the programme, the Minister recommended that contraceptives be dispensed to women over 17 and under 40, for purposes of child-spacing ("inter-gestational counselling"), to those who have had an abortion or still-birth, and to those suffering from specifically identified illnesses or disabilities. There is to be no coercion, and even with the high-risk pregnancies, religious convictions, culture and personal choice must be respected. This programme is due to start in 1978 and continue for four years, during which time it is estimated that over 50,000 women will be treated, 10 per cent of whom will be "high-risk" cases. There are certain restrictions on methods of contraception: for example, no IUDs except for women in certain categories of age, parity and ill-health, no sterilisations or abortions except those permitted by law and no free issue of the Pill except under medical supervision (although prescriptions for the Pill which run for 12 months are now allowed).

The success of this programme will depend on the means for its delivery, specifically whether there are enough health centres, clinics or dispensaries to bring health services into the interior and whether there are sufficient trained personnel to carry it out. Between 1978 and 1981, it is hoped that 5,800 doctors, nurses and social assistants and 2,775 other para-medical personnel will be trained to diagnose and treat high-risk pregnancies and to provide family planning advice and services.

At present, within the health service in general and the MCH sector in particular, a major bottleneck hindering implementation is the ill-distribution and inadequate training of health personnel. Specifically, there are numbers of well-qualified doctors but a desperate shortage of auxiliary health workers[5]. Moreover, nearly half the professionals work in two States—Sao Paulo and Rio de Janiero. The Federal Government cannot simply redistribute its doctors, nor, if it could, would there be support for diverting qualified professional resources from the immediate needs of curative medicine to long-term preventive activities such as family planning. As it is considered that 70 per cent of Brazil's health problems could be dealt with by specially-trained para-medical personnel, the MCH training programme is an important first step to better health care generally.

DELIVERY OF FAMILY PLANNING SERVICES THROUGH THE STATES' HEALTH SERVICES

The Federal Government has not only given the States the freedom to initiate family planning policies if they wish, it can also itself provide budget allocations for specific projects—for example, the MCH programme. Whether or not a family planning element has been included in a State's health programme has been, in practice, very much a matter of whether the particular Governor is convinced of its necessity, and whether he feels that the people and the Adminis-

---

5. "The published information shows that in the year 1971, the Health Service had a total of 116,345 professionals of university level, of whom 49 per cent were doctors, 29 per cent dentists, 12 per cent pharmacists, 5 per cent veterinary surgeons and 5 per cent nurses. In population terms, that meant that for each 10,000 inhabitants, there were 5.9 doctors, 3.5 dentists, 1.4 pharmacists, 0.6 veterinary surgeons and 0.6 nurses." (Ministerio da Saude Fundacao Instituto Oswaldo Cruz, Instituto Presidente Castello Branco, Relatario Grupo de Trabalho sobre Recursos Humanos para la Saude, November 1974, p. 3.)

tration at municipal level are ready to accept family planning. The first State to introduce family planning information and services into its health services was the Rio Grande do Norte—before Bucharest—in 1971[6]. It co-operated with BEMFAM, which was given the responsibility to mobilise resources within the framework of the State's health infrastructure. The responsibilities of the State, on the one hand, and BEMFAM on the other, are defined in a contract which states that the aim is, first, to decrease maternal and infant mortality and, second, to discourage induced abortions by offering family planning advice and means of contraception (for the welfare of the family and the community). Funding can now come, in part at least, from the Federal Government, but it also comes from the State budgets and, where possible, outside donors. (BEMFAM has the right to organise outside funding where the donor does not require that the request must come from the Government. This effectively limits its source of major funding to the IPPF.)[7] By the end of 1976, three other States in the north had followed the example of Rio Grande do Norte—Alagoas, Paraiba, Pernambuco— all using BEMFAM support in the same way.

ENCOURAGEMENT TO BEMFAM

The activities of BEMFAM have had increasing support from both the Federal Government and the States since it was first set up in 1965. It has played an important role in the States' efforts to implement their own family planning policies (see above).

At Federal level, the role of BEMFAM has been less important. However, it has cultivated its contacts at the highest levels of Government, since, in its view, only the Government will be able to create the climate and the framework for family planning activities throughout the whole country. It has been rewarded with the policy *volte-face* announced at Bucharest.

COMMUNITY-BASED DISTRIBUTION

Large-scale CBD programmes are operating in several States run in conjunction with BEMFAM and with funding from IPPF (which contributes approximately $4 million per annum). These have the tacit support of the Federal Government. As elsewhere, the CBD approach is potentially very attractive, especially if it can be made self-supporting financially. In a country as large as Brazil, where supplying contraceptive pills only to the women of fertile age who are on social security would be extremely costly, this is particularly true.

SUPPORT FOR RESEARCH

The Federal Government encourages and supports research relevant to population problems. An example is the work of the IBGE (Fundacao Instituto Brasileiro de Geografie e Estatistica) one of whose programmes is a survey of 55,000 families nation-wide, in order to study how demographic variables interrelate with other socio-economic variables. Family planning and population-related research is also now carried out by a number of State universities within their respective departments of Medicine, Biology, Social Science, etc.

---

6. Before taking the decision, the Governor held meetings and discussions in every municipality to make sure that both the local people and the local executives and mayors agreed with the policy.

7. BEMFAM has received some small-scale assistance from the Pathfinder Fund and other sources.

The Government has not yet embarked on any action to motivate people to *want* family planning: action is limited to provision of services to meet already existing demand. Moreover, delivery is limited mainly to the Government's health services. No use has been made to date of the social security system, which, with its several million beneficiaries, could provide access to family planning to a large section of the "vulnerable" population. However, the Government is now beginning to study this possibility.

PROGRAMMES AFFECTING POPULATION INDIRECTLY

The Government is embarking on many large-scale programmes of social development which are likely to have eventually an indirect effect on population.

Its efforts to balance the urban and rural populations are one example. With 65 per cent of the population concentrated in towns whose average growth rate was 5.2 per cent per year between 1960 and 1970 (as compared with a rural growth rate of 0.7 per cent in the same period), the idea is to "fix" the rural population and develop middle-sized townships to contain the drift to the urban areas around Rio de Janiero and Sao Paulo. There is also a big increase in spending on education—not simply to provide the economy with a qualified labour force, but as part of the broader social aim of giving people better living conditions and prospects.

It is difficult to say at this stage whether Brazil, which entered the field of population policy relatively late, but which has very able and sophisticated economic analysts and planners, will do things in the same way as other developing countries. Brazil's conversion to the cause of a population policy was announced at a time and in a milieu when the "development approach" was very much to the fore. Its Development Plan recognises the inter-relationship between population and all aspects of socio-economic development, but this recognition has as yet had very little influence in practice. When it gets going, it will be interesting to see whether the Brazilian approach will be more classical than developmental after all, since its main strategies so far have been focussed on the MCH programmes.

AID

Brazil has received very little external aid for population so far. This is partly because the official policy has not been translated into large-scale programme action and partly because the Federal Government's identification with the official policy that it announced at Bucharest has since been far from active. There is the further feeling in Brazil that aid in any sector is not really a necessity (although it might in certain cases be a convenience), and that since Brazil is a rich and powerful nation, it does not need to ask for help from outside. In the case of aid for population, although the need is recognised at Federal level, the Government has been anxious not to appear as initiating programmes and forcing them on the States. But although the States (and BEMFAM) have the right to ask for aid, many of the international donor organisations insist that the request comes from the Federal Government. Thus many possible sources of aid (for instance, aid from UNFPA) are blocked.

Apart from IPPF's funding of BEMFAM, the only significant aid for population to date has been grants from the Ford Foundation for experimental MCH/family planning services and for bio-medical research.

MEXICO

Total population[1]	59,204,000
Population under age 20[1]	56.8%
Population density per sq. km.[1]	30
Rate of growth[1]	3.34%
Crude birth rate (per thousand)[1]	41.7
Crude death rate (per thousand)[1]	7.6
Life expectancy (total)[1]	65.5 years
Per capita national income (1970)[2]	$632
Literacy rate[3]	76%

Sources:
1. UNFPA, *Inventory of Population Projects 1975-76.*
2. U.N., *Statistical Yearbook,* 1976.
3. IBRD, *Comparative Education Indicators,* 1978.

INTRODUCTION

The Government of Mexico's decision in 1972 to adopt a national policy to limit the country's population growth was hailed as a significant event in the history of population policies in the Western Hemisphere. As an enthusiastic new convert, Mexico played an active part in the Bucharest Conference. The interest of the Mexican experience in the field of population since that time is to see how the Government has set about translating its population policy into programme action and what it has been able to achieve.

For most of the first half of the present century, the rate of population growth had remained low[1], due primarily to the high mortality rate. Economic boom and expansionist policies had led the Government to follow consistently pro-natalist policies right into the 1970s. In fact, in his 1969 election campaign, President Echeverria even adopted a pro-natalist stance as part of his platform and, when elected, effectively halted the initiatives in favour of family planning which had already begun under private auspices in the 1950s. It is significant therefore that only three years later, he was to completely reverse this policy.

The introduction of Mexico's national population programme has been accompanied by a decline in the population growth rate. The Mexican Authorities estimate that the crude birth rate, which was 45 per 1,000 in 1970, had fallen to approximately 41 per 1,000 by 1975-76. They reckon that the annual growth rate had thus fallen from 3.5 per cent to 3.2 per cent[2].

---

1. In the 1940s, population growth was 2.72 per cent per annum, in the 1950s it was 3.13 per cent, in the 1960s it was 3.43 per cent. (T.O. Sanders, Mexico 1974, *Demographic Patterns and Population Policy, American Universities Field Staff,* N. America Series, Vol. II, No. 1.)
    2. Figures taken from 1978 Work Programme of FEPAC.

POPULATION POLICIES

The decision to attempt to control Mexico's population growth was precipitated by many factors, but primarily by the drop in the rate of national economic growth—from 6 per cent per annum in the decade 1960-1970 to 4 per cent in 1971. At the same time, it was recognised that the steadily climbing population growth rate (which reached peaks of 3.5 per cent per annum and more in the early 1970s) was diluting development efforts and aggravating the various problems the country was facing in its process of modernisation: viz. the rapid rates of urbanisation (over 5.4 per cent per year), the high infant mortality (65 per 1,000), a high dependency ratio, serious health and nutritional deficiences, high unemployment, unequal income distribution and extreme regional disparities.

Mexico's official family planning programme began in 1973. In November of that year, a General Law on Population (effective as of January 1974) authorised the Government to take steps to "regulate the phenomena that affect the volume, structure, dynamics and distribution of the population in the country". The objective was defined as that of "regulating rationally and stabilising the growth of the population so as to achieve the best utilisation of the human and natural resources of the country". A National Population Council (CONAPO) was created for the purpose of formulating national demographic policy and coordinating demographic planning with social and economic development programmes.

Although Mexico is a strongly Catholic country, the separation of Church and State has allowed the Government to pursue its population policy. When the policy was first announced in 1972, the Bishops of Mexico even expressed their support for the principle of "responsible parenthood", i.e. the right of couples to make their own decision as to family size and spacing[3]. Leftist opinion has on the whole kept quiet, since it sees the population policy as part of an overall policy of more equal income distribution and elimination of poverty. The Government has sought to minimise any potential opposition by maintaining that it is seeking to control population not as an alternative, but as an aid to development. It has also made use of the publicity afforded to the population issue by the Bucharest Conference and the World Population Plan of Action to emphasize that its population policies have "international sanction".

Mexico's national population policy as defined by the Law of 1974 is very wide-ranging. Its scope includes, in addition to considerations of population size, the population's "structure, dynamics and distribution". The policy is intended to cover not only reduction of fertility, but also lowering of infant mortality, improving the status of women, control of emigration and geographical redistribution. The reduction of fertility has, however, until recently been the principal consideration, and despite the broad conceptual definition of population problems, the national population programme has been primarily concerned with family planning, MCH designed, in particular, to reduce infant mortality, and family planning motivation activities.

---

3. On occasion, the Church has made some mild criticism of the Government's extensive use of public media for promoting artificial contraception.

DEVELOPMENTS SINCE BUCHAREST

In the light of the first few years of the programme's operation, the Mexican Government has made a reappraisal of its policies and achievements and has decided on a number of shifts of emphasis.

First, there is a new determination to bring family planning to the rural areas. In terms of overall acceptances, the Government's family planning programme can claim no small success: from fewer than 29,000 family planning acceptors in 1971, the number had risen to over 600,000 by 1975[4]. Most of this effort, however, has been concentrated in the towns, and very little has yet been done in the rural areas, where very large families are still the accepted pattern. It is now official policy to make good this deficiency, by strengthening the rural health infrastructure and making greater use of para-medical personnel.

Second, the Government has now announced specific demographic targets. The General Population Law was essentially concerned with qualitative goals, i.e. improving the quality of life and human dignity, and the national population programme was not accompanied by targets of any kind. In 1977, in an attempt to make the programme more effective, the Government announced targets for the overall rate of population growth, the level of fertility and population redistribution. The new National Family Planning Programme announced in July 1977 aims to reduce the population growth rate to 2.6 per cent by 1982.

Third, the Government is making a greater effort to coordinate its population policies with development activities in other sectors. New administrative machinery has been set up for this purpose.

The President of Mexico, Senor Lopez Portillo, has given signs of being much more committed to the whole population question than was his predecessor. His concern covers not only the need to limit population growth, but the pressing urgency of dealing with the many serious problems that stem from it—namely the frightening rate of urban growth, youth unemployment, migration, etc. A fourth trend that may be noted, therefore, is a greater attention to the distributive aspects of population by measures to check urban growth and to exercice some control over the huge continuing migration of Mexican labour to the industrial cities of Mexico and to the United States.

STRATEGIES FOR IMPLEMENTING POPULATION POLICIES

The main focus of the Government's population activities has been devoted to getting family planning services spread among as wide a sector of the public as available resources and infrastructure would permit.

FAMILY PLANNING AND HEALTH SERVICES

Family planning services have been available in Mexico through private family planning associations since the 1950s, at first through the Association for Maternal Health and, since 1965, through the Foundation for Population Studies (FEPAC), an affiliate of the IPPF.

The Government entered the field in 1973, and began offering family planning as part of the public health services. The Ministry of Health and Welfare has official responsibility for supervising the Government's family

---

4. Population Council: Population and Family Planning Programmes—Factbook 1976.

planning programme, but provision of family planning services is split between the Ministry and Mexico's two powerful social security institutions, the Mexican Institute of Social Security (IMSS) and the Institute of Social Security for Government Workers (ISSTE).

This pattern has given the Mexican family planning programme its strong initial bias towards the urban population. IMSS, which is financially stronger than the Ministry of Health and serves twice as many people, operates primarily in the urban areas; ISSTE is also largely urban-based. The facilities of the Ministry of Health and Welfare are intended to provide medical care for the 90 per cent or so of the people in the rural areas who are not covered by social security. In fact, however, a considerable part of the rural population is still without reasonable access to modern health facilities of any kind.

IMSS began in 1973 by offering family planning services to its insured members, but almost immediately extended them to uninsured people also. All IMSS health facilities now offer family planning; its maternity services include post-partum programmes, and IUD insertion and sterilisation are provided free. In January 1977, a new Department of Family Planning was set up to improve its coverage and standard of service. ISSTE, which offers family planning services in 80 per cent of its larger urban-based clinics, also has plans to extend its family planning coverage, especially in the semi-urban areas.

Through the Ministry of Health and Welfare, which provides the contraceptives, the Government is trying to introduce the practice of contraception to large groups of the population organised in the army and major Governmental and semi-Governmental institutions. Contraceptives are now issued to the military, railway workers, the staff of the Federal Electricity Commission, the National Petroleum Company, etc.

In Government clinics, etc. contraceptives are provided free of charge. Those sold through private-sector outlets, however, do not have any Government subsidy. The Population Council is currently undertaking a study of commercial distribution of contraceptives in Mexico and this may lead to changes in the pricing policy.

These various initiatives are addressed to a very largely urban clientele. A Mexican study undertaken in 1976[5] found that 9 out of 10 contraceptive acceptors under the Government programme were urban dwellers; 9 out of 10 of those obtaining their contraceptives from private-sector outlets were also urban. The study reckons that use rates in the urban areas may run as high as 40-50 per cent of the eligible female population, whereas of women in the rural areas, probably not more than 5-10 per cent have any form of contraceptive protection.

The urban areas are the logical place to start a Government family planning programme. The urban population, often poor, living in over-crowded and insanitary conditions, is where the need is most urgent, and where changing economic, social and cultural patterns make it the most receptive. The urban areas are also those where the medical facilities and personnel are to be found.

The move to bring family planning to the rural areas of Mexico, where none of these factors are to be found, has barely begun. It will involve a considerable strengthening of health infrastructure, greater use of mobile health units for dispersed rural communities, and an efficient corps of para-medical and auxiliary personnel. Expansion of health care in the rural areas of Mexico and the introduction of family planning services will need to be tackled as a single objective.

---

5. Studies in Family Planning, by Alfredo Gallegos.

Family planning information and education occupies an important part of the Mexican Government's population programme. The Government runs extensive publicity campaigns, using media of all kinds to build up public awareness of the problem of over-population and the advantages of smaller families. (There is no attempt to recommend an ideal family size: family planning is presented as a means of child-spacing.)

CONAPO and the three major public health institutions have between them run a number of campaigns on these themes using television, radio, newspapers, posters, etc. The Government feels they have already been effective in breaking a number of taboos traditional to popular culture which are obstacles to acceptance of family planning in Mexico. (The publicity slogans show an interesting progression in approach. The first was "Let us become less numerous", followed by "The small family lives better", followed by "Senora, it is you who decides when you will become pregnant".) It is interesting that the emphasis is on the societal implications of high fertility rather than the personal[6].

Despite the ubiquity throughout Mexico of the transistor radio, and the use (supported by UNFPA on a pilot basis) of community theatre groups, mobile information units, etc., most of this informational activity has been directed at largely urban audiences. CONAPO is currently preparing new informational campaigns among the rural population, but feels that person-to-person contact, albeit costly in terms of training, is likely to be the most effective method.

The Mexican Government has taken energetic steps to introduce sex education in schools. The National Programme for Sex Education (carried out by the Ministry of Education under the general supervision of CONAPO) has financial assistance from UNFPA and SIDA and has developed rapidly. The necessary educational reforms have already been completed to introduce sex education into the school curriculum, and a start has been made at primary and secondary school levels (Government schools only—private schools are generally reluctant). Significantly, sex education includes not only human biology, but an attempt to inculcate the idea of a more equal role for men and women.

As the coverage of family planning services depends on the effectiveness of the vehicle provided by the health service, so population education depends for its success on the strength of the national educational system. At the present time, the total drop-out rate is extremely high (estimated by the Mexican Authorities at some 50 per cent at primary school level). Moreover, the rates are obviously still higher among the most deprived groups: peasants, people living in less developed areas, and girls[7].

Demographic Research

Mexico enjoys a very high quality research capacity in demography and related subjects in the Colegio de Mexico (Centre for Economic and Demographic Studies) and in CONAPO and FEPAC, which undertake research related to the operation of actual population programmes in Mexico. A National Fertility Survey (as part of the World Fertility Survey) is being undertaken by the Mexican Bureau of Statistics and the Census, supervised by CONAPO.

---

6. Government television programmes were followed by the slogan: "While you listened to this programme, 500 Mexicans were born", leading into an explanation of family planning as a solution to national and family problems.

7. Report by Ester Corona, President of the Mexican Association for Sex Education.

PROGRAMMES AFFECTING POPULATION INDIRECTLY

The Mexican Government's recognition of the relationship between population trends and the need to equalize opportunities, raise the status of women, improve levels of health and education, create new employment possibilities for the young, etc. is a theme frequently heard in public speeches[8]. The Government is trying to tackle these various problems by means of rural development activities of various kinds, creating new centres of economic activity in the rural areas and improving health care and schools in the countryside.

Budget expenditures on economic and social projects intended to infuse fresh life into the depressed rural areas have increased greatly since the beginning of the decade. Particular objectives are the increase of food production (Mexico is currently unable to produce enough food to keep up with the population increase, and nutritional levels are declining, particularly among the rural and urban poor); the development of agricultural industries and small-scale industrial production in depressed rural areas; improved health services (including family planning); and reduction of the high school drop-out rate and poor school performance.

The Government is also turning serious attention to the problem of the desperate over-crowding in the capital (Mexico City is now the most populous capital city in the world), and other major industrial cities. It is hoping to set an example by re-locating some government administrative services in the provinces.

Measures to deal with Mexico's urban problems may perhaps be considered as dealing with the *consequences* of high fertility rather than its determinants. One problem, however, which is recognised both as an important issue in itself and as a very direct determinant of fertility is the status of women. In Mexican popular tradition, the concept of "machismo" is still a powerful obstacle to limitation of family size, especially among the rural areas and the less educated urban poor. The Government took a significant first step in 1975 by passing a constitutional amendment declaring the equality of men and women before the law. To translate this legal move into popular acceptance of sex equality will require a lengthy and intensive preparation through education, backed by practical measures to offer women new opportunities for economic and social self-assertion. Perhaps the first step of all must be to raise living standards generally —so that poor families can afford to keep their daughters in school.

MACHINERY FOR IMPLEMENTING POPULATION PROGRAMMES

A national body at ministerial level for the purpose of integrating population policy with other policy objectives was created in 1974 when the Government announced its national population policy. CONAPO is chaired by the Secretary of the Interior and made up of the Ministers of Education, Health and Welfare, the Treasury, Foreign Affairs, Labour and Social Welfare, Finance and Public Credit, Programming and Budget, and Agrarian Reform.

Despite the wide scope of "population" policy, the responsibilities of CONAPO have been limited to strictly demographic matters, notably the preparation of family planning and population education programmes.

---

8. In the speech at the inaugural meeting of the IUSSP Conference in Mexico City in August 1977, President Lopez Portillo stressed that Mexico's population problem was not solely a matter of numbers, but rather of the Government's capacity to respond to "qualitative change", e.g. increasing urbanisation, the young age structure, etc. by providing adequate opportunities for employment, education and social services.

CONAPO's task is to integrate policy at the ministerial level. It may be relevant here to mention a small but practical step taken recently to facilitate co-ordination between socio-demographic development and planning at the *working level*. A new unit (CONFRONTA) has been set up in the National Statistical Office to analyse data and make recommendations to the relevant ministries on the demographic implications of national development trends. It represents an attempt to introduce demographic considerations into development planning as a regular part of the planning process.

New machinery has also been set up to co-ordinate the programmes of the several different governmental and private bodies involved in family planning. The Inter-Institutional Council for Family Planning was created in January 1977 to co-ordinate all family planning activities in Mexico. It is presided over by the Minister of Health and Social Welfare, but its membership (from CONAPO, the principal health and social security institutions and other relevant bodies) is at senior executive level.

POPULATION ASSISTANCE

When Mexico adopted a national population policy, the international community would have been more than willing to help launch it. In practice, however, Mexico has proceeded with a certain caution in accepting foreign aid for population, so as to avoid creating any suspicion that its policies were being influenced by outside interests. To date, only assistance from the U.N. is acceptable[9]. There is no bilateral assistance for population so far: the Swedish aid for sex education (approximately $2 million—Government of Mexico contribution approximately $22.5 million) is given through a funds-in-trust arrangement with the UNFPA.

Until now, therefore, Mexico has chosen a policy of "self-reliance" in its population activities. (CONAPO officials have stressed the desirability of not building up programmes on the supposition that aid will be forthcoming to fund them.)

The Mexican Authorities look to aid less as a source of funding than as a potentially valuable catalyst to sponsor innovative activities, to stress the need for regular evaluation of population programmes, and to provide exchanges of experience in the areas of socio-demographic and bio-medical research.

Up to the end of 1977, Mexico has received only small amounts of financial assistance. Apart from IPPF contributions to FEPAC, the only significant funding is from UNFPA, to assist the Ministry of Health and Welfare in the expansion of its MCH and family planning services (evaluation, training, education and supervision), the fertility survey, and in population communication (research and training). In most of these activities, the aid input is very small indeed compared to that of the Government.

---

9. A World Bank loan for population was under discussion for some time but the Government eventually decided against outside help.

AFRICA

KENYA
TANZANIA
ZAIRE

Officials in the African countries were interviewed by Julien Condé, OECD Development Centre.

KENYA

Total population[1]	13,251,000
Population under age 20[1]	56.8%
Population density per sq. km.[1]	23
Rate of growth[1]	3.38%
Crude birth rate (per thousand)[1]	48.0
Crude death rate (per thousand)[1]	14.3
Life expectancy (total)[1]	52.5 years
Per capita national income (1975)[2]	$209
Literacy rate[3]	40%

Sources:
1. UNFPA, *Inventory of Population Projects 1975-76.*
2. U.N., *Statistical Yearbook,* 1976.
3. IBRD, *Comparative Education Indicators,* 1978.

INTRODUCTION

Kenya, unlike most African countries, recognises that its high overall rate of fertility poses a national population problem. The Government of Kenya has accordingly formulated a national population policy designed to bring about a reduction in the birth rate, and has established a National Family Planning Programme for the purpose.

Kenya was the first African country south of the Sahara to adopt an official family programme. The rate of population growth has been increasing for the past three decades: the census returns showed that the annual growth rate had risen from 2.8 per cent to 3.3 per cent between 1962 and 1969 and to 3.5 per cent in 1974. But the problem for Kenya was not only the fast rate of growth, but the pressure that this implied on the available land resources. Although Kenya has a low average population density (23 inhabitants per square kilometer), the 90 per cent of the population which is rural is concentrated into the 17 per cent of the land area that is suitable for cultivation. In consequence, Kenya suffers from a disproportion of population to land resources to a greater extent than most African countries.

In 1967, the Government of Kenya announced the start of an official Family Planning Programme to supplement the work already being undertaken on a small scale by private family planning groups. In fact, however, there has been very little commitment to the Programme at ministerial level, and until recently, the main impetus has come from the international community who provided most of the finance and the necessary technical guidance.

137

BEFORE BUCHAREST

In 1965, the Kenyan Government made a request to the Population Council to study the population problems of the country and recommend solutions. A mission from the Population Council followed shortly thereafter and reported that the rate of population growth was incompatible with the Government's economic development targets. The report also suggested possible ways to reach an "ideal" population growth rate[1].

Following upon this report, in 1966, the Government declared its intention of pursuing policies to reduce the rate of population growth by means of voluntary family planning. It further announced the principle that family planning would henceforth be part of the National Development Plan. The Five-Year Development Plans drew attention to the impact of the high rate of population growth on economic development in general and on the standard of living of the individual Kenyan family. (Kenya is, to date, one of only seven African countries to take account of population in its development plans.)

The responsibility for carrying out the National Family Planning Programme was given to the Ministry of Health. The Ministry announced that it intended to make family planning information and services available as part of the maternal and child health care provided in government hospitals and public health centres. It did not, however, go into details of how it was planning to deliver these services.

The Government did not adopt the quantitative goals recommended by the Population Council and indeed set no specific demographic targets at the time aiming only at a "maximum" reduction of infant mortality and a "realistic" decrease in fertility. The approach was to be on child spacing ("make every child a 'free-choice' child") rather than on limitation of family size, and treatment for sterility was to be provided as well as contraceptive services. Participation in the Programme was to be entirely voluntary, with no incentives offered[2].

Official statistics show an impressive development of the Programme between 1967 and 1974: the number of Government dispensaries delivering family planning services increased from 58 to 298 and the total number of contraceptive users grew from 18,000 to 233,000. By 1974, one-third of the country's health centres were involved in the Programme.

Nonetheless, in spite of the Government's declared support, the Programme seems to have had very little real impact up to the time of Bucharest. As of 1974, no sign of a decline in population growth or in fertility was perceptible.

One of the reasons for this may be that, although the Ministers of Health and of Development Planning[3] strongly supported the Programme, there was little real commitment on the part of the President of the Republic or the rest of the

---

1. Specifically, the report recommended trying to reduce fertility by one-half within 10 or 15 years. To achieve this goal, IUDs were the most recommended means. For example, 25,000 insertions of IUDs were to be aimed at for the first year of the Programme and 150,000 by the end of the fourth year. Fifty thousand new acceptors of other contraceptive methods each year were to be added to the IUD acceptors.

2. The Authorities insist strongly upon the voluntary aspect of family planning. Individual customs, values and beliefs are fully respected. Since Kenya is divided into several ethnic groups, sometimes hostile to each other, this approach is very important and avoids creating social tension. Emphasis is not put on family limitation but on planning for desired family size, by means of birth spacing. Each couple is left to determine its own preferred family size, and the Government does not recommend any ideal "norm".

3. The name of the latter Ministry has since been changed to the Ministry of Finance and Planning.

Government.   Because of so many other development priorities, the Government was not able to finance the Programme adequately, and the major impetus came from the international community.   The Programme was accordingly started as a foreign-sponsored activity and did not build up the necessary infrastructure and personnel to enable it effectively to absorb large aid inputs.

In addition, the socio-economic conditions of the country were not conducive to the success of a large-scale national family planning programme.   Infant mortality was too high to allow rural mothers to think of using any contraception. Illiteracy prevented the mass of the rural population from understanding the family planning message.   Moreover, because of tribal animosities, no ethnic group would agree to control its fertility for fear that the other groups would out-number it.

A further problem was the inadequate health infrastructure, and, in particular, the shortage of medical and para-medical personnel qualified to deliver family planning and maternal and child health services.   Most of the patients in the dispensaries and health centres came for medical attention and not for family planning services, and there were so many that family planning services could only be offered once a week and sometimes even only once a month.   Further-more, there were far too few health centres in the rural areas.

SINCE BUCHAREST

Since Bucharest, the family planning programme has made some progress. It still, however, suffers from a lack of commitment at the highest levels of government.

Shortly before the World Population Conference, the Kenyan Government announced a new national population policy, which was included in the Third Plan (1974-78) (entitled "Third Development Plan and Equality in Kenya"). This, for the first time, represented a serious attempt to relate population programmes to development objectives in other economic and social sectors (in contrast to the earlier Plans which had simply referred to population in general terms). A new Five-Year Population Programme was announced in 1975 and incorporated in the Development Plan.

The new population policy marks a real step forward.   "Population" is no longer to be solely a matter of providing family planning, but is now officially recognised as part of a broad spectrum of social programmes, beginning with health (and reduction of infant mortality) and embracing also a broader develop-ment effort intended to raise the standard of living by reducing unemployment and income disparities, accelerating rural development and improving access to economic opportunities.   Kenya's official statement at Bucharest was an extract from the text of this policy.

Despite the broadening of context, the focus of Kenya's population activities remains reduction of fertility by means of family planning activities.   The new FiveYear Population Programme (1975-79) for the first time includes demo-graphic targets: natural increase is to be reduced from 3.5 per cent per year in 1974 to 3.0 per cent in 1979 and to 2.8 per cent by the year 1999.   The 1979 goal is based on plans to recruit 640,000 family planning acceptors, prevent 150,000 births, lower the birth rate by 5.5 per thousand and reduce the death rate by 2.5 per thousand.   The Government intends to set up some 400 full-time and 190 part-time service delivery points by 1979.   It is hoped that the Programme will slow the rate of population growth so that by the year 2000 the total popu-lation of Kenya will be 27 million instead of 30 million.

Family planning remains a low-key activity, treated not as an end in itself, but as an aspect of maternal and child health care.   The Government has accordingly changed the name and the emphasis of the Programme from Family Planning to Family Welfare. This is part of an information and education campaign in which the Programme is presented as part of a general policy to improve the socio-economic condition and the well-being of Kenyan families.

The costs of the current Five-Year Population Programme are estimated at US $38.8 million. The Kenyan Government has committed $11.8 million, or around 30 per cent of the total budget, the rest being financed by a large group of different aid donors.

POPULATION STRATEGIES

Recognising that social and economic conditions in Kenya may not be favourable to widespread acceptance of family planning, the Government is giving priority to the creation of the appropriate conditions and attitudes. The Five-Year Population Programme accordingly emphasizes the importance of providing people with information and education about the need for family planning, as well as making the actual services available in all Government health facilities. The new Programme builds upon the Family Planning Programme introduced in 1967, but endeavours to solve some of the difficulties it encountered, such as lack of high and middle-level manpower, the need for better co-ordination of disparate family planning efforts, and the traditional bias towards large families. Improving the coverage and distribution of health services throughout the country is to be achieved by means of increased nursing training facilities, and greater use of para-medical and field personnel. The Programme calls for the establishment of an appropriate national institution for planning, implementing and evaluating the Population Programme. This has now been created in the National Family Welfare Centre.

The principal means of recruiting eligible women to the Programme and delivering family planning services is through the MCH care network. It is felt that mothers are always sufficiently motivated to bring their children to MCH centres for care and that, once there, they can be approached by the nurses or trained para-medical personnel with information about family planning.

Family planning services have been available in Kenya long before Government involvement, through private sources. Some private physicians began providing contraception in 1950 in the two main cities, Nairobi and Mombasa. After 1955, voluntary family planning associations were formed in those two cities. In 1961, these associations were merged to form the Family Planning Association of Kenya (FPAK), which affiliated itself to the International Planned Parenthood Federation in 1962, becoming the first African member of that Organisation. When the Government took over the Programme, the FPAK was operating in 40 dispensaries and delivering family planning services to about 140,000 women, mostly in urban areas.

The official Programme set up in 1967 has the support of private and municipal activities. FPAK is now able to concentrate on providing family planning information to the rural areas. It also trains its own and some Government personnel, and conducts information and publicity campaigns. It has eight clinics of its own which supplement the services of the Ministry of Health. The IPPF has subsidised seven well-equipped mobile clinics staffed with doctors, nurses, midwives and field workers, to serve 90 dispensaries in the remote areas. The City Council of Nairobi was responsible for establishing 43 dispensaries, which serve about 20 per cent of all the country's acceptors. Other dispensaries delivering family planning services were run by the City Council of Mombasa, missionaries and various other private organisations.

By 1974, however, still only one-third of the nation's health centres were involved in the Programme and most of these were located in the two major cities of Nairobi and Mombasa. A vast programme of construction, reconstruction and expansion of the rural family planning network has been envisaged. Some 400 family planning/MCH service points are to be established by 1979 (of which 250 are currently in operation) to provide daily services. At the same time, an effort will be made to train manpower for these centres and to improve the training of the nurses and para-medicals employed in the National Population Programme. Specialised training to be given at the National Family Welfare Centre, will emphasize a broad approach to family planning, including health education. In addition, the Health Education Unit of the Ministry of Health will provide space and equipment for the production of family planning and health education materials.

INDIRECT MEASURES AFFECTING POPULATION

There are at the present time a number of concurrent plans to endow Kenya with a better health infrastructure. There is a Ten-Year Health Development Plan and a separate Ten-Year Rural Health Master Plan. The latter, which has been prepared with the assistance of FAO, covers integrated rural development and health activities; the former covers medical and health programmes. The National Family Welfare Programme is part of these Health Plans and will use the extended outreach provided by them to achieve greater family planning coverage, particularly in the rural areas. At the same time, the Health Plans, by reducing the high rates of infant mortality, are expected to contribute to the success of the Family Planning (Welfare) Programme.

An experiment in raising the standards of rural life has been carried out by the Kenyan Government with the assistance, primarily, of the FAO. Entitled "Programme for Better Family Living", the intention was to develop education and action programmes aimed at such target audiences as field workers, women's groups, adult education groups, etc. Its long-range objective was to help raise the level of rural welfare by educating families and communities. The programmes mainly provided educational materials which illustrate the relationship between family size and other areas of family and community welfare, and help communities to make the most effective use of the various social services that are available to them. This was not itself a family planning programme, but it carried the family planning message through various community and educational activities.

INSTITUTIONAL MACHINERY

In order to provide the operational and technical support needed to administer an expanded family planning/MCH programme, the Government established in 1975 a National Family Welfare Centre (replacing the National Family Planning Programme Centre). The Centre is responsible for the day-to-day administration of the National Population Programme and the organisation of family planning and MCH activities and their co-ordination with other aspects of development. The Centre has four Divisions—Clinical Services, Information and Education, Training, and Evaluation and Research.

There exists also, in theory, special machinery for co-ordinating population programmes with development in other sectors. An Interministerial Working Committee was created in 1975 with representation at high level from the relevant Ministries (Health, Finance and Planning, Information and Broadcasting, Co-operatives and Social Services, Education, Agriculture, and Lands and Settlement) and the University of Nairobi, FPAK and the National Council of Social Services. This Committee is backed up by three Advisory Working Committees to provide technical support in the fields of evaluation and research, information and education, and medical matters. It was intended that the Committee would meet every three months to help formulate population policy and review the developments of the National Population Programme: in point of fact, however, is met for the first time in 1977.

The administrative machinery of the National Population Programme thus appears adequate for implementing the family planning programme that Kenya has now planned. So far, however, lack of sufficiently trained personnel has prevented this machinery from actually functioning.

EXTERNAL ASSISTANCE

As the first African country to adopt a national family planning programme, Kenya has been the focus of an extraordinary amount of attention from the population donor community. The DAC reported that for 1975, among 118 recipient countries, population commitments to Kenya were exceeded only by those to India, Pakistan and Bangladesh[4]. When taken on a per capita basis, Kenya has received more population assistance than any other country in the world[5].

During the past ten years, some dozen multilateral, bilateral and private agencies have provided financial and/or technical assistance to family planning programmes in Kenya: US AID, SIDA, UNFPA, ODM, the Population Council, Ford Foundation, IPPF, Population Services International, World Education, World Assembly of Youth, and the African Medical and Research Foundation. Although some bilateral donors and private foundations have lost some of their initial enthusiasm, the country remains a prime favourite for both institutional and bilateral donors[6]. In March 1977, a Joint Evaluation Mission was undertaken by a number of donor agencies to study the situation and the effective possibilities for renewed population assistance.

Thus, the current Five-Year Population Programme is being financed as to 70 per cent of its total cost by foreign aid. In 1974, UNFPA agreed to provide $3.5 million for general support of the family planning programme to supplement aid from a number of other donors totalling over $30 million. The donors have agreed to divide between them the various components of the programme.

In addition to this large health and family planning "package", Kenya is receiving help from US AID (nearly $2 million) to establish a Population Studies and Research Centre at the University of Nairobi (through a contract with the Population Council). The Kenyan Family Planning Association is continuing to be funded by the IPPF.

---

4. *Assistance to Population Programmes 1975*, DAC, OECD, Paris, 11th June 1977.
5. *Ibid.*
6. The Netherlands, the United Kingdom and a few other donors with small projects phased out their direct involvement in family planning in Kenya. The United Kingdom has since reactivated its interest in helping Kenya in the population field.

Until an adequate infrastructure has been created and the coverage greatly extended, the main focus of Kenya's population assistance will remain for some time the "core" family planning and health activities. The very keenness of foreign assistance donors to help Kenya to establish this basic infrastructure and services does, however, pose considerable problems of organisation. In view of the very large number of funding agencies participating in Kenya's Health and Family Planning Programmes, there is a pressing need for close co-ordination, both of on-going activities and new plans, in order to avoid duplication of effort and ensure orderly follow-up and evaluation of progress.

In principle, the Ministries of Health and of Finance and Planning are responsible for co-ordinating external aid. The donors themselves combined forces effectively in 1977 to organise an External Mid-Term Review mission to report on the progress of the population programme.

A further constraint to the effective use of population assistance in Kenya has been the limited absorptive capacity of the relevant Government services. The Government of Kenya is well aware of this problem and recognises that its lack of qualified personnel and adequate infrastructure have hampered the best use of foreign aid possibilities.

In order to get the new Programme off the ground, the first need is for substantial technical assistance. The National Family Welfare Centre needs personnel qualified to analyse family planning service statistics and carry out the expanded information and education activities envisaged under the Programme. The National Family Welfare Centre is looking to foreign experts[7], both medical and in a management capacity, as well as to shorter-term advisors to strengthen its own capacity. It recognises, however, that it will eventually have to run the Programme without foreign personnel, and is hoping that aid will meanwhile provide fellowships for the necessary training of Kenyans.

A survey being undertaken by the United Nations in co-operation with the Kenyan Government on the quality of life in rural areas is expected to determine more accurately specific aid needs in the social and health fields and ensure more efficient use of resources. By measuring such factors as access to water, medical facilities and markets, and the availability of amenities, this survey should enable precise information to be provided on the extent and nature of the problems of different areas of the country. This data will make it possible to set realistic development goals and give precise estimates of the actual needs in terms of foreign aid.

---

7. As expressed at the time of the Development Centre mission in October 1976.

TANZANIA

Total population[1]	15,438,000
Population under age 20[1]	57.1%
Population density per sq. km.[1]	16
Rate of growth[1]	3.13%
Crude birth rate (per thousand)[1]	49.3
Crude death rate (per thousand)[1]	18.0
Life expectancy (total)[1]	47 years
Per capita national income (1975)[2] [Tanganyika only]	$162
Literacy rate[3]	63%

Sources:
1. UNFPA, Inventory of Population Projects 1975-76.
2. U.N., Statistical Yearbook, 1976.
3. IBRD, Comparative Education Indicators, 1978.

INTRODUCTION

Tanzania is sometimes held to have no official population policy because the Government does not seek to limit the country's overall population growth. However, the Government's deep concern with the principles of equality and social justice brings with it the desire that the number of children born should be commensurate with the effective ability of parents and the State to provide them with a decent start in life. The Government accordingly supports family planning, not in order to reduce population growth, but in the hope of improving the standard of living for each family.

Tanzanian development policies are designed to influence the three basic components of population movement: fertility, mortality and geographical distribution. In this sense, Tanzania may be said to have an implicit national population policy which forms an integral part of its whole development approach. Indeed, Tanzania had given to the concept of "population" the broad connotation of a population enjoying a satisfactory level of nutrition, health, education and employment, well before the Bucharest Conference gave these ideas international publicity and made them the basis of the WPPA.

POPULATION POLICIES

Tanzania, with a small population (approximately 15½ million) and a large land area (940,000 sq.km.), has no long-term problem of population growth outrunning land resources. The average population density is very low (16 per

144

sq.km.) and the population is concentrated in nine widely separated areas, leaving large tracts of potentially good agricultural land either totally empty or very sparsely populated. Although the population is 95 per cent rural, the chief constraint for the country's development is lack not of land resources, but rather of capital and human resources.

The Tanzanian Government has stated on several occasions (before Bucharest, at Bucharest, and after Bucharest) that there is plenty of unused land and that the size and trends of the country's population growth are acceptable. Nonetheless, from the time that President Nyerere first announced his development philosophy in the famous Arusha Declaration in 1967, it has been accepted that the success of the national development policy is predicated on the growth of the population not outrunning the country's economic possibilities. Tanzania's Second Five-Year Plan for Economic and Social Development (1969-74) states the position clearly:

"It is very good to increase our population because our country is large and there is plenty of unused land. But it is necessary to remember that these 350,000 extra people every year will be babies in arms, not workers. They will have to be fed, clothed, given medical attention, schooling, and many other services for very many years before they will be able to contribute to the economy of the country through their work. It is important for human beings to put emphasis on caring for children and the ability of looking after them properly."

The aspect of the country's population profile that the Government considered to be of first importance for the realisation of its development objectives was its geographical distribution. Policies of rural settlement and village development, designed to regulate population distribution, are, accordingly, the heart of Tanzanian socio-economic planning. Measures to affect the fertility and mortality aspects of population by means of health programmes and later through family planning, although very important, are to be regarded rather as supporting elements of the Government's rural development policy.

So far, the Tanzanian Government has not felt it necessary to try to limit the rate of population growth. Indeed, it has not considered "population" as a problem separate from that of achieving the overall social and economic objectives laid down in the National Development Plan. Family planning, however, is accepted as a means of reducing infant mortality, by means of birth spacing, and improving the health of mothers and children. For a time, the Government maintained an attitude of benevolent neutrality towards private family planning initiatives. Since 1973, it has itself begun providing some family planning services as part of maternal and child health care.

Although it has so far resisted the implications in terms of population policy, it is evident that President Nyerere is well aware that a continuance of the country's present rate of population growth may jeopardise the realisation of the economic and social objectives of the Plan. In 1973, he declared: "Whatever we produce has to be divided between an increasing number of people every year... it's no use saying that these extra 380,000 people have hands as well as mouths. For the first few years of their life, at the very least, children eat without producing".

In 1977, reviewing the country's progress in the ten years following his original Arusha Declaration, President Nyerere referred to population only once, but to make the significant point that population growth was holding back improvements in the standard of living: "National income has increased by only 4.6 per cent a year, but as the population is increasing by about 2.8 per cent per year, this means a negligible real improvement in the per capita standard of living"[1]. Already the education programme has been held back for two years because of the unexpectedly large number of school-age children.

In many respects, Tanzania presents a picture which is the reverse of that of other developing countries. In countries which have a population policy, the emphasis has tended to be first on the "direct" approach, i.e., limitation of fertility through family planning, and only later has it broadened out to include some "development" activities with a view to eventually influencing fertility behaviour. Tanzania, on the other hand, has effectively started with the development approach and has been pursuing it single-mindedly for the past decade. Direct Government action in the family planning field came later and is still on a relatively small scale.

STRATEGIES TO TRANSFORM THE TANZANIAN POPULATION

"VILLAGISATION"[2]

In Tanzania as in most developing countries, the towns and a few areas of concentrated economic activity have tended to develop at the expense of the rest of the country. Unlike other countries, however, Tanzania is striving strenuously to arrest this trend by developing the potential of the rural areas and improving the conditions of life of the rural population.

The means chosen was to group the scattered rural population into economically viable village units. The first approach was through the principle of Ujamaa. A traditional principle of social and economic organisation of Tanzanian society, Ujamaa means basically that people should live together in groups, work together and share jointly in the means of production and the fruit of their labour. Since, however, the principles of self-help did not prove as effective an economic driving force as the Tanzanian Government had hoped[3], Ujamaa was subsequently reinforced by a second, more organised measure of population grouping. The 1975 Village Act provided for the grouping of Tanzania's rural population, much of which lived in isolated homesteads, into villages (each to have a maximum of 600 households and a minimum of 2,500 inhabitants) (cf. President Nyerere, in his speech reviewing ten years of progress after Arusha: "The purpose of villagisation is to lay the foundation for a permanent improvement in people's lives")[4].

The villages were to be created by a judicious mixture of self-help and government support to provide the necessary infrastructure and social services[5]. The idea was that by revitalising rural life and bringing to the countryside the basic services previously available only in urban areas, further rural-urban migration will be checked[6].

---

1. The World Bank has estimated that if population growth continues at its present rate, the cultivated area will have to expand 64 per cent by 1992 just to supply the same amount of food per capita as is grown today.
2. The name by which the Programme is known in Tanzania.
3. The principles of common ownership of the means of production and equal distribution implied in Ujamaa have met with popular resistance and the results in terms of agricultural output have been disappointing.
4. The Arusha Declaration Ten Years After, January 1977.
5. The Government surveys and maps the area, provides water for irrigation and domestic purposes, agricultural extension and credit. It also pays the salaries of extension workers, health workers and school-teachers. The settlers do most of the land clearance, prepare the fields, build their own houses, the communal buildings and dwellings for the school-teacher and health worker.
6. The Government intends also to shift the capital from Dar-es-Salaam to Dodoma, a small city in the middle of a poor and under-populated rural area.

The "villagisation" plan had achieved its target of covering the whole country with such settlements by 1977. President Nyerere announced at the TANU[7] Conference in April that year that 13 million Tanzanians were now living together in 7,684 villages (compared to 2 million in 1973). Seventy per cent of the nation's population had thus moved their homes in the space of about three years.

HEALTH POLICIES

Despite the socialist orientation of Tanzania's development from 1967 until 1974, the Ministry of Health concentrated its efforts on providing curative services, with the major effort concentrated in the urban areas. There accordingly developed the familiar pattern, of highly expensive, Western-style medicine, with the scant resources available for health applied to hospitals in the towns, leaving the rural areas still without basic health services.

In 1974, occurred a major shift of emphasis, at the initiative of the TANU Congress, which gave the Government explicit directives for health development. Henceforward, the emphasis was to be put on preventive medicine, with the aim of reaching as many people as possible. Each village was to have its own health centre, which should include a maternal and child health unit and a kindergarten; the MCH care should include family planning in the interests of child-spacing. Environmental hygiene was to be an important part of the drive for better health; a rural water programme was to be established to provide water to the whole of the rural population by 1980 (by means of self-help labour); nutrition was to be improved through nutrition education and a more balanced crop production. Programmes to carry out these objectives were incorporated in the Third Development Plan.

In order to achieve a measure of health coverage for the whole country, the Government relies heavily on para-medical personnel. Eighteen training centres have been set up to provide courses for public health nurses in maternal and child health care, family planning and elementary nutrition. The plan is to train 2,600 MCH workers and assign them to 900 rural health centres and 2,000 rural dispensaries by 1980[8].

FAMILY PLANNING

Although family planning has been provided by the Family Planning Association of Tanzania (UMATI in Swahili)[9] since 1959, there was considerable resistance to the idea of family planning among members of the TANU Party, the Government and members of Parliament. Accordingly, the Government did not feel able to introduce it into the MCH Programme of the Ministry of Health until 1973. TANU has since requested that all relevant Government institutions should provide family planning services.

UMATI, as a voluntary and private organisation, still plays a significant role in family planning activities in Tanzania. Following a directive from TANU, the Ministry of Health has assigned to UMATI three important functions in the new MCH Programme: family planning information, education and communication

7. TANU is the sole political party in Tanzania. All the Tanzanian Government's policies are decided by the Party: the Government's role, through the Ministries and technical services, is to implement them.
8. Tanzania also has initiated some very interesting experiments to train village workers, with only a minimum of education, to recognise the most common ailments and health problems and to present simple remedies.
9. The Association began as the Family Planning Association of Dar-es-Salaam and became the National Association in 1966, when it joined the IPPF.

at the national and local levels; training personnel both for the Government and the Association's programmes; and the provision of supplies.

The Government sends its health personnel for training on UMATI courses in Dar-es-Salaam and Moshi, and UMATI also provides the family planning courses in the medical curriculum at the University of Dar-es-Salaam. IPPF provides UMATI with all the contraceptives needed by the Government for its rural health clinics. Its own clinical activities are limited to Dar-es-Salaam and the immediate hinterland. In the rural areas, its activities are primarily training and information. A certain amount of information work is done through the mass media (though very discreetly); it prefers more selective communication work through seminars for special groups (political leaders, doctors, health advisers, trade unions, women's organisations). For example, the Government and UMATI are jointly sponsoring a programme to assess the needs of women. In many of these activities, UMATI has a valuable ally in the Christian Council of Tanzania.

Family planning in Tanzania is offered to encourage child-spacing as a means to better family life. There is accordingly no attempt to prescribe any particular ideal family size, or even to advocate smaller families. Abortion is against the law, and sterilisation is only permitted on medical grounds.

There have, however, recently been certain indications that the concern with child-spacing may develop into a programme of fertility limitation. Since March 1975, women (whether married or unmarried) have been allowed maternity leave (three months with pay) only once every three years. (If a working mother, therefore, has two births within two years, she will not get paid leave.) More significant still, tax allowances for *all* children have now been entirely abolished.

At present, the whole issue of population is still very sensitive in the eyes of many members of the Tanzanian Government. It is significant, for example, that there is no move to introduce sex education in schools. Indeed, books on sex education are banned by the Government.

DEMOGRAPHIC RESEARCH

The Government, recognising the importance of accurate information on the country's demographic trends and related social changes, set up a Demographic Unit in the University of Dar-es-Salaam in 1972 (with aid from the Population Council). It has carried out a National Demographic Survey (which includes micro-level information), and a National Household Budget. It also trains demographers. A national census is to be held in 1978 by the Central Bureau of Statistics.

ACTIVITIES AFFECTING POPULATION INDIRECTLY

In the case of Tanzania, the distinction between "direct" and "indirect" relevance to population of the Government's social and economic policies tends to become blurred. Thus, "villagisation" has been described above under direct population strategies.

Faced with an acute shortage of trained manpower (at the time of Independence, Tanzania was among the least educated countries of Africa), the Tanzanian Government, in its First Development Plan, made education its first priority. The emphasis was placed on primary education, and the aim was to provide free compulsory education for all children between the ages of 7-14, and by means of adult education and functional literacy campaigns, to eradicate illiteracy by 1975. The goals proved impossible to attain, partly because the Government had underestimated the effects of population growth[10], partly because of hesitancy as to whether the emphasis should be on primary or secondary education, and partly for lack of teachers. The attainment of universal education has been deferred until 1977—a postponement of two years; a massive campaign of functional literacy is under way, involving more than 2.5 million (school) students and some 70,000 adult teachers, and almost 20 per cent of the Government's budget for recurrent expenditure is devoted to education.

The purpose of the intensive national education effort is to produce the trained manpower that the country needs for its socio-economic development. Manpower planning is carried out very systematically in Tanzania (there is a Ministry in charge of Manpower Development, and a Manpower Planning Division in each Ministry and in each District), and it is intended that education at all levels should be geared to meet the specific needs indicated by surveys of manpower requirements and resources[11].

THE ADMINISTRATION OF POPULATION POLICY

Since Tanzania admits to no specific "population" policy separate from its national development policy, there is no special body charged with overall responsibility for population matters.

Nevertheless, since the Government's policies of integrated development touch on population at so many points, it may be said that Tanzania has achieved a degree of co-ordination of population concerns with policies for socio-economic development greater than in any other developing country to date. This result has been achieved almost unconsciously rather than by a deliberate attempt at "co-ordination". Problems of co-ordination, in fact, will only arise when there is an identifiable separate population policy to be harmonised with other government intentions.

EXTERNAL AID FOR POPULATION

Although Tanzania receives substantial foreign aid (President Nyerere stated in 1977 that it amounted to 59 per cent of the development budget[12], by far the bulk of this is for major infrastructure projects. This is in accordance with the Government's philosophy that "assistance should be reserved for really major

---

10. The Second Plan states: "... expansion in the number of primary school places has held back. We have done very little more than expand at the same rate as the number of Tanzanian children was increasing because of the population growth. Indeed, the census has revealed that the chances of a 7-year old Tanzanian going to school are worse now than we thought they were when we drew up the First Plan. At that time, we used to say that about 50 per cent of our children went to school. The much larger population of the country which was revealed in the census figures showed up that the actual percentage in 1964 was nearer 46 per cent, and even now, at the end of the Plan period, only about 47 per cent of our children can find a primary school place."

11. The techniques for making the manpower planning exercise sufficiently flexible to be a sound guide for educational planning are everywhere still far from perfect, though the Tanzanian Government has been seeking to improve them through three successive Plan periods.

12. 1977 speech to TANU.

projects which we could not do without". Aid for strictly population activities has consequently been very limited (on average, between 1969-78, $3 million per year, except for 1973, when the Government's MCH programme started and US AID contributed over $5 million towards the construction of training centres and field stations for rural health workers).

The rural health programme is receiving bilateral aid from Finland and Norway—the former, building training facilities and the latter, rural dispensaries. Other bilateral aid has been received from Canada, Denmark, Sweden, Switzerland and the U.K.[13]. Some of this goes to support the villagisation programme. UMATI receives funds from IPPF. There is also some Population Council support for demographic research and training. There is virtually no multilateral assistance for population, apart from a very modest FAO programme (Programme for Better Family Living) financed by UNFPA.

It would seem that Tanzania could usefully absorb more aid than it is presently receiving[14], particularly since the Government's high degree of commitment to its programmes of rural development make effective absorptive capacity for aid in this field greater than that of some of its neighbours. Tanzania is reluctant, however, to rely too much on aid, primarily for ideological reasons, on the grounds that continued external assistance is inconsistent with its emphasis on self-reliance.

This reluctance carries the attendant risk of slowing down the execution of the Government's programmes. Foreign aid is badly needed to help fill two major gaps: shortage of foreign exchange for imported materials and shortage of certain professional skills. Although Tanzania does not wish to accept foreign "advisers", selective support for demographic and social science research, project management, evaluation, etc., could greatly speed the implementation of the development programme.

It is reasonable to speculate that in the future, either or both of two things may happen. First, if improvement in the standard of living does not proceed fast enough, the discrepancy between population growth and economic growth may force the Government into a more deliberate policy of fertility limitation. The second is that the development activities may gather sufficient momentum to have an effective influence on fertility levels. In either case, the result will be an increasing need for family planning services. Clearly, neither Tanzania nor the donor community would wish a situation to arise where need for family planning could not be fully satisfied for lack of foreign exchange to purchase the necessary contraceptive supplies and services. It is therefore possible that over the next few years, aid for family planning activities will come to occupy an increasing share of Tanzania's foreign aid requests.

---

13. Although Tanzania receives considerable aid from the People's Republic of China for infrastructure projects, it has no Chinese aid in the rural health field, despite China's wellknown experience in this area.

14. Tanzania is in the group classed as Least Developed Countries by the United Nations.

ZAIRE

Total population[1]	24,485,000
Population under age 20[1]	53.5%
Population density per sq. km.[1]	10
Rate of growth[1]	2.65%
Crude birth rate (per thousand)[1]	44.9
Crude death rate (per thousand)[1]	18.5
Life expectancy (total)[1]	46.0 years
Per capita national income (1974)[2]	$124
Literacy rate[3]	15%

Sources:
1. UNFPA, *Inventory of Population Projects 1975-76.*
2. U.N., *Statistical Yearbook*, 1976.
3. IBRD, *Comparative Education Indicators*, 1978.

INTRODUCTION

Zaïre, the largest country in Central Africa, has a low population density and there is no shortage of cultivable land. There is also a wealth of minerals. Thus, although the exact demographic situation of the country is unknown for lack of reliable census data, the Government does not consider that the growth of population presents a problem[1].

It recognises, however, that there is a population problem on the family level. Accordingly, in 1972, two years before the Bucharest Conference, it announced a policy of "Desired Births" prompted by concern for family health and welfare, and intended to help families to space the number of their children in order to improve the health of mothers and infants.

Although the francophone countries of Africa tend generally to be reticent about family planning (the 1920 French law against contraceptives is still widely observed), the Government of Zaïre has defined a national population policy and created a Health and Population Programme. It has been slow, however, in setting up the MCH network which will provide family planning services, although some progress is now being made. Foreign aid could usefully provide substantial support, if the Government now maintains a continuing commitment to the Programme and provides the infrastructure and administrative arrangements necessary to put it into effect.

1. According to US AID, however, Zaïre is among the 20 developing countries having the most serious population problems and the most urgent need for assistance.

POLICIES

The President of Zaïre announced that the country would have a national population policy, in a speech made in December 1972. Described as a policy of "Desired Births", it is concerned essentially to improve the health and welfare of the family, considered as the basic "cell" of the nation. The intention is that, by means of contraception, couples will be able to decide the spacing and number of their children, thereby limiting family size to the number of children than they can care for adequately (five children is generally accepted to be "ideal" family size in Zaïre).

The Programme to implement this policy aims to reduce the appallingly high rate of infant mortality (one out of every three children dies before age five) and also the high rate of induced abortion. By the practice of contraception, which would permit resumption of conjugal life soon after childbirth, it is hoped also to reduce the high rate of divorce and polygamy, which are also considered as threatening the stability of the family. The Programme also includes treatment for sub-fertility and sterility, of which (a typically African phenomenon) there is a high incidence in certain regions of the country.

The statement made by the President in announcing this new concern of Government policy merits quoting in extenso:

"According to our Bantu philosophy, the ultimate purpose of marriage is procreation. But child-bearing is not without its limits. In our traditional society, small family size created a sense of insecurity, and the high prevailing rate of infant mortality was compensated by a desire for numerous pregnancies. A couple who wanted 5 children, for example, was led to have 10 or 15 in the hope that at least 5 would survive. In modern society, however, well-off families, who lose fewer of their children in infancy, are able to keep down the overall number of their births. The State should therefore endeavour to reduce infant mortality to a minimum so that the number of actual births corresponds as closely as possible to the number of desired births.

This problem commonly goes under the name of 'family planning', although we prefer to use the term 'desired births' since, in fact, the high rate of induced abortion in our society reveals that many women prefer to terminate their pregnancies—even at the risk of their lives—rather than go through with a birth which is undesired. The State has the duty to explain and to facilitate the use of contraceptives in order to protect our citizens from the necessity to resort to abortion.

Having such a measure of control over the evolution of our population will also permit us to control our national development, since we will be able to adapt population growth to economic growth.

We should also be aware that our duty is to bring up our children well, and that people who have many children without sufficient means run the risk of their suffering from an inadequate mental and physical develop-ment."[2]

The policy is thus squarely a concern for family health and welfare. To implement it, a special National Committee for the Principle of Desired Births was set up a few months later (February 1973), and placed under the authority of the already existing National Council for Health and Welfare. Until 1975, however, the Committee existed in name only.

---

2. Unofficial translation.

The Desired Births Programme purports to be a specifically African approach ("authenticité africaine"), and implies rejection of anything foreign to the African context. In view of the capital importance of procreation in African society (sub-fertility and sterility being frequent causes of divorce), the Programme avoids any implication of birth *control*, emphasizing instead birth *planning* in the strict sense of the term.

There are some indications, however, that behind the concern with family welfare, Government opinion is aware also of the need to ensure that population growth remains in reasonable balance with natural resources, viz. the third paragraph of the President's speech and the statement of the Minister of Health at a seminar organised by the Government on the Desired Births Programme in March 1974[3]: "We believe... that a moderate demographic growth limited to desired births is part of the basic equilibrium of a modern country in full development".

On the other hand, in the absence of reliable census data or a national development plan, population policy is still largely at the level of theory. A distinct step forward, however, has recently been taken with the elaboration of the country's first development plan[4] as well as the decision to plan for a national population census[5].

POLICIES SINCE BUCHAREST

Although represented at both the World Population Conference and the Regional Consultative Conference held in Lusaka the following year, Zaïre made no official declaration concerning its population policies. However, these Conferences and ensuing debates on population issues may have helped to sensitize the opinion of intellectuals and, more especially, of the country's leaders, concerning population problems. In any case, there have since been signs of a new Government determination to make the Desired Births policy operationally effective.

In November 1975, the National Committee for the Principle of Desired Births was finally made operational with the appointment of its seven members. At the same time, its name (and rationale) was changed to "National Committee for Desired Births", perhaps reflecting the feeling of the Zaïrian Authorities that the "principle" of Desired Births had now been accepted and that it was time to move into the stage of implementation.

The Government has subsequently drawn up a Six-Year National Health Programme (to begin in 1978). This will include the Desired Births Programme which will be integrated with the Government's MCH services.

POPULATION STRATEGIES

The implementation of a population programme, as of other social development policies, got off to a slow start in Zaïre, because of the problems the

---

3. "Naissances désirables basées sur la maternité."
4. At the time of our visit, the plan was not yet available for consultation. It was, however, expected to integrate the activities of the Desired Births Programme with other sectoral policies.
5. A national demographic survey had been taken in 1957, before Independence, but is no longer applicable, and a more recent 1970 administrative census, although carried out with demographic objectives, has proved to be largely unusable.

country faced in the first years of Independence. Although the colonial system had left a certain infrastructure (administration, roads, railroads, water transport, etc.), these were totally disorganised by internal troubles. With the return to political stability about ten years ago, the first priorities were to maintain national unity, re-establish an effective administration, restore the national economy, build up the school system, etc. There were inevitably a number of false starts, and in the absence of a development plan, the various initiatives sometimes lacked co-ordination. The public announcement of a national population policy therefore was, perhaps unsurprisingly, not promptly followed up by vigorous programme implementation.

After the Presidential declaration of December 1972 announcing the Desired Births policy, a few modest steps were taken towards putting the intentions into practice. However, the only significant commitment was that of foreign agencies who financed the few clinics.

The recent integration of the Programme into the regular activities of the Ministry of Health (Commissariat d'Etat à la Santé) and the appointment of the National Committee for Desired Births represented the first real steps towards official action. The Committee has subsequently been enlarged and given independent quarters as well as, for the first time, a Government budget. The Zaïrian Authorities are aware that a national effort must be made before foreign aid can be expected, and that the volume of this aid will depend upon the input of both material and financial resources by the country itself.

A second symposium on Desired Births[6] was held in October 1976 under the sponsorship of the IPPF and the Committee for Desired Births. It brought together doctors, para-medical personnel and journalists. Its purpose was largely to spread information about family planning and to try to clear up popular misapprehensions. At that meeting, the Chairman of the National Committee defined the Programme's goals in the following terms:

— Development, co-ordination and standardization of all Desired Births clinics in the country, establishment of a central administrative machinery, and extension of MCH and family planning services and infertility counselling.
— Information and education drives through the press, radio and television, and creation of a programme of sex education for youth.
— Family planning training for medical and para-medical personnel.

To achieve these goals, the Government has carried out or envisages actions in the following areas:

1. PROVISION OF MCH/FAMILY PLANNING SERVICES

Family planning services are to be offered as an integral part of basic health services, and it is planned to make them available through all existing public and private hospitals, clinics, maternity hospitals, and at pre-marriage, pre-natal, and post-partum consultations. The Government feels that the health-based approach facilitates access to family planning services while at the same time removing some of the psychological barriers to their acceptance.

Health services are provided through three sources: the Fonds Médical de Coordination (FOMECO), which is directly responsible to the Office of the President, the Commissariat d'Etat à la Santé, and various Christian missions. The budget of FOMECO and of the Commissariat comes mainly from the State; the missions' health centres function with outside financing. At the present time, the health programme is overwhelmingly urban-oriented. The budget of

---

6. "Desired Births, Family Welfare and National Development."

FOMECO, which covers only the Mama Yémo hospital (1,800 beds) and a few other dispensaries in Kinshasa, is larger than that of the Commissariat d'Etat à la Santé, which is nevertheless responsible for all the country's health centres and its entire health policy.

The first dispensary under the Desired Births Programme was set up at the Mama Yémo hospital in February 1973. Consultations initially given twice a week soon had to be given daily to cope with a growing clientele. In the following year, two other MCH dispensaries offering family planning were set up in Kinshasa, and certain health centres run by religious groups in the interior of the country began to offer family planning services also. However, there are still only a very few health centres in the country which provide family planning services, and these are primarily in the capital. As of October 1976, only five clinics and the hospital dispensary were operating in Kinshasa, serving a total average of 150 clients a day. No statistics were available for the interior of the country.

The weakness of the actions undertaken so far may be explained, in part, by the inadequacy of financial and material resources. However, the Government is planning a considerable increase in the budget of the Health Ministry over the next two years.

2. INFORMATION AND EDUCATION ON POPULATION ISSUES

The Government has declared its intention to use all means available to see that the population is informed about the Desired Births Programme and about the various contraceptive methods available through it. Information will be provided routinely at medical examinations, pre- and post-natal consultations, school inscriptions, public meetings and informal gatherings. The Party structure and organisations (women's, youth and workers' groups) are also to be utilised to help diffuse these ideas. The national radio-television agency is presently preparing MCH/family planning radio tapes and films for national distribution.

Within the formal education system, a programme of sex education and family life instruction for all levels of public school is being worked out by the National Committee for Desired Births, in collaboration with parents, education officials, doctors, psychologists and religious groups.

3. TRAINING

In order to put the Desired Births Programme into effect, efforts are now being made to train a technical corps (doctors, nurses, midwives) in the methods (professional and psychological) of family planning delivery. The corps is to be responsible for recruiting and motivating contraceptive acceptors, prescribing and administering contraceptive methods, and ensuring follow-up of users. Training is given either at courses overseas (particularly in the United States) or in the Mama Yémo clinic. In addition, all medical students now receive instruction on contraceptive techniques as a matter of course. However, the execution of the Programme will depend increasingly on the work of nurses and of para-medical personnel who are being given considerable responsibility.

4. RESEARCH

Socio-demographic and household budget studies have been carried out in most of the chief cities of Zaïre since 1967. As part of the World Fertility Survey, the International Statistical Institute in 1974 made a pilot study on fertility in the city of Kananga. A national demographic survey was begun the following year with the aim of providing information on demographic variables, but had to be abandoned for lack of funds.

A research capacity in Zaïre in demographic studies was established in 1974, with the assistance of the Population Council, by the creation of a National Centre for Scientific Research and a Department of Demography at the University of Zaïre. With the Government's renewed interest in the Programme of Desired Births, attention is being given also to research on socio-economic aspects of population and family planning. The National Commitee for Desired Births is itself setting up a unit to study problems such as abortion and attitudes and practices concerning contraception.

STRATEGIES LIKELY TO AFFECT POPULATION POLICIES INDIRECTLY

Since Zaïre is only now embarking on overall development planning, no attempts have been made so far to co-ordinate population policies with other development objectives. When the Ministère du Plan (Ministry of Planning) was set up in 1971, its priorities were development of agriculture, housing, health, education and transport. Although only the Health Programme will have a direct effect on population, the programmes for developing some of the other sectors may have a spin-off effect on population, even if this was not the prime intention.

The programmes, for example, to try to create employment and stem the flow of people from the rural areas to the towns will have an influence on population distribution. Since 1960, many parts of the country have regressed from an export agriculture to a subsistance economy, and production as well as the GNP has decreased. The Government has tried to alleviate the situation: laws have been passed (and backed by police action) to persuade the urban unemployed to return to the countryside; agricultural co-operatives have been created to provide work for the unemployed; the "Salango" movement attempts to recruit voluntary manpower for works of public interest. There was also an attempt to limit the number of foreigners working in Zaïre and owning factories, shops, plantations, etc. (a policy of *Zaïrianisation des emplois*), but this was so unsuccessful that it has since been reversed and the confiscated businesses handed back. Nonetheless, the increase in the populations of cities like Kinshasa and other urban centres is still very high—about eight per cent yearly. Kinshasa's population has trebled since Independence. The effect of urbanisation on behaviour and attitudes may be expected to lead in time to changes in the demographic variables.

The education programmes will also have an indirect effect on population. One-quarter of the national budget is devoted to education. In 1972-1973, 60 per cent of children between 7 and 15 years were at primary school: the number of secondary school students has expanded nearly ten-fold since 1960.

It is perhaps significant that in the secondary and higher education sectors, only 20 per cent of the students at present are female. This suggests that the development of alternative roles for women has hardly begun in Zaïre and it will take some time for education to affect acceptance of family planning and smaller family size.

156

ADMINISTRATIVE MACHINERY

The recently created Ministry of Planning has been given the task of intregrating the activities of the Desired Births Programme with the other economic and social policies of the country. The National Committee for Desired Births, which is responsible for co-ordinating and supervising the execution of the Programme, has had its membership expanded to include not only doctors but demographers, sociologists, economists and lawyers. This attests to the intention that the Programme will make a broader contribution to the national life than simply the provision of family planning services.

Although the Committee has the direct responsibility for the Desired Births Programme, the ultimate authority for both health and population matters is the Health Ministry. The Government now recognises that it will be difficult to carry out a vigorous Desired Births Programme without simultaneously strengthening and expanding the health infrastructure, and training personnel at all levels to staff it.

ASSISTANCE FOR POPULATION ACTIVITIES

The Desired Births Programme has so far benefited very little from outside aid[7]. The little that it has received comes for the most part from US AID and is in the form of materials (contraceptives) and technical assistance for developing the MCH/family planning system (training, IEC, contraceptive distribution and development of model clinics). The IPPF assists the current expenses of the Committee for Desired Births. There is, however, no IPPF affiliate at present in Zaïre ready to take up a supporting role for the Programme. A limited amount of assistance has also been contributed by the Pathfinder Fund (training and equipment), Population Council (seminars, research and training), Church World Service and Family Planning International Assistance (family education), and IDRC (research and demographic surveys). In addition, some funds and technical assistance have been provided through UNFPA (for the demographic and rural fertility survey, the civil registration system, and strengthening of the Demographic Division of Zaïre's Department of Statistics).

The assistance received by Zaïre has been small chiefly because the Programme has remained so long in an undeveloped state. Moreover, the Government's own commitment in the way of budget, infrastructure, personnel, and social planning was so minimal that donors have been hesitant to commit themselves extensively.

The problem may have been compounded by the extensive centralisation of all decision-making and executory powers in Zaïre, which tends to hinder the sector departments from making their needs known to the outside.

Now that Zaïre has a Development Plan, donors can feel more assured that there will be a coherent policy framework for aid activities in the different sectors of the economy. The new Six-Year Health Plan, if its proposals for building up a health infrastructure and qualified personnel are effectively implemented, should also give Zaïre a real absorptive capacity for population assistance for the first time.

---

7. For 1975, the DAC reported a total disbursement of $ 392,000 in population aid to Zaïre, of which $328,000 was from the US and $64,000 from private agencies (commitments were reported at $99,000 from multilateral sources and $100,000 from private agencies, of which 88 per cent for family planning and the rest for basic population data).

POPULATION ASSISTANCE AGENCIES

INTERNATIONAL ORGANISATIONS
United Nations Fund for Population Activities (UNFPA)
World Bank
United Nations Population Division

NON-GOVERNMENTAL AGENCIES
International Planned Parenthood Federation (IPPF)

FOUNDATIONS
Population Council
Ford Foundation
Rockefeller Foundation

BILATERAL DONORS
United States Agency for International Development (US AID)
Sweden
Norway
Federal Republic of Germany
Canada
Japan
United Kingdom
Denmark

The interviewing of some of the donor agencies was undertaken by Mr. Ralph Susman, consultant, the others by the author.

159

INTERNATIONAL ORGANISATIONS

UNITED NATIONS FUND FOR POPULATION ACTIVITIES
(UNFPA)

INTRODUCTION

The UNFPA is the largest source of multilateral population assistance for developing countries and, with the World Bank and US AID, one of the three "great powers" among population assistance donors. Assistance provided by UNFPA currently represents approximately 30 per cent of total aid for population[1]. By the end of 1977, it was providing financial support for almost 750 projects in 106 countries.

UNFPA was created in 1967 in response to concern among UN Member countries, and particularly the donor community, that rapid population growth in the developing countries was tending to nullify development efforts. It was their feeling, partly that the population problem was of such importance that it called for a special UN effort to provide assistance in this field, and partly that in this particularly sensitive area, aid channelled through a UN organisation might be more acceptable than when provided through bilateral arrangements.

The UNFPA functions essentially as a "broker" of funds: it collects contributions from, at present, almost 80 UN Member governments[2] and disburses them to countries and specialised agencies requesting assistance for population activities. Many bilateral donors in fact prefer to channel an increasingly large part of their population assistance through a "disinterested" international agency such as the UNFPA. The Fund's role is mainly to bring projects and funds together. While it does the choosing, coordinating and evaluating of projects itself, the actual operational work is increasingly carried out by the recipient governments themselves or, at their request, by the UN and UN organisations, or occasionally by non-governmental or private organisations. UNFPA's Secretariat is therefore relatively small; it includes a field staff of project co-ordinators who assist the UNDP resident representatives in overseeing the Fund's projects.

FUNDING CRITERIA AND CHOICE OF COUNTRY

The bulk of UNFPA funds are allocated for direct country assistance, with a smaller percentage for regional, interregional and global projects. The Fund also contributes to the population programmes of the UN Organisations and a few non-governmental organisations (NGOs) and private agencies, most notably the IPPF.

---

1. If account is taken of assistance it provides through the UN and UN organisations. (OECD, *Assistance for Population Programmes 1975*.)
2. Almost two-thirds of these are also UNFPA aid recipients, and make only a small, symbolic contribution to the Fund.

In allocating its resources, the UNFPA does not exert its own policy preferences but responds to what requesting countries see as their own population problems and the best approaches to solving them. Thus it is prepared to support programmes designed to combat sterility or stimulate population growth as well as programmes of population limitation.

Recognising that in some developing countries the need is no longer for the traditional types of assistance (advisory services, seminars, fellowships, research support) but for continuing operating funds for projects which are already under way, the UNFPA is able to cover, where necessary, essential local costs such as equipment, contraceptive and medical supplies, vehicles, and, to some extent, local salaries.

In spite of some early concern with its slowness in processing requests and with the gap between funds committed and those eventually disbursed, the UNFPA has always been given a great amount of discretion by its donor members in allocating their contributions to specific projects. It has therefore been able to take a flexible approach, and its interpretation of population-related activities has been a broad one. Thus, during its earlier years of operation, when projects were slower in being formulated and implemented, the UNFPA was already supporting work in a wide range of areas, such as population aspects of employment, food supplies, etc., as well as more direct population activities. Moreover, recognising that the requests of countries reflected their culture as well as their social and economic needs, the UNFPA did not impose its own views in its response to governments' requests. Thus, for example, in spite of reservations about the rhythm method, it funded such projects as a part of family planning programmes in countries where culture and religion resisted other methods.

It may be said that the Fund has always, to an extent, implicitly taken a "development" approach to population, since its projects are executed by the United Nations Organisations: proposed major projects of an innovative character are submitted for the approval of the UNDP Governing Council.

CHANGES SINCE BUCHAREST

As official "sponsor" of the World Population Year and provider of both financial and promotional support to the Conference, the UNFPA has been particularly sensitive to changing ways of thinking about population. The year of the Conference was also marked by a dramatic increase in the volume of requests for assistance received by the Fund, which threatened to outstrip even the growing amount of resources available to it. This high volume of requests has been maintained since and is continuing to grow.

Immediately after Bucharest and several times since, the Fund has carried out a serious examination of its programme and priorities to consider whether they should be modified in the light of the Conference recommendations and in the face of increased demand for assistance. The outcome of these examinations has been UNFPA's decision to maintain its programme along the same lines as before but to "tighten up" its criteria for project funding.

The UNFPA has thus decided that it should most usefully continue to provide the bulk of its funding for activities forming the "core" of population work. These are defined as "collection and analysis of basic population data", "population dynamics", "population policy", "family planning", and "population communication and education"[3].

UNFPA's funding for "family planning", for instance, has jumped from 39 per cent of its budget in 1969-1975 to a projected 51 per cent for the 1977-1980

3. UNFPA, 1975 Report of the Executive Director, p. 11.

period, in order to respond to increasing requests for assistance of this type[4]. Within these traditional categories of population assistance, however, UNFPA is increasingly funding projects which use innovative social and economic activities as channels for family planning information and supplies (e.g. the integration of population education into agricultural programmes, provision of family planning through industrial health services, etc.).

Another decision taken in response to the sharp upsurge of requests received from governments since 1974, has been to considerably increase the proportion of assistance provided directly to countries instead of through other agencies for regional, inter-regional and global projects[5]. Country projects now account for over 70 per cent of the total budget, as against 46 per cent in 1973, and are expected to rise even further to 80 per cent by 1979[6]. At the same time, UNFPA is reducing the proportion of infrastructural support it provides to the population programmes of the UN and the UN Organisations.

In a document published in 1977[7], the UNFPA defined the recently adopted funding criteria it will apply in allocating its resources. It intends to concentrate its funds in 40 countries having the greatest need for population assistance, with emphasis given to activities designed to strengthen the recipient countries' self-reliance in population matters. Aid will be given especially for establishing national population policies and implementing them within the framework of basic needs programmes in the population field. Within these countries, highest priority will be given to activities benefiting the most disadvantaged population groups, with population action programmes aiming at popular participation at the grass-roots level. Particular emphasis will be given to the involvement of women in the planning and decision-making process at all levels.

An interesting innovation since Bucharest is the development of joint or "multi-bilateral" funding arrangements with other donors. The advantages of this type of collaboration are several. It will increase the financial input into population projects and will provide the opportunity for close co-operation among donors. The UNFPA would, in most cases, be responsible for the overall appraisal, monitoring and evaluation of joint projects, although other donors may do this on their own if they so wish. Most important, donor contributions to the multilateral budget of UNFPA remain unaffected. Multi-bilateral funding is particularly suited to "integrated" projects, for which the UNFPA would limit its contribution to the specifically "population" component, with other donors funding the rest.

In order to ensure the best use of its limited resources, the UNFPA is particularly concerned with monitoring the quality and effectiveness of its projects and, to this end, a number of independent evaluations have been undertaken of various programmes and projects.

The experience of the three years since Bucharest seems to have confirmed for the UNFPA the continued relevance of its original categories for population assistance. The demand for specific "population" assistance continues to grow; it is also becoming more closely related to broader concepts of development planning.

---

4. Requests from Latin American countries for projects in MCH and family planning have increased sevenfold since 1974, and this trend is being noted also in other parts of the world. (*World Population Growth and Response*, Population Reference Bureau, April 1976, p. 198.)

5. The Fund continues, however, to provide a major part of the funding of the World Fertility Survey, an inter-country project.

6. New projects are also being undertaken in Arab countries with funds recently made available for this purpose by the League of Arab States.

7. *Priorities in Future Allocation of UNFPA Resources.*

THE WORLD BANK (IBRD)

INTRODUCTION

The World Bank entered the population field in 1969 because it became convinced that development efforts to raise the standard of living in developing countries were, in many cases, being seriously undermined by rapid population growth. It therefore took the position that efforts to reduce fertility, added to overall development programmes, would both accelerate economic progress and benefit the condition of the poorest groups in developing countries. This approach has been strongly advocated in a number of public statements by the President of the World Bank.

Lending for population began in 1970 when the Bank made its first loan to Jamaica for US $2 million. Early in 1978, the Bank approved its fifteenth population loan—$33.1 million as part of a $68.6 million project in Thailand. Over the period 1970-1976, the Bank has committed $197 million to support population projects costing a total of $400 million.

In terms of total Bank activities, the input into population has been very small (less than 1% since 1947), although since 1975, it has been increasing. In 1976, the Bank's commitments to population ($34.3 million)[8] represented slightly over 10 per cent of total commitments to population from all sources.

FUNDING CRITERIA AND CHOICE OF COUNTRY

The Bank considers that in terms of impact on the global population problem, its population activities would be most fruitful if concentrated in 17 "key" developing member countries with sizable populations and major population problems. There are another 19 countries with serious population problems not considered priority countries. Before the Bank can assist such a country, however, it is necessary, first, that its government should want a Bank population project and, second, that the Bank should be satisfied that the project will have a significant impact. The Bank is prepared to support population projects in countries outside the key group of 36 countries with population problems, if there are special grounds for Bank assistance.

The Bank has brought to population assistance its traditional project lending techniques applied in other sectors of activity. These generally begin with a "sector review"[9] to analyse the country's population problems and identify possible areas for Bank assistance; this is followed by the preparation of very detailed project design and cost estimates, and finally by loan negotiations. As this process generally takes at least two years, the Bank is sometimes criticised for the length of time that elapses before any Bank funds begin to flow for population projects. The Bank maintains that for a country which is in the early stages of a population programme, careful planning is necessary if funds are not to be wasted and in particular, that it is essential to create suitable administrative machinery for planning and carrying out a population programme. This problem of the long "gestation period" arises mainly in the case of a first loan in the population sector[10].

Loans for population projects, as for activities in other sectors, are made on terms appropriate to the economic situation of the country concerned, i.e., either at the Bank's normal lending rate or, for poorer countries, at IDA rates.

---

8. Excluding Nutrition, included in some earlier population projects (DAC, Assistance to Population Programmes, 1976).

9. Except in cases of "second generation" projects in the same country.

10. The World Bank indicates that recent comparisons with the major population programmes of other donors show that the gestation periods are now closely comparable.

The Bank likes to associate other aid agencies with its population activities in some form of co-financing arrangement. This has the advantage of making more funds available for population activities (particularly from bilateral donors) and is particularly useful as a means of providing funds on softer terms than those available under either IBRD or IDA lending. Very often the contribution of the other agencies is in the form of outright grants. To date, the Bank has participated in nine co-financed projects, with varying modalities of partnership. Although co-financing tends to compound problems of administration[11], the Bank feels that it offers a valuable means of co-ordinating the objectives and programmes of different donors. In addition, the Bank generally seeks close co-operation with the international and other agencies working in the population field. In the case of WHO, it has signed a Memorandum of Understanding concerning co-operation between the two agencies (1973).

The Bank's population projects have tended to concentrate on extending the health infrastructure of a country as providing the readiest means of delivering family planning services. As a consequence, the earlier Bank population projects included substantial "hardware" components for the construction of health centres, MCH clinics, and training facilities for para-medical personnel.

Recently there have been two shifts of emphasis in the Bank's population activities. First, although MCH is still regarded as the core of government-provided family planning programmes, the Bank is now prepared to support the provision of family planning services (particularly those not requiring close medical supervision) through other networks, both governmental and non-governmental, including community-based distribution systems (CBD).

The second shift is that increasing attention is being given to activities that not only meet the existing demand for contraception, but are intended to create demand. While IEC components have been included in Bank population projects from the outset, they are becoming increasingly sophisticated, and are supplemented by monitoring and evaluation components which measure the effectiveness of family planning programmes with a view to improving them.

CHANGES SINCE BUCHAREST

At the request of the President of the World Bank, an External Advisory Panel was set up late in 1975 to review the Bank's activities in the population field and suggest ways in which they might be made more effective. The Report of the Panel was submitted in 1976, and the Bank has accepted practically all its recommendations.

The Panel recommended that the Bank should concentrate its population assistance on the 17 "key" countries. It further emphasized that, while the Bank should continue its family planning projects, which concentrate on the supply side of the "fertility equation", it should give greater attention to the demand side where its status and prestige could enable it to have a substantial impact. It should therefore continue and extend its recent emphasis on the social sectors, such as rural and urban development and education, where development can be especially significant for fertility, and look for opportunities to introduce "population components" into projects in these sectors. Such components, the Panel notes, offer a way of introducing population activities in countries which have not requested direct population assistance. "Population components" in this context are defined very broadly. They could cover supply of contraceptives through both the health network and CBD, family planning services, motivational

---

11. "Project Co-financing and Aid Co-ordination in the Population Sector", IBRD Discussion Paper prepared for the Meeting of Population Donor Agencies, December 1977.

activities (including training in person-to-person motivation), IEC, female literacy, and community-based activities (for example, youth groups, mothers' clubs, etc.). The Panel also recommends that the Bank, which has hitherto financed health facilities only to the extent that they provided family planning services, should bear in mind the potential effects of better health and nutrition on fertility when appraising such projects.

Significantly, the Panel's recommendations include the proposal that the country concerned need not necessarily have formulated a national family planning programme in order for population activities to be included in a Bank project. Indeed, offering "population" activities through other development activities is likely to be particularly valuable in the case of larger developing countries which, for political or cultural reasons, are unwilling to establish national population programmes. It is one way of initiating a dialogue with the government concerning the harmful consequences of rapid population growth.

The Panel recognizes that the Bank has its internal constraints as regards a stepped-up population assistance programme. These are due partly to manpower resources, partly to procedures (designed originally for lending activities of a very different nature), and partly to the departmental organisation of the Bank, which is not easily conducive to integrated or multi-sectoral approaches. It recommends that the Bank review procedures used in its earlier "hardware" projects with a view to increasing their flexibility and suitability for innovative activities. The Bank and the Panel both recognize the desirability of approaching population problems in a much broader context than has generally been the case hitherto, but agree that multi-sectoral activities need to be very carefully designed and implemented so as not to complicate operations and impose a heavy management burden.

With the endorsement of the Panel, the Bank will continue to provide loans for conventional family planning programmes and will also continue to devote a considerable proportion of its funding to "hardware". This is partly on the grounds that funds for this purpose are in short supply from other donor sources, and partly because strengthening basic infrastructure continues to be a critical need in many developing countries. At the same time, there is a new interest in a wide variety of "software" activities which are quite unrelated to construction, and these are expected to occupy a larger share of Bank-supported projects in future.

UNITED NATIONS POPULATION DIVISION

INTRODUCTION

The UN Population Division is the most venerable of the international population assistance agencies. Its origin dates back to the creation of the UN and the necessity to provide technical services within the UN Secretariat to carry out the programmes recommended by the Population Commission, by the Economic and Social Council (ECOSOC) or the General Assembly in the population field. It thus constitutes the "substantive" arm of the UN in respect of population matters.

The primary role of the Population Division has always been the preparation of projections of regional and world population trends and demographic analyses, especially studies designed to show how various demographic factors were inter-related with social circumstances, culture and economic conditions. However, with the increasing concern of the international community about world population growth which led to the creation of the UNFPA, the Population Division has broadened the scope of its activities in order to provide technical support to the population assistance programmes carried out by the UNFPA, as have the UN Regional Commissions and the Specialised Agencies.

In 1970, the Population Division was given the task of organising the World Population Conference to be held in Bucharest in 1974 and of preparing the draft World Population Plan of Action to be presented to the Conference. It was this involvement, and notably the preceding regional conferences and symposia, which led the Population Division even before Bucharest to broaden its definition of population-related subjects. Thus, in the early 1970s, its work programme already included study of such subjects as the role of women in development, the relationship of family structure and function to fertility, and the relevance of population factors for human rights and the environment.

CHANGES SINCE BUCHAREST

Certainly the Conference itself, and the strong emphasis which both the developing and the developed countries placed upon the inter-relations of the population factors with development, obliged the Population Division, in common with the UNFPA and the whole of the UN system, to reappraise its work programme and priorities in order to see how best to implement the World Population Plan of Action and the new approaches and new ideas that it embodied. It is difficult, however, to determine to what extent the work of the Population Division has actually changed in practice. The Division's traditional research into demographic conditions and trends, dissemination of population information and provision of relevant services was confirmed as being among the priorities established by the Conference. Such shifts as may be discerned, therefore, would seem to be rather a matter of emphasis than changes of substance. In particular, research is becoming rather more policy-oriented: population projections are being calculated according to different possible government population policies; there is more concern with the inter-relationship between population and other variables, etc.

The Bucharest Conference gave a mandate to the Population Division (as the "appropriate body" in the UN system) to undertake the continuous monitoring and biennial reporting of population trends and policies. This task is not new to the Division which has been monitoring and reporting population trends to ECOSOC on a regular basis since 1968[12] and periodically since 1947. (Before the Bucharest Conference, the Division had already issued several major reports on the world population situation, and had conducted two enquiries among governments, one on population changes and economic development (1963), and one on attitudes and policies affecting population trends (1972-73).) The official mandate given at Bucharest and included in the WPPA may be said, however, to have confirmed the Division's monitoring role and to have given it increased importance. The regular demographic studies have accordingly been intensified and broadened, with emphasis placed on catching up on the previously neglected field of mortality, nuptiality and international migration. New work is being done on the aged and, for the first time, research priorities include studies of other special population groups (youth, working women) and the development of quality-of-life indicators. Most notable is the greatly increased emphasis upon studies of population and development. Indeed, one post-

---

12. When ECOSOC requested the Secretary-General to prepare, on a biennial basis, a concise report on the world population situation for presentation to the General Assembly. This work has been implemented by the Population Division.

Bucharest phenomenon has been the establishment, within the Population Division, of a new unit that will deal exclusively with questions of the inter-relationships between population and development. The Bucharest mandate has also been a means of reviving interest in the Division's demographic data bank and the information bank on population policies[13]. Since the Bucharest Conference, the Division has conducted a third enquiry among governments—on population policies in the context of development—and a fourth is planned on problems of integrating population-related measures into development plans. The first post-Bucharest biennial reports on population trends and population policies were published in 1976. The Division has also been requested to report to the Population Commission in 1979, presenting a review and appraisal of the progress made towards achieving the goals and recommendations of the WPPA.

In its capacity as a technical division of the UN, the Population Division provides substantive support to some 80 experts in the field. Most of the technical assistance activities are funded by UNFPA. In 1975, they amounted to programmes of the order of $13 million. Many of these are concerned with building up institutional capacity in demography in developing countries, in training and in research. Two new UN demographic institutions have been created since 1974—one in Bucharest itself and the other in the Soviet Union. The training programme at the Bucharest Centre, for francophone students from developing countries, concentrates particularly on the inter-relationship between population and development, and the recently established Centre in Moscow is also to emphasize interdisciplinary training.

It is expected that in the next few years the technical co-operation activities of the Population Division will alter somewhat in nature, due primarily to the constraints posed by rising expert costs within a reduced programme budget. The Division will therefore tend to encourage mutual assistance between the developing countries themselves. Increasing numbers of trained researchers and teachers are now beginning to graduate from the various demographic institutes established by the UN in various parts of the developing world, which will make possible this new form of co-operation.

A concrete expression of the new pre-occupation with the inter-relationship between population and development factors since Bucharest is the issue by the Population Division in May 1976 of "Guidelines on Population-Related Factors for Development Planners". This will be followed by publication of a number of co-operative studies already underway in selected countries on ways to incorporate population factors in development planning under different conditions and circumstances.

---

13. Plans are now in progress to change these into a computer-based operation, with terminals at each of the regional economic commissions, which will store and make easily available linked data on demographic levels and trends, on population policies, and on the whole complex of relationships between social and economic factors and population.

NON-GOVERNMENTAL AGENCIES

THE INTERNATIONAL PLANNED PARENTHOOD FEDERATION
(IPPF)

INTRODUCTION

Established in 1952 for the purpose of promoting and assisting family planning activities, the IPPF is constitutionally different from other population assistance agencies in that it is an international federation of a large number of national family planning associations. The individual associations, 91 in all, embracing developed countries as well as developing countries, are themselves autonomous, although many of them receive funding from the federal organisation. This federal structure has important implications for the formulation of IPPF policies, which are the result of a continuing and subtle inter-action between the views of the IPPF Secretariat in London and the programmes and wishes of the national Associations (voluntary) in the different countries.

Under the terms of its constitution, IPPF has two main purposes: to provide individuals with family planning information and services, and to increase awareness of demographic problems among both people and governments. This second is the only part of IPPF's mandate which links it to "population" in the broad sense. "Population" has always, however, been a sensitive issue, particularly among the European Associations. Although "demographic problems" do not necessarily imply a need to reduce the birth rate, a number of the national Associations feel that population policies are a concern of governments, and not of voluntary organisations[1]. The main concern of the IPPF, therefore, unlike that of most of the international agencies engaged in population assistance, is still "family planning" rather than "population".

FUNDING CRITERIA AND CHOICE OF COUNTRY

IPPF provides funds (including general budgetary support) to the national Associations. Although IPPF mainly supports private voluntary associations, it also renders some assistance to other organisations and, in some cases, to governments, especially if there is no private association in the country.

The IPPF has grown considerably in recent years. Its 1961 budget totalled $30,000: by 1975, expenditures amounted to $42.6 million. The increase reflects both the growing number of national Associations and the increase in the scope and strength of their respective activities. IPPF provides all of its financial assistance in grant form, although loans and special contracts are technically

---

1. Family Planning Associations have been set up in a number of countries where official population policy is pro-natalist. The concern of these Associations is with such matters as illegal abortion, maternal health, child spacing, etc., rather than national "population" problems.

possible. Commodity assistance represents an important part of IPPF's activities: this includes world-wide provision of contraceptive supplies, both to family planning associations and to individual hospital units and other organisations; IPPF also provides medical and audio-visual equipment and materials.

The level of IPPF provision of both financial and commodity assistance to individual countries varies widely (within a range of $10,000 and $4 million per year). In the case of Brazil, for example, the National Family Planning Association (BEMFAM), financed almost entirely by IPPF, has been the only major agency delivering family planning services.

In addition to providing its member Associations with funding and with supplies and equipment, IPPF's support also covers a wide range of technical assistance services in medical, legal, educational and other relevant fields.

Since a large part of the programmes that the Associations put up to IPPF for funding are regular on-going activities (clinics, motivational campaigns, etc.), and the extent to which the Associations are able to generate local funding is highly variable, IPPF assistance will normally cover local currency recurrent costs as a matter of course. Cost-effectiveness and operational efficiency, however, are becoming increasingly important considerations in IPPF's approval of Association project requests.

CHANGES SINCE BUCHAREST

Since Bucharest, the IPPF has undertaken a series of major re-appraisal exercises with a view to determining what should be its most appropriate role and objectives in the situation of today. The initial impetus was not Bucharest, but rather IPPF's normal internal review process. Already before Bucharest, it was felt that there was need to re-examine the relationships between the national Associations and their respective governments, now that governments were themselves becoming actively involved in family planning programmes and the Associations were losing, in consequence, their earlier pioneering role. From there to an examination of the role of the IPPF itself was but a logical step. A major re-appraisal study on IPPF and its future was completed in November 1977, undertaken by IPPF's own volunteer leaders and Secretariat staff with the advice of a panel of outside experts[2].

One of the major questions to which the study was addressed was that of the priorities and criteria to be followed by the IPPF in allocating resources to the Associations. Quite independently, however, of the eventual recommendations of this study, the past few years have seen a considerable evolution in the scope of IPPF activities, partly the result of deliberate management decisions and partly in response to programme changes at the national Association level. Indeed, in many cases, a formal policy decision by IPPF's Governing Body had already been preceded in fact by the actual programmes of a number of national Family Planning Associations.

The question of overall resource allocation breaks down into several subsidiary questions, each of them highly significant for the future role of IPPF, not only in relation to the national Associations but also in relation to the work of other international agencies concerned with population assistance.

The main questions are: first, to what extent should IPPF go beyond family planning and get involved in other kinds of development activities; second, where there is such involvement, should IPPF resources be applied to the financing of all or part of these other activities, or should they be limited to the family planning

---

2. Suggested at the IPPF Donors' Meeting in November 1975, and decided by the IPPF Management and Planning Committee in April 1976.

and related components; third, should resources be concentrated on those countries of greatest need, or those where the government is not yet active in the population field; and fourth, should responsibility for provision of clinical services be progressively transferred to the governments concerned, leaving to IPPF to concentrate on training, informational and motivational work (IEC), and other programmes of an innovative nature?

The actual experience of the past few years provides a partial answer to some of these questions. The most significant trend has been in the direction of *integrated* activities, i.e. the association of family planning with community development and similar social programmes. At first, the decision was that the financing of the non-family planning elements should be left to other bodies. Subsequently, this view was modified, and in certain circumstances, at the discretion of the IPPF, these other elements can receive IPPF funding. The project "Planned Parenthood and Women's Development" is a good example[3]. In other cases—an interesting new departure—IPPF funds have allowed the local Associations to provide community services other than family planning *first* in the expectation that demand for family planning will eventually follow.

Another aspect of IPPF's recognition that family planning alone is not the answer is the inclusion of *nutrition* among its official approaches. This has not yet been developed very far and in no case has IPPF agreed to fund a nutrition programme unless it is associated with a family planning element. The intention is to collaborate with other agencies (e.g. UNICEF, World Food Programme) in integrated projects in which IPPF funds the family planning component. (The joint parasite control/nutrition/family planning projects initiated by JOICFP[4] are interesting examples.) The association of family planning work with youth programmes is an increasingly common form of such integration.

The study of IPPF's future endorses the move towards integrated projects, and recommends that IPPF should advocate "more rapid socio-economic development including a better quality of life through the more equitable distribution of wealth, improvement in the status of women, response to the needs of the poor and the under-privileged". The study acknowledges that in many situations it is not possible or realistic to isolate family planning from the physical, cultural, social and economic aspects of fertility, but calls for a clearer definition of integration in planning and programme terms.

It may be noted in this connection that while the term "integrated projects" is relatively new in the parlance of international development assistance, several of the national Associations have in fact been engaged in various forms of joint community development/family planning endeavour for some time, but without calling them "integrated".

One potentially very important development in IPPF strategies in the post-Bucharest period has been to promote *joint funding* with other agencies. The idea is to try to insert a family planning element into programmes of other agencies intended for other development purposes. Joint funding is still very much at the idea stage (only 2 per cent of total funding in 1976). It offers, however, a promising approach for the future, whereby IPPF can participate in the "wider" approach while maintaining its own appointed role.

The problem of *geographical allocation* and national self-sufficiency is far from clear-cut. IPPF would like the National Family Planning Associations to become financially independent (as some of them have). However, even in

---

3. The actual form that the women's development activity is to take is left to the determination of the individual country.

4. The Japanese Organisation for International Co-operation in Family Planning is partly funded by IPPF and UNFPA, but receives substantial support from private Japanese sources.

countries with a strong national programme, the National Associations either find it more difficult to attract voluntary local financing just because of the vigour of the national programme, or they feel it expedient to preserve a degree of independence from government and the increased flexibility of action that this implies. Other donor agencies also sometimes find it convenient to have strong independent local Associations with which they can work easily and quickly—particularly in the case of new and experimental activities.

A few years ago, IPPF activities showed a distinct *trend away from clinical services* in favour of training, IEC, and innovative approaches. While the interest in these latter activities is developing steadily, it seems that the decision to phase out the clinical side was in many cases premature (either because governments cannot do everything, or because their procedures are more bureaucratic). The study of IPPF's future found "unexpectedly strong evidence" of a need for the private sector to continue to provide family planning services. It suggested that national Associations could demonstrate simple and economic delivery systems for the benefit of governments, and that they should give priority in their activities to the poor, the illiterate, the young, and immigrants. The family planning services provided by IPPF are themselves changing in nature, often taking some form of community-based distribution instead of being clinic-based.

There was at one time a feeling that IPPF's activities tended to be too urban-oriented, providing services for an urban elite rather than the rural masses. More recent experience, however, indicates that many Family Planning Associations have been successful in their efforts to reach rural areas and that many governments now expect them to be more active in these areas.

In the field of research, the policy of IPPF has been to leave basic research to other agencies—the findings of which it closely monitors—and to concern itself more with action-oriented research, whether in bio-medical or social sciences.

Some of the recent developments in IPPF's activities are consistent with the WPPA (e.g. greater concern with the position of women, youth, legal change) but they are largely a reflection of prevalent attitudes towards both population and development questions generally. The fact that IPPF is a non-governmental, private organisation, embracing a wide range of both national and international operations, and in particular, the fact that it draws on the services of large numbers of volunteers should be conducive to a flexible and imaginative approach.

FOUNDATIONS

POPULATION COUNCIL

INTRODUCTION

The Population Council is an independent, non-profit organisation created for the specific purpose of addressing the problems of population. Established in 1952, it was one of the first organisations to focus on the consequences of rapid population growth.

The Council's principal funding comes from the Rockfeller and Ford Foundations and US AID, though it also receives support from UNFPA, the World Bank, and the International Development and Research Organisation (IDRC) of Canada. The Council, in its turn, provides financial support for population projects and for institutions and individuals world-wide. It is currently funding activities in over 50 countries.

The main task which the Council has set itself has been to stimulate awareness and concern on the part of governments of the problems posed by rapid population growth. The Council has played an important pioneering role in this respect, by encouraging governments in developing countries to sponsor national family planning programmes and providing operational and substantive support for carrying them out. It has also helped provide training for some of the world's population specialists and has built up institutional capacity for research and training in demography and bio-medicine, particularly in poorer countries. The research sponsored by the Council has developed new techniques of fertility regulation, and the Council's technical co-operation activities have facilitated their delivery to the people who needed them. The Council has also taken a lead in the evaluation of family planning programmes, and in particular, in the scientific assessment of their impact on fertility.

FUNDING CRITERIA AND CHOICE OF COUNTRY

The Population Council's original programme emphasis was on training and research in the demographic and bio-medical fields. In the early 1950s, the Indian Government invited the Council to send a mission to provide advice on the formulation of its family planning programme. Similar invitations followed from other governments, and soon the provision of technical assistance to developing countries became a major Council activity.

In the years immediately preceding Bucharest, direct operations in developing countries accounted for only a very small proportion of the Council's total budget. But, in addition, much of the research and training undertaken by universities and research institutions in the United States to which the Population Council provides support is of relevance to the population problems of developing coun-

173

tries. The publications[1] issued by the Population Council, disseminating the results of research in the population field world-wide, provide a further important technical service of benefit to the growing body of population specialists in developing countries.

CHANGES SINCE BUCHAREST

The Population Council, through the Chairman of its Board of Trustees[2], itself provided one of the surprises of the Bucharest Conference through a speech putting forward the view that the objective of population programmes should be not reduction of fertility, but the enhancement of human welfare. The statement held that family planning was not a need in itself: accordingly, problems of population could only be solved within the context of economic and social development. The fact that the "development not family planning" approach was now being put forward by the head of the foremost professional body in the population establishment caused a considerable stir. To some observers, it was interpreted almost as a repudiation of the previous twenty years of effort in the cause of fertility limitation.

Following Bucharest, the Council undertook a very searching re-examination of its purposes and programmes in order to redefine its role. The outcome has been a very considerable broadening of the scope and orientation of its work.

As now re-stated, the Council's primary purpose has moved from its initial concern with fertility, to a remarkably wide concept of "population". The Council now defines its objective as "to contribute to knowledge and capacity for improving human welfare". The Council's Statement on Future Directions spells this out clearly: "To our long-standing emphasis on population growth, we must add related concerns with economic, social and cultural factors, such as resources, income and capital, consumption, productivity, the role and status of women[3], health, education, housing, employment, social security and institutional structures; and we should pay greater attention to issues related to migration, urbanisation and mortality."

Within this broad context, the Council will continue to sponsor research on the demographic and bio-medical aspects of population, areas that it still considers of critical importance. It will now, however, also support research in the social sciences, in order to explore the complex inter-relationships between fertility, the development process and human behaviour and motivation. The Council's technical co-operation services will similarly deal henceforward not only with questions relating to the causes of fertility, but—a significant addition—to their consequences also. (The Statement speaks of the problem of how to "ease the adverse *consequences* of demographic patterns".)

The programme and structure of the Council have been reorganised to reflect this new wider perspective. There are now three major programme divisions, plus an administrative services division (which includes publications and information). Two of the divisions continue some of the long-standing interests of the Council. Thus the Centre for Bio-medical Research has as its goal the improvement of contraceptives. Wide-scale clinical studies and laboratory research are devoted to evaluation of new contraceptive leads. These efforts

---

1. *Studies in Family Planning; Reports on Population/Family Planning; Country Profiles; and Current Publications in Population/Family Planning.* The Council also publishes a quarterly journal, *Population and Development Review.*
2. Mr. J. D. Rockefeller III.
3. The status of women was singled out for particular emphasis ("We can no longer regard women in developing countries as statistics, merely as 'users' or 'acceptors' ").

are complemented by a programme to monitor the safety, effectiveness, and health effects of methods now in use.

Through its international programmes, the Population Council is continuing to provide technical co-operation to developing countries. There are four regional area offices: Latin America and the Caribbean, West Asia and North Africa, South and East Asia, and Sub-Saharan Africa. This decentralised network helps identify programme initiatives and assists local, national and regional institutions in the design, implementation, and evaluation of research and action programmes. Researchers, technical advisers and Council representatives are located in 16 countries.

The widening of the scope of the activities of the Population Council is reflected in the creation of the third division, the Centre for Population Studies, which will promote research into the relationships between demographic change and social and economic development. At the same time, it will seek ways of better applying this knowledge to the design of social policies that are responsive to the needs of people in developing countries.

The Council is making determined efforts to bring to bear a multi-disciplinary approach on its future population work by recruiting people from a wide variety of disciplines and backgrounds. The intention is to develop a world-wide network of professionals.

Subjects identified for addition to the range of professional and technical services in the late 1970's and early 1980's now include the role and status of women; project-level inter-relationships between population and other development activities; sterilisation and abortion; safety and health effects of fertility regulation methods, and transfer of appropriate fertility regulation technology.

THE FORD FOUNDATION

INTRODUCTION

Since the Ford Foundation is a multi-purpose institution, population assistance represents only a small part of the total budget. Moreover, of the Foundation's expenditures on population activities, a considerable proportion is applied to building up institutional capacity in developed countries (notably the Population Council and multi-disciplinary study centres in the US engaged in population work). Nevertheless, the Ford Foundation's population activities in developing countries absorb about 20 per cent of its total budget for international activities, a higher proportion than for any other multi-purpose aid agency.

The Ford Foundation's budget is allocated among the different programmes on a bi-annual basis. Population, together with agriculture, has always been a priority activity and the allocations have remained fairly constant. For the five fiscal years ending 1976, population expenditures have averaged about $13 million a year. Although financial stringency has compelled the Foundation to cut its budget by half, the amount allocated to population, now $8 million per annum, has not been cut proportionately.

Ford sees its prime function in the population field as strengthening capacity to understand and thereby control demographic factors, and to influence governmental policies accordingly. This it does, to a large extent, through direct grants for research and training, but it also seeks to associate itself with other donors in these activities[4].

---

4. One example of this is the International Review Group of Social Science Research on Population and Development (IRG), set up at the end of 1974 to advise donors on priority areas for social science research.

Traditionally, the major focus of Ford Foundation population work has been on the reproductive sciences, which have accounted for over half the population budget. The social sciences and related studies have taken second place (something over a quarter of the budget), and the application of management sciences to population programmes[5] third place (about 12 per cent). Information and communication activities make up the balance (4 per cent). It should be noted that the Foundation has no family planning programmes of an operational nature, except for small experimental efforts.

The Ford Foundation's support for population activities is provided on a grant basis and can be used for local as well as external expenditures. No commitment, however, is made for more than about five years—not so much to encourage self-reliance in the receiving country as to avoid tying up funds for too long in any one activity.

In principle, funds allocated for population activities could be applied to projects in other sectors with an indirect rather than a direct bearing on fertility, e.g. education, if the Foundation staff felt that this was indeed the most desirable way of tackling a particular population problem. In practice, however, it is not likely to occur very frequently as the Foundation feels that no evidence yet exists which clearly establishes the inter-relationships between population and the other variables. There is, however, particular interest in the increasingly important new problem of *managing* comprehensive population programmes, and especially those at community level.

Changes Since Bucharest

The Foundation has recently made two shifts of emphasis in its population work. The first is a reduction in the support given to institutions in developed countries in favour of those in developing countries. The second is a move away from bio-medical research towards increased concern with the social science aspects of population problems. Both these changes were prompted initially by financial constraints. The decision to increase activities in the social sciences rather than the reproductive sciences reflects also the nature of the Foundation's own expertise which gives it a comparative advantage in the former field[6]. At the same time, however, the result of the Foundation's new look at its population activities is in line with the general spirit of Bucharest, since it gives a new priority to examining the inter-relationships between the population factor and other economic and social variables.

The Foundation is well placed to explore ways of integrating population activities with those in the other sectors in which it operates, such as agriculture and rural development, education, development planning, promotion of the role of women, etc., since its staff organisation is very decentralised. Its "Population Office" (the only part of the Foundation to be organised on a functional basis) collaborates with the regional and field staff[7] who decide the actual programmes to be financed. The fact that staff members sometimes work both in the Population Office and the regional programmes, increases the likelihood that population considerations will be taken into account.

---

5. Ford helped create ICOMP (the International Committee for the Management of Population Programmes).
6. Ford also considers that its role is to assist innovative and "risk" activities. Whereas in the early 1960s, the Ford Foundation was financing some 40 per cent of all bio-medical population research, a decade later many new agencies have entered the field.
7. Retrenchment has recently cut the number of field staff and shut down some of the regional field offices.

Despite the financial limitations on its assistance for population projects, the Ford Foundation's work in the population field is significant in that it is not aimed at immediate and visible results. The Foundation is unusual among donors of population assistance in that it is not only prepared to take the long view, but prefers to give its support to activities which are by their nature long-term and speculative.

THE ROCKEFELLER FOUNDATION

INTRODUCTION

The involvement of the Rockefeller Foundation in population matters has developed considerably since the Foundation was established in 1913 with the express aim "to promote the wellbeing of mankind throughout the world". The Foundation provides grants for research to academic and scientific institutions world-wide, scholarships to individuals and funding of training programmes. The Foundation has prided itself on being forward-looking and innovative, and as the ideas that it has sponsored at their inception become more widely adopted, has a policy of moving on to support new activities.

The early programmes of the Foundation were concerned primarily with public health, demographic research and bio-medicine. Interest in broader population questions began in 1948, when the Foundation made a report into the problem of food supply and population in five countries in the Far East. One of the findings of the report was that the reduction of human fertility was the most difficult and, at the same time, the most important problem the area had to face. Since 1952, the Rockefeller Foundation and the Ford Foundation have supported the Population Council as a separate body to be concerned solely with population issues. Both Foundations also began giving financial support to training in demography at the Office of Population Research at Princeton, as well as to other university research programmes in reproductive biology and human genetics.

In the early 1960s, the Foundation reoriented its priorities and its programmes overseas in order to give greater emphasis to the special needs of developing countries. Its Population and Health Programme had the special purpose of seeking to stabilise population growth in these countries.

FUNDING CRITERIA AND CHOICE OF COUNTRY

The setting up of the Population and Health Programme by the Foundation had coincided with two major breakthroughs in contraceptive technology (the Pill and the Inter-Uterine Device), both of which looked as though they would make birth control a possibility for whole populations. The Foundation gave its support to organisations already working in these areas, primarily the IPPF, and continues to fund research in reproductive science in universities throughout the world.

The Foundation was one of the first institutions to recognise the inter-relatedness of population with economic factors and to organise its work on this basis. The Foundation has therefore supported research in the social sciences, specifically to explore the social and economic determinants of fertility behaviour and its consequences, and to provide training in these fields.

In 1972 the Foundation reviewed its Population and Health Programme and, in view of the increase of funding from other sources, decided to shift away from two of its original goals: support for family planning service programmes and for IEC activities. It continued to finance bio-medical research and research into contraceptive methods (through the International Committee for Contraceptive Development, which is under the auspices of the Population Council), its principal aim being to find new contraceptive methods that would be suitable for the needs of developing countries. At the same time, it began to expand its work on the social science aspects of population and in particular on the interrelations between population and other development sectors.

The whole budget for the Population and Health Programme is some $7 million per annum. Funding of population activities, as for all Foundation programmes, is on a grant basis. (Grants may vary from $2 million for a single activity to $1,000, and may include local costs as necessary.)

CHANGES SINCE BUCHAREST

The Rockefeller Foundation had thus been increasingly concerned with the wider aspects of population policy and, in particular, the inter-relation of population and development since well before Bucharest. Bucharest did not, therefore, give rise to any particular changes in overall policy or the organisation of the Foundation's work. It is, however, giving increased attention to the exploration of the highly complex problem of how population and development in fact interact. In 1977 a further review of the Population and Health Programme led to a decision to concentrate on research into reproductive biology and, in particular, into safer, more effective and cheaper methods of contraception, and on policy studies (to be carried out by scholars in both developed and developing countries) of the determinants of fertility and of the socio-economic factors that affect the growth of population and acceptance of contraception.

BILATERAL DONORS

(In order of magnitude of programme)

UNITED STATES (AGENCY FOR INTERNATIONAL DEVELOPMENT)

INTRODUCTION

The US Government, through the US Agency for International Development (US AID), the agency under the State Department responsible for foreign aid, has provided more population assistance than any other donor since the problem of population growth first received international attention in the mid-1960s. In the decade 1965-1975, of a total of $1,054 million of international population assistance, $732 million was provided by US AID[1]. Although during this period, a number of institutional donors have entered the field to become major contributors of population assistance, the most important are themselves generously funded by US AID which continues to be by far the largest source of population assistance. In 1976, it accounted for 53 per cent of all DAC commitments for population and 31 per cent of total population assistance.

Population was the first individual sector to be accorded a special allocation in the Agency budget. This type of assistance currently represents some 15 per cent of the Agency's development assistance programme, but less than 3 per cent of US total official development assistance (ODA). This proportion has remained more or less constant since 1975.

One-third of US AID's population assistance funds is provided in the form of direct bilateral aid. It represents a massive input. For example, in 1976, US AID's bilateral[2] population assistance amounted to $96.9 million or 75 per cent of all bilateral population assistance from DAC countries.

The greater part of US AID's population assistance goes to support other agencies, notably UNFPA, IPPF, the Population Council, Pathfinder Fund, Association for Voluntary Sterilisation, Family Planning International Assistance, and a number of other voluntary organisations, universities and institutions. The major beneficiary is UNFPA, which through 1976 had received a total of nearly $117 million from US AID or about 12 per cent of total Agency population funding to date. IPPF had received $79 million through 1976. In addition, US AID funds a very considerable amount of research activity world-wide, part of which is carried out by American universities and other US research institutions. This includes demographic data collection and analysis, policy development and social science research, bio-medical and operational research. One of the most important of US AID-supported research activities is the World Fertility Survey, which it finances jointly with UNFPA.

---

1. *World Population Growth and Response 1965-1976,* Publication of the Population Reference Bureau.
2. Including inter-regional assistance.

179

As a matter of policy, US AID has focussed its aid on those countries "whose national population increase poses the most serious problems for the world as a whole"[3]. These are Pakistan, Bangladesh, Indonesia, the Philippines, Nepal and Thailand, in Asia; in Africa, Zaïre, Kenya, Egypt, Morocco; and in Latin America, Colombia. (A few of these countries are now felt to be passing into the "self-sustaining" stage, or are expected to do so shortly.)

In addition to this group, the Agency has a particular interest in countries which, although their population policies are currently weak, are nonetheless important demographically (e.g., Nigeria, Ethiopia, Afghanistan), or where the prospects for fertility limitation appear especially encouraging, or where there appear to be opportunities for developing prototype programmes that may prove useful for other countries.

The forms of assistance provided cover information and education, training and institutional development, contraceptive supplies and equipment, and experiments in the retail sale of contraceptives. US AID's underlying philosophy has been that there exists in developing countries a large unsatisfied demand for family planning. The focus of the Agency's population assistance, therefore, has largely taken the form of efforts to improve the supply and the delivery of contraceptive services to the rural and urban poor.

US AID has been since 1966 the developing countries' leading source of contraceptive supplies. Through 1977, US AID has provided almost $162 million of contraceptives and other fertility-control materials[4]. While much of this has been provided through government-to-government aid agreements, the Agency has also an extensive programme for provision of contraceptive supplies to private family planning organisations in developing countries. Commodity support thus accounts for about 16 per cent of US AID's total population assistance.

Project assistance, as opposed to general programme support, similarly reflects the priority concern with family planning. Within this general area, however, there is considerable variety regarding the form of the project, the beneficiary agency, the size, etc. US AID is usually willing to finance local costs (salaries, operating expenses, etc.) as part of the project. Use of aid funds for construction of physical facilities, however, is not encouraged. The preferred emphasis is on the strengthening of human resources (through training programmes and advisory services), although this often includes liberal provision of technical equipment. The fact that aid can be provided on a 3 to 5-year basis (with possibility of renewal) assures an important element of continuity, both for the individual project and for government planning.

In the field of research, US AID's support again reflects the importance accorded to family planning. Major efforts ($60 million through 1977) have concentrated on bio-medical research and the search for improved methods of contraception, and in the development and testing of innovative and inexpensive delivery systems ($30 million). Population research in the social science fields, $53 million through 1977, has been concerned with problems of motivation, the determinants of fertility, KAP studies and evaluation of the results of different types of programmes.

Although recognising that it is the national government that must finally determine its own policies, US AID undertakes "to discover and elaborate lines of informal national self-interest that, in turn, can buttress an adequate fertility

---

3. *World Population Growth and Response, 1965-1975.*
4. $100 million of orals, $44 million condoms, $3 million IUDs, $9 million medical kits, $4 million aerosol foam and $1 million of other commodities.

control policy"[5]. The means of doing this is by "research and persuasion". The Agency accordingly seeks to act as an "information broker", organising country studies and conferences in order to bring together population experts and decision-makers[6].

US AID's assistance in the field of population reflects two important factors. One is the size and organisation of the agency. Within the Agency, the Office of Population is responsible for population assistance. With a staff of 90 people, it is itself part of a Bureau for Population and Humanitarian Assistance. In addition, US Missions in developing countries with significant population pro-grammes have a special officer for population assistance. As a consequence, US AID is able to exert a more systematic concern with considerations of cost-effectiveness, monitoring and evaluation than is generally feasible for smaller donor agencies.

The second factor is the influence of the US Congress. The requirement to seek annual aid appropriations makes the aid policies and programmes of US AID particularly sensitive to Congressional opinion. Congress has generally been in favour of population assistance, on the ground that unrestricted population growth frustrates economic aid designed to raise standards of living. However, it stipulates that the Agency should not support abortion or any coercive form of family planning.

CHANGES SINCE BUCHAREST

US AID has given greater attention to the need to supplement family planning services by activities designed to influence the socio-economic determinants of fertility. Although family planning remains the core of the Agency's population work, efforts are being made to expand and extend the health and nutrition programmes.

Recent policy directives within US AID seem to reflect the general trend in development philosophy that "population" problems need also to be tackled as part of a package of social measures. These measures include, notably, improving the status of women, better nutrition and health care, especially in the context of overall rural development. There seems to be an emerging awareness of the "population implications" of development activities in parts of the Agency outside of the Office of Population. This is so particularly in respect of rural development activities[7], and of US AID-sponsored "impact" research which studies the indirect effect on population of other forms of development activity.

Additional impetus towards using developmental assistance to influence reduction of growth rates was given in 1977 by Section 104(d) Foreign Assistance Act, which urged that *all* future development assistance should be examined from the view-point of its likely impact on population (reflecting recommendations of paragraphs 31-32 of the World Population Plan of Action). A similar provision had been made in 1975 in respect of the effect of development projects on women ("The Percy Amendment").

US AID appropriations for population assistance, which remained stationary for a period after Bucharest, are now increasing again and further increases are

---

5. *World Population Growth and Response, 1965-1975.*

6. Examples are the agreements with the Inter-Disciplinary Communications Pro-gramme (ICP) of the Smithsonian Institute to study social and economic determinants of fertility; the American Academy for the Advancement of Sciences (AAAS) studies of cultural factors in population dynamics; GE-TEMPO's series of country studies to measure the consequences of rapid population growth and assist development planners in weighing the policy alternatives. Most of these studies are carried out in collaboration with researchers of the country concerned.

7. Guidelines have been issued underlining the population aspects of rural development.

sought for 1978 and 1979. Although the broad categories for population assistance remain largely as previously (family planning delivery services and supplies), major changes in programme are expected within these categories. There are likely to be substantial increases for the training and use of para-medicals and auxiliaries in family planning delivery programmes, increased training of physicians and management personnel, expanded support for voluntary sterilisation programmes, and operational research to test innovative delivery systems to reach the rural and urban poor.

SWEDEN

INTRODUCTION

The Swedish International Development Authority (SIDA) is the central body under the Ministry of Foreign Affairs responsible for Sweden's bilateral aid programme. Multilateral assistance is handled direct by the Ministry of Foreign Affairs. In 1958, SIDA made an agreement with Sri Lanka to contribute personnel and material to a family planning project. This made Sweden the first and, for several years, the only Government to provide family planning assistance on an official basis to a developing country.

As a mark of its particular interest in population, SIDA has a special budgetary allocation for population assistance. (Swedish aid programmes generally have a strong bias towards the "social" sectors, of which family planning is one—the others being rural development, education and health.) Currently, Sweden is allocating between 4-5 per cent of its total ODA budget for population activities, the highest percentage after Norway among DAC countries. In 1976, expenditures on population totalled $14.5 million, of which 47 per cent went to multilateral support, and 51 per cent to bilateral programmes. Sweden also participates in multi-bilateral population projects. An additional sum of $13.1 million was disbursed in 1976 by the Ministry of Foreign Affairs directly to UNFPA and WHO.

FUNDING CRITERIA AND CHOICE OF COUNTRY

In earlier years, when Sweden was alone in providing assistance to what it considered an area of "vital importance in the present world situation"[8], SIDA departed from its usual policy of geographical concentration of aid in favour of satisfying as many requests for population support as possible, especially for bulk supply of contraceptives.

Thus, over the course of time, Sweden has supported projects in family planning and population policy in some 25 countries. However, as various international bodies and more donor countries have entered the field, Sweden has come to feel that its assistance would be most effective if concentrated on a smaller number of countries where SIDA's previous experience has been positive.

Most Swedish bilateral assistance is given under long-term co-operation agreements with selected developing countries made on a rolling three-year basis. The majority of these programme countries are in the low-income group, Swedish aid being specifically intended to promote development for poor people in poor countries. In exceptional cases, Sweden has been prepared to go outside of the programme countries, for example, if it is felt that countries have population

---

8. SIDA, *Swedish Development Aid*, 1968.

problems which are particularly challenging and serious, or if they are likely to gain particular benefit from the assistance provided. (Thus Sweden has been providing population assistance to South Korea, although it is not a low-income country, because there are good chances that aid can achieve a considerable population impact.)

SIDA makes a point of not imposing its own views, but follows the policies and priorities of the programme country. (The only exception is a firm stand against the use of coercive methods: SIDA would not support a programme that included compulsory sterilisation.)

SIDA is very liberal about meeting local currency operating and recurrent costs (including, if necessary, salaries and salary supplements), and has even agreed, in certain circumstances, to provide aid to cover the local costs of an activity originally started by another donor.

CHANGES SINCE BUCHAREST

Since Bucharest, SIDA has doubled the funds available for population assistance from $14.4 million to $29.2 million. It also made significant efforts to broaden the scope of the activities it was prepared to support.

Whereas SIDA's assistance was earlier concerned primarily with family planning activities (supplies, delivery, research, motivation and training), there has in the past few years been increasing interest in a broader, more integrated approach to population problems. Since Bucharest, Sweden has explicitly required that a national population programme for which Swedish assistance is requested should form part of a package of general social development and welfare policies. While Sweden fully endorses the message of Bucharest[9] that "the population problems of the developing nations are, to a large extent, a function of under-development"[10], it does not interpret this to mean that it should move away from traditional "population assistance" to development activities with supposedly higher, if longer-term, indirect demographic yields. Its view is that there is need for both.

SIDA gives particular support to efforts to develop new strategies, methods and innovative techniques through co-operation with international organisations. Concrete efforts are being made to link family planning assistance with health activities such as improvement of rural health infrastructure, preventive medicine, mother and child health care, etc., and with broader social programmes in fields such as nutrition, education, improvement of the status of women, rural development and employment promotion. By 1976-1977, Swedish population assistance was being applied to such varied activities as studies in futurology and ecology and the preparation for the International Year of the Child, as well as supporting pilot field projects in India in integrated rural health cum family planning (through the World Council of Churches)[11].

To provide better structural support to this wider approach, in 1976 SIDA merged the Population Division and the Health and Nutrition Section into a single Division dealing with a wide range of welfare-oriented activities, including family life and sex education, demography and related research, etc. At the same time, SIDA is making a special effort to train its staff in areas and sectors complementary to their own particular competence in order to inculcate a wider approach to development problems.

---

9. In the preparation of which, officials of SIDA played an active part.
10. Report of the Commission on Sweden's Future Development Co-operation Policy.
11. The Jam Khed Project.

SIDA is well aware of the need to adapt its aid to changes in international inter-relationships and developing country attitudes and requirements. A special Commission was appointed to evaluate Sweden's assistance programme overall and make suggestions as to how it might be modified or improved. The Commission's Report generally endorses current policies and programmes. In respect of population, it reiterates that it is for the developing countries themselves to formulate the economic and social policies which will best contribute to a reduced birth rate: the role of Swedish aid is to respond, and support such policies when requested to do so.

NORWAY

INTRODUCTION

Norway has a notable record among DAC countries for the seriousness of its concern with the problems of the developing world in general and with the problem of population in particular[12]. The Norwegian Parliament has also shown a particular interest in aid for population activities. In 1971, it decided that about 10 per cent of Norway's total development assistance should be expended for family planning. Actual expenditures on population assistance programmes ($23.9 million in 1976) have now exceeded this level (they represented 12.7 per cent of Norway's total ODA)[13]. The proportion of Norwegian aid going to population is far ahead of that of any other DAC country and, in absolute terms, places Norway third after the USA and Sweden.

The political responsibility for aid policy formulation and aid programming is concentrated in the Department of International Social and Economic Development in the Ministry of Foreign Affairs. The Norwegian Agency for International Development (NORAD) has since 1968 been the executive agency for the bilateral programme. Within NORAD, there is a special Division for Health, Family Planning and Education. The principal instrument for co-ordinating programmes in the population field with other programmes is the country programming procedure, which is under the administrative responsibility of the Ministry of Foreign Affairs.

FUNDING CRITERIA AND CHOICE OF COUNTRY

As a matter of policy, Norway's population assistance has been divided more or less equally between multi—and bilateral channels. In addition, Norway has entered into co-financing or "multi-bilateral" arrangements with eight UN agencies (including UNFPA), the World Bank, and the African and Asian Regional Development Banks.

Norway's bilateral assistance is concentrated on a limited number of recipients (Tanzania, Kenya, Zambia, Botswana and Mozambique in Africa, and India, Pakistan, Sri Lanka and Bangladesh in Asia), with which it has entered into revolving co-operation agreements providing for aid up to an agreed

---

12. Norway was one of the first DAC countries to declare its readiness to meet the target set by the UN Second Development Decade for official development assistance (0.7 per cent of GNP). This target was reached in 1976 and even slightly exceeded in 1977 (0.82 per cent—the third highest figure among DAC members). In 1978, Norwegian aid appropriations will reach 1.0 per cent of GNP. It is the intention of the Government to maintain this level in the medium term, despite the world economic crisis.

13. *Assistance to Population Programmes 1976*, DAC (not yet published).

mount for purposes to be determined annually by joint consultation. However, in a number of fields (maritime transport, scholarships, multi-bilateral assistance, emergency aid and family planning), assistance may be given to countries outside this group. This is also the case with family planning, on the grounds that, as the Norwegian Government has stated, "still only a minority of the developing countries have effective programmes in this field, which is, at the same time, one of those to which Norway attaches prime importance" (cf. Parliamentary Report 29).

Generally speaking, Norway confesses itself disappointed that there is not greater demand for population assistance.

Norwegian population assistance is given on a grant basis and is not tied, which makes its programme support particularly appreciated. Norway also has one of the most liberal procedures among DAC countries as regards local and recurrent cost financing.

The emphasis of Norwegian population assistance has been very much on the family planning approach, together with other traditionally-associated activities. The Norwegian Government's concern about the rapid population growth in developing countries, which it sees as a major obstacle to their aspirations for a better life, is matched by its firm conviction that the initiative in population matters must be left to the countries themselves. The role of aid is thus to be purely supportive. (Norway has indicated that it would not wish to get involved in advising on population policies or even in project formulation.) It is, however, prepared to be flexible in responding to requests, and if these become more broadly-based or innovative, so, presumably, will the nature of Norway's population assistance.

CHANGES SINCE BUCHAREST

Norway still remains firmly committed to what it calls the "extended concept of family planning"[14], which emphasizes the integration of family planning activities with broader programmes in the health field particularly MCH and nutrition. There does not, however, seem so far to have been any attempt to extend the concept of integrated approaches further in order to include population activities in, for example, programmes of agricultural development or rural development, areas where Norway is particularly active.

FEDERAL REPUBLIC OF GERMANY

INTRODUCTION

Population represents only a small element in the Federal Republic's aid programme (0.68 per cent of total ODA disbursements in 1976). Nonetheless, starting with small contributions to UNFPA in 1969, by 1976 Germany was providing population assistance to the amount of over $16 million (commitments), the fourth highest contribution among DAC Member countries. Over recent years, interest in bilateral population assistance has also been growing rapidly, and by 1976 represented over 50 per cent of Germany's total commitments to population assistance.

The formulation of German aid policy is now the responsibility of the Federal Ministry for Economic Co-operation. Capital assistance is implemented

---

14. Parliamentary Report No. 94 on "Norway's Economic Relations with Developing Countries", Ministry of Foreign Affairs, 1975.

by the Kreditanstalt für Wiederaufbau (KFW) and technical assistance (since 1975) by the German Agency for Technical Co-operation.

FUNDING CRITERIA AND CHOICE OF COUNTRY

It is the declared policy of German development assistance to give preference to the "Least Developed Countries" and to those most seriously affected by the increase in the price of oil and and other major commodities. Since these are often also the countries where the problem of rapid population growth is most serious, the Federal Government is prepared to give increased support to population programmes, if these countries so request. By 1976, 10 countries were receiving population assistance under bilateral agreements: Kenya, Tunisia, Togo, El Salvador, Honduras, Colombia, Bangladesh, Pakistan, India and Yemen. Total commitments amounted to $9.3 million, of which Bangladesh accounted for 64 per cent.

The role of development assistance, as interpreted by the Federal Ministry of Economic Co-operation, is strictly responsive, and particularly so in the area of population assistance, which it considers especially sensitive. (There are, however, certain limitations on activities that it would agree to support under bilateral assistance—for example, abortion or sterilisation programmes—although it recognises that it is indirectly supporting them through multilateral channels.)

Most German bilateral aid for population is for specific projects rather than general programme support. Although German aid would not take the initiative in proposing innovative activities, it is prepared to be flexible in response to innovative proposals if the developing countries present them for financing. It is prepared for example, to finance pilot projects, including local costs (salaries and incentive payments as well as recurrent costs). It is also prepared to provide the facilities for local production of contraceptives in developing countries. Where German aid covers the import of supplies and equipment, it is untied.

Population assistance is provided either in grant form (technical co-operation) or in the form of loans on concessional terms. In the case of the least developed countries, all population assistance can be given on grant terms.

CHANGES SINCE BUCHAREST

The most significant change in German population assistance to have occurred in recent years is the fact that the German Government now provides aid for population activities directly to developing countries as part of its bilateral aid programmes. Previously, there was no direct bilateral population assistance programme as such, although Federal funds were channelled via German non-governmental organisations, which used them to support their own development activities in developing countries. (German religious and missionary organisations have a long tradition of service in developing countries, and the Federal Government has assisted these efforts, as well as those of German universities, research institutions, labour organisations, etc.) This has enabled Germany to support family planning activities in developing countries, while maintaining a low donor profile on the Federal level. Germany has welcomed the "multi-bi" approach, and is one of the 6 donors participating in the major population project in Bangladesh.

The German Ministry for Economic Co-operation recognises a need to broaden its population assistance programme and to achieve a closer co-ordination of family planning with other kinds of services[15]. This broader approach to population activities has not yet, however, been translated into actual aid programmes. Although within the Ministry, there is a single Division responsible for health, family planning and nutrition activities, it is the "area desks" which give the final decision on particular country programmes. The German Authorities maintain that if requests were made for integrated activities, they would be treated sympathetically, but it is not for the Ministry to take the initiative. To date, therefore, projects assisted by the Federal German Government in such areas as land settlement, rural development, industry or vocational training have not usually included a family planning element.

CANADA

INTRODUCTION

The Canadian International Development Agency (CIDA), the official development assistance agency of the Canadian Government, began providing population assistance in 1970, soon after Canadian legislation removed a long-standing legal prohibition against dissemination of contraceptive information and services and set up a Federal Family Planning Programme within Canada itself. The Agency tends to maintain a low profile in aid-giving generally, and in the highly sensitive area of population assistance seeks to act with particular discretion. (A strong element of public opinion within Canada is hostile to family planning.)

Canada has accordingly provided most of its population assistance through multilateral channels (primarily UNFPA, IPPF and WHO). These contributions have been steadily increasing and by fiscal year 1976/1977 amounted to $9.4 million, representing 1 per cent of Canada's total ODA.

FUNDING CRITERIA AND CHOICE OF COUNTRY

Despite a marked preference for the anonymity of multilateral channels, Canada does provide some bilateral aid for population. In fiscal year 1976/1977, $3.6 million were allocated for this purpose (for activities extending over 2-3 years) mostly in India and Bangladesh. (Canada prefers to concentrate its population assistance on a few large-scale projects.) The project in Bangladesh is undertaken under "multi-bi" financing arrangements with the World Bank, UNFPA and five other bilateral donor agencies.

Most Canadian aid is tied, although exceptions are increasingly being made for certain priority projects. CIDA recognises that for population assistance, its aid-tying requirements often represent a practical constraint. On the other hand, CIDA is prepared to finance the local costs of a project, to the extent that this appears necessary.

Canada's bilateral assistance may sometimes include activities very closely related to population which are, nonetheless, not officially classified as population assistance. For example, CIDA is assisting urban-regional planning projects in

---

15. "The task of reducing the growth of population is made more difficult by the traditional patterns of behaviour of the people concerned and by inadequate social security in developing countries. In order to help ensure that family planning programmes are successful in the long term, it is necessary to further the economic and social security of the individual so that the people are no longer so heavily dependent on having a wealth of children", *Revised Report on the Development Policy of the Federal Government, 1975.*

Brazil and in Indonesia. In Indonesia, redistribution of population is part of the national population policy: it is therefore an open question whether the individual donor similarly chooses to consider such activities as part of its "population assistance". In this case, Canada does not do so.

Canada also provides some population assistance through non-governmental organisations. Under these arrangements, CIDA provides matching grants to such organisations to be used in their projects in developing countries. Originally limited to Canadian agencies, since 1974 these grants can now be made to non-Canadian organisations. CIDA's Non-Government Organisation Division particularly encourages innovative and experimental proposals.

CHANGES SINCE BUCHAREST

Since Bucharest, Canada has further increased its support to multilateral population assistance agencies. The Canadian Government is looking for ways to increase its bilateral assistance to population, although misgivings about direct intervention in the population field seems to be as strong as ever. Parallel financing arrangements with the World Bank appear to offer a useful compromise, permitting Canada to pick up particular components of a major population activity which is associated with an international donor agency.

The conceptual approach to population would not seem to have moved significantly since Bucharest, although CIDA's official Strategy for International Development Co-operation 1975-1980 stated that it considered population as an area of priority concern. The "Strategy" also indicated commitment to the idea of integrating population into a broad programme of other social development activities (rural development, public health, education, food production, energy, etc.), but so far, this has not been translated into actual programme terms.

JAPAN

INTRODUCTION

Assistance to the population sector has been a very marginal part of the Japanese Government's official aid programme (about half of one per cent in 1976). Much the greatest part of this (over 90 per cent) is given through UNFPA, to which Japan is the second ranking donor after US AID.

Japan entered the field of international population assistance with a certain circumspection. The Japanese Authorities feared that there might be some political sensitivity to the Japanese providing developing countries with aid for the purpose of limiting the growth of their populations. There also seems to have been some feeling of modesty—a notion that the Japanese experience was perhaps not particularly relevant to developing countries seeking to limit their fertility through governmental action.

Population assistance through multilateral agencies seemed, therefore, the solution. Japan's contribution to UNFPA, beginning with $200,000 in 1969, has risen since 1974 by $2 million each year, reaching $11 million in 1977. A small amount also goes to support the Intergovernmental Co-ordinating Committee (IGCC) in Kuala Lumpur.

The administration of the Japanese Government's population assistance is the responsibility of the Ministry of Foreign Affairs. (There is no separate aid Ministry.) Contributions to the UNFPA are handled by the UN Bureau, and bilateral aid by the Economic Co-operation Bureau. There is some possibility of sectoral co-ordination at the operational level through the Technical Co-operation Divisions, but prima facie, the administrative structure does not favour integrated approaches either to population or to other social development activities. The Japanese Authorities report that new measures intended to facilitate inter-sectoral co-ordination are currently under study.

FUNDING CRITERIA AND CHOICE OF COUNTRY

Japan would like to see its contribution to UNFPA used particularly in Asian countries. Approximately one-third of its contribution to UNFPA is transferred to IPPF, which in turn applies part of the funds to support the Japanese Organisation for International Co-operation in Family Planning (JOICFP). JOICFP is a private body but works in close collaboration with the Japanese Government. Established in 1968, its objectives are:

a) to increase Japan's role in international co-operation in the population/family planning fields;

b) to share Japanese family planning experience with other countries;

c) to introduce world population issues to the Japanese people; and

d) to promote population education in Japan.

Bilateral population assistance from the Government of Japan (also beginning in 1969, at the same time as Japanese support to UNFPA), was, until 1974, confined to Indonesia. It has since been extended to Thailand, the Philippines and Bangladesh, but the very modest amount of funds applied to bilateral population assistance has not been increased.

Bilateral aid to population has primarily taken the form of supplies (of Japanese manufacture)—notably, contraceptives, vehicles and audio-visual training equipment for IEC[16]. Assistance is provided in grant form and is limited to foreign exchange costs only. To date, the Japanese Government has not been willing to provide assistance for the establishment of local production of contraceptives in developing countries (it maintains that the conditions are not yet ready for it). It is, however, currently exploring technological advances in the manufacture of contraceptive materials in Japan which may eventually be of great interest to developing countries.

Although it provides little technical assistance in the form of expert personnel, the Japanese Government has built up specialist training expertise, notably in the field of population information and education. Quarterly seminars on these subjects are organised in Japan for family planning workers throughout the world.

CHANGES SINCE BUCHAREST

In the period since Bucharest, notably in the past two years, there have been signs of a certain quickening of interest in Japan in international action on population. This has involved political leaders, the Administration and some leading Japanese business men and philanthropists[17].

The Government of Japan has not yet broken away from its traditional pattern of population assistance (i.e., supplies), but it is now beginning to consider a more project-oriented approach. There is a feeling that future projects should be clearly defined and aimed at specific target groups, and that there should be realistic evaluation of their results. In particular, the Japanese Authorities are

---

16. This latter is something of a favourite among Japanese aid items.

17. A notable example was the "Tokyo Initiative", an international seminar on population launched jointly by some prominent private citizens in the US and Japan in 1977 for the purpose of stimulating private funds and public interest in international population assistance.

beginning to think in terms of activities that would create greater *motivation* for family planning.

One possibility being considered is to associate family planning with agricultural development, a field where Japan has recognised expertise. Another might be some form of regional population projects, possibly jointly financed by Japan and other donors. (Japan is not a participant in the "multi-bi" financing arrangements for the Bangladesh Population Project, as the Government's interest in broadening its population assistance has developed only recently.)

The Japanese Authorities seem now to be convinced that their earlier reticence about giving bilateral population assistance was needless. The developing countries of Asia are sufficiently strongly committed to their national population programmes to welcome assistance from Japan just as much as from any other quarter. Moreover, the developing countries and the donor community feel that Japan's own experience in curbing her population growth can be of help to developing countries who are still looking for solutions.

In this new and more relaxed attitude to population assistance, the Japanese Government is examining how it could make its population programmes more dynamic. It accordingly commissioned (in 1976) a private Japanese research body (the International Development Centre of Japan) to prepare a study of the matter.

Meanwhile, an innovative approach to population assistance initiated by Japan has come from JOICFP. In collaboration with IPPF, JOICFP has organised a number of pilot projects which combine family planning activities with improved nutrition and parasite control. The treatment for parasites (a field where Japan has considerable experience) has immediate and visible effects on the community and can thus help establish credibility for the family planning activities which follow. The first pilot project began in Taiwan in 1975 and showed encouraging results. The following year, programmes were begun in Thailand, Indonesia and the Philippines. Other countries in the Asian region (Republic of Korea, Malaysia and Nepal) are about to start or have started projects, while Latin America countries (Colombia, Mexico) have shown interest. The projects are providing valuable experience of "integrated" population activities, both as regards the psychological approach and project organisation and management.

UNITED KINGDOM

INTRODUCTION

The United Kingdom was one of the first DAC countries to be concerned with the population problem in developing countries and to include it as part of its development assistance effort. In 1964, the Ministry of Overseas Development (ODM)[18] announced that it was willing to provide assistance for population activities under its bilateral aid programmes. It has contributed substantially to the work of the IPPF, and since 1966, when the United Nations entered the field of population assistance, to the population programmes of the UN agencies also. Although there is no set allocation for aid to population, the British Aid Administration has always been strongly committed to population assistance.

---

18. Currently the Secretary of State for Foreign and Commonwealth Affairs has overall responsibility for the ODM. It is, however, separate from the Foreign and Commonwealth Office. Full day to day control is exercised by a Minister of State in the Foreign and Commonwealth Office with the title of Minister for Overseas Development.

The major part of UK aid for population is given through its contributions to multilateral agencies. Annual commitments to UNFPA currently account for approximately half of total population assistance, those to IPPF a further 25 per cent. The amount spent on bilateral population assistance is, therefore, very small.

In view of its sympathetic approach to population, it has long been a source of disappointment to the British Authorities that there has not been more demand for the bilateral aid that Britain is ready to provide in this field. They attribute this to the special sensitivity of the population issue in many developing countries[19].

FUNDING CRITERIA AND CHOICE OF COUNTRY

British bilateral aid has traditionally concentrated on the countries of the Commonwealth, but in recent years the amounts going to some non-Commonwealth countries have been increasing. Current policy is set out in the 1975 White Paper "More Help for the Poorest"[20] under which the aim is to give increasing emphasis in bilateral aid to the needs of the poorest countries, especially those most seriously affected by the rise in the price of oil and other commodities. (The White Paper gives high priority to population assistance, on the grounds that it is difficult to help these countries to better their condition if their population continues to increase more rapidly than their resources.) UK population assistance has, in fact, been widely spread geographically. Since 1969, the UK has provided population assistance of some kind to over 40 different countries.

The UK is very careful to keep its role as an aid donor responsive. Accordingly, the criteria of the activities supported by UK aid tend to be determined by the nature of the requests received rather than by ODM's own views. The terms applied to population assistance are those applying to bilateral aid as a whole: that is to say, technical co-operation (including equipment where appropriate) is provided on a grant basis, as is all capital aid to the "poorest" countries (and all multilateral contributions). In fact, practically all UK population assistance is in grant form.

Aid funding can be used to cover local salary costs and other recurrent expenses. ODM is also now sympathetic to the use of aid funds to foster the manufacture or packaging of contraceptive supplies in the developing countries themselves.

CHANGES SINCE BUCHAREST

Since Bucharest, the ODM has taken a number of measures intended to make its population assistance programme more dynamic and effective. It has increased contributions to multilateral agencies and is seeking to increase its bilateral population assistance also. Further efforts have been made to acquaint developing countries with the possibilities of population assistance that Britain is prepared to make available.

ODM has also shown considerable enthusiasm for the wider possibilities offered by joint financing of projects with multi-lateral agencies (which, among other advantages, offers a way of "defusing" the sensitivity problem). The UK is one of the participants in the Bangladesh Population Project and would welcome an opportunity for similar joint funding arrangements in other large-scale population projects.

---

19. In the past this reticence was perhaps shared to a certain extent in British diplomatic circles, which may have sometimes hesitated to press "population assistance" because of its sensitivity.
20. Cmd. 6270, October 1975.

There has been some development of funding population activities through support to UK voluntary agencies. In addition, the UK is building up a British expertise in population matters for the benefit of developing countries. In 1974, ODM helped set up the Centre for Overseas Population Studies in London—now the overseas section of the broader-based Centre for Population Studies—(under the aegis of the London School of Hygiene and Tropical Medicine). Its purpose, "to provide an official British base for consultancy, research and training in the field of population science and *its application to health, social welfare and economic development* in non-industrialised countries", attests to a new, broad approach to population problems.

The official approach to population has, in principle, broadened since Bucharest to cover the need for "an inter-disciplinary approach" outlined in the White Paper. This envisages population as covering not only family planning information and services, but a wider range of social development activities.

Structurally, the ODM, which has a Special Population Bureau, would seem well adapted to implement a broad-ranging population assistance programme. Moreover, responsibility for population policy lies with the Bilateral Aid and Rural Development Department, which has general oversight of "poverty-focussed" aid programmes.

In practice, however, progress towards a multi-disciplinary approach is proceeding only slowly. Perhaps the reason is in part the traditional reticence to push what might be interpreted as "donor bias". In any case, when a new definition of "population assistance" was issued by ODM in an internal guidance note in July, 1977, the activities that it listed as eligible for population assistance were all in the classic "family planning" categories, i.e., they included population information and education, demographic data gathering, and evaluation of population programmes, but *not* programmes to enhance the status of women, improve nutrition, diminish infant mortality, etc.

The paper does, however, reiterate the importance of such programmes for population, and ODM maintains that the distinction between them and the orthodox type is essentially administrative. They are dealt with under British bilateral aid programmes, even if they are not presented to developing countries as part of Britain's population assistance.

DENMARK

INTRODUCTION

In spite of serious economic difficulties, Denmark has maintained one of the most vigorous and effective aid programmes among DAC countries. Disbursements of official development assistance corresponded in 1976 to 0.56 per cent of GNP and are planned to reach 0.76 per cent in 1981. Bilateral and multilateral contributions are approximately evenly balanced and roughly half of bilateral aid consists of grants. Other characteristics of the programme are its highly concessional terms, the concentration of bilateral aid on the poorest countries and the emphasis on agriculture and rural development.

Support for population activities, on the other hand, is relatively small and dates back to an initial grant to India in 1966. Since then, most of it has been extended through multilateral channels (mainly UNFPA, WHO and IPPF). Total disbursements amounted to $4.8 million in 1976 (2.2 per cent of Danish ODA), placing Denmark eight among DAC countries.

The executive agency for the aid programme is the Danish International Development Agency (DANIDA) which is a Department of the Ministry of Foreign Affairs. A Board of International Development Co-operation and a Council serve in an advisory function. Within DANIDA, there is no single administrative unit responsible for population activities. Multilateral contributions are administered by the Multilateral Division, and bilateral contributions by several bilateral divisions, notably the geographic "country" desks.

FUNDING CRITERIA AND CHOICE OF COUNTRY

Of Denmark's total population assistance, only a minute fraction is provided bilaterally (4 per cent of disbursements in 1976). This reflects mainly:

a) the heavy administrative burden imposed on DANIDA by the great increase of activities relative to staff in recent years;

b) lack of requests by recipients; and

c) the concentration of Danish grant project aid on a very narrow range of recipients.

On the other hand, Denmark has a liberal approach with regard to local cost financing and is also prepared to provide programme assistance (e.g., contraceptive supplies and medical equipment), although a definite preference is given to the support of specific and well-designed projects. The totality of assistance in the population field is provided in the form of grants.

The bulk of Danish grant assistance in all fields is concentrated on only four recipients (Bangladesh, India, Kenya and Tanzania), for which multi-year country programming has been established. (Other recipients are Botswana, Malawi, Vietnam and Zaire, but without a pluri-annual planning procedure.) Out of these eight major recipients, only India and Bangladesh have so far asked Denmark for aid in the population field. (DANIDA is also a co-financing partner with the World Bank—in the amount of $0.6 million— in the Kenyan population project.)

The largest Danish population project is in India, where Denmark is providing $3 million for new premises for the National Institute for Health and Family Planning in New Delhi. The primary task of the Institute is training of administrators, physicians, nurses and social workers. The Indian Government has recently decided to merge the Institute with a training institute for public health administrators, in line with its general policy of integrating family planning with health services. Denmark also supports a family planning project in the slum areas in Calcutta, administered by the National Family Planning Association of India, and a Medical Research Institute at Lucknow in Northern India (Central Drugs Research Institute), which is in charge of the development of new contraceptive methods.

Preliminary approval has been given to a $32 million health project in India. The project covers ten rural districts and will set up integrated health services, consisting of preventive and curative services, family planning, mother and child care and nutrition programmes.

Assistance to Bangladesh is of a more recent date and consisted in 1976 of a commitment of $397,000 for the supply of 1.5 million cycles of oral pills.

CHANGES SINCE BUCHAREST

There do not seem to have been any significant changes in Danish aid to population since the Bucharest Conference.

OECD SALES AGENTS
DÉPOSITAIRES DES PUBLICATIONS DE L'OCDE

ARGENTINA – ARGENTINE
Carlos Hirsch S.R.L., Florida 165,
BUENOS-AIRES, Tel. 33-1787-2391 Y 30-7122

AUSTRALIA – AUSTRALIE
Australia & New Zealand Book Company Pty Ltd.,
23 Cross Street, (P.O.B. 459)
BROOKVALE NSW 2100   Tel. 938-2244

AUSTRIA – AUTRICHE
Gerold and Co., Graben 31, WIEN 1. Tel. 52.22.35

BELGIUM – BELGIQUE
LCLS
44 rue Otlet, B 1070 BRUXELLES . Tel. 02-521 28 13

BRAZIL – BRÉSIL
Mestre Jou S.A., Rua Guaipà 518,
Caixa Postal 24090, 05089 SAO PAULO 10. Tel. 261-1920
Rua Senador Dantas 19 s/205-6, RIO DE JANEIRO GB.
Tel. 232-07. 32

CANADA
Renouf Publishing Company Limited,
2182 St. Catherine Street West,
MONTREAL, Quebec H3H 1M7 Tel. (514) 937-3519

DENMARK – DANEMARK
Munksgaards Boghandel,
Nørregade 6, 1165 KØBENHAVN K. Tel. (01) 12 85 70

FINLAND – FINLANDE
Akateeminen Kirjakauppa
Keskuskatu 1, 00100 HELSINKI 10. Tel. 625.901

FRANCE
Bureau des Publications de l'OCDE,
2 rue André-Pascal, 75775 PARIS CEDEX 16. Tel. 524.81.67
Principal correspondant :
13602 AIX-EN-PROVENCE : Librairie de l'Université.
Tel. 26.18.08

GERMANY – ALLEMAGNE
Alexander Horn,
D - 6200 WIESBADEN, Spiegelgasse 9
Tel. (6121) 37-42-12

GREECE – GRÈCE
Librairie Kauffmann, 28 rue du Stade,
ATHÈNES 132. Tel. 322.21.60

HONG-KONG
Government Information Services,
Sales and Publications Office, Beaconsfield House, 1st floor,
Queen's Road, Central.   Tel. H-233191

ICELAND – ISLANDE
Snaebjörn Jönsson and Co., h.f.,
Hafnarstraeti 4 and 9, P.O.B. 1131, REYKJAVIK.
Tel. 13133/14281/11936

INDIA – INDE
Oxford Book and Stationery Co.:
NEW DELHI, Scindia House. Tel. 45896
CALCUTTA, 17 Park Street. Tel. 240832

IRELAND · IRLANDE
Eason and Son, 40 Lower O'Connell Street,
P.O.B. 42, DUBLIN 1. Tel. 74 39 35

ISRAËL
Emanuel Brown: 35 Allenby Road, TEL AVIV. Tel. 51049/54082
also at:
9, Shlomzion Hamalka Street, JERUSALEM. Tel. 234807
48, Nahlath Benjamin Street, TEL AVIV. Tel. 53276

ITALY – ITALIE
Libreria Commissionaria Sansoni:
Via Lamarmora 45, 50121 FIRENZE. Tel. 579751
Via Bartolini 29, 20155 MILANO. Tel. 365083
Sub-depositari:
Editrice e Libreria Herder,
Piazza Montecitorio 120, 00 186 ROMA. Tel. 674628
Libreria Hoepli, Via Hoepli 5, 20121 MILANO. Tel. 865446
Libreria Lattes, Via Garibaldi 3, 10122 TORINO. Tel. 519274
La diffusione delle edizioni OCSE è inoltre assicurata dalle migliori
librerie nelle città più importanti.

JAPAN – JAPON
OECD Publications and Information Center
Akasaka Park Building, 2-3-4 Akasaka, Minato-ku,
TOKYO 107. Tel. 586-2016

KOREA · CORÉE
Pan Korea Book Corporation,
P.O.Box n° 101 Kwangwhamun, SÉOUL. Tel. 72-7369

LEBANON – LIBAN
Documenta Scientifica/Redico,
Edison Building, Bliss Street, P.O.Box 5641, BEIRUT.
Tel. 354429–344425

MEXICO & CENTRAL AMERICA
Centro de Publicaciones de Organismos Internacionales S.A.,
Av. Chapultepec 345, Apartado Postal 6-981
MEXICO 6, D.F. Tel. 533-45-09

THE NETHERLANDS – PAYS-BAS
Staatsuitgeverij
Chr. Plantijnstraat
'S-GRAVENHAGE. Tel. 070-814511
Voor bestellingen: Tel. 070-624551

NEW ZEALAND – NOUVELLE-ZÉLANDE
The Publications Manager,
Government Printing Office,
WELLINGTON: Mulgrave Street (Private Bag),
World Trade Centre, Cubacade, Cuba Street,
Rutherford House, Lambton Quay, Tel. 737-320
AUCKLAND: Rutland Street (P.O.Box 5344), Tel. 32.919
CHRISTCHURCH: 130 Oxford Tce (Private Bag), Tel. 50.331
HAMILTON: Barton Street (P.O.Box 857), Tel. 80.103
DUNEDIN: T & G Building, Princes Street (P.O.Box 1104),
Tel. 78.294

NORWAY – NORVÈGE
Johan Grundt Tanums Bokhandel,
Karl Johansgate 41/43, OSLO 1. Tel. 02-332980

PAKISTAN
Mirza Book Agency, 65 Shahrah Quaid-E-Azam, LAHORE 3.
Tel. 66839

PHILIPPINES
R.M. Garcia Publishing House, 903 Quezon Blvd. Ext.,
QUEZON CITY, P.O.Box 1860 – MANILA. Tel. 99.98.47

PORTUGAL
Livraria Portugal, Rua do Carmo 70-74, LISBOA 2. Tel. 360582/3

SPAIN – ESPAGNE
Mundi-Prensa Libros, S.A.
Castellò 37, Apartado 1223, MADRID-1. Tel. 275.46.55
Libreria Bastinos, Pelayo, 52, BARCELONA 1. Tel. 222.06.00

SWEDEN – SUÈDE
AB CE Fritzes Kungl Hovbokhandel,
Box 16 356, S 103 27 STH, Regeringsgatan 12,
DS STOCKHOLM. Tel. 08/23 89 00

SWITZERLAND – SUISSE
Librairie Payot, 6 rue Grenus, 1211 GENÈVE 11. Tel. 022-31.89.50

TAIWAN – FORMOSE
National Book Company,
84-5 Sing Sung Rd., Sec. 3, TAIPEI 107. Tel. 321.0698

UNITED KINGDOM – ROYAUME-UNI
H.M. Stationery Office, P.O.B. 569,
LONDON SEI 9 NH. Tel. 01-928-6977, Ext. 410 or
49 High Holborn, LONDON WC1V 6 HB (personal callers)
Branches at: EDINBURGH, BIRMINGHAM, BRISTOL,
MANCHESTER, CARDIFF, BELFAST.

UNITED STATES OF AMERICA
OECD Publications and Information Center, Suite 1207,
1750 Pennsylvania Ave., N.W. WASHINGTON, D.C.20006.
Tel. (202)724-1857

VENEZUELA
Libreria del Este, Avda. F. Miranda 52, Edificio Galipàn,
CARACAS 106. Tel. 32 23 01/33 26 04/33 24 73

YUGOSLAVIA – YOUGOSLAVIE
Jugoslovenska Knjiga, Terazije 27, P.O.B. 36, BEOGRAD.
Tel. 621-992

Les commandes provenant de pays où l'OCDE n'a pas encore désigné de dépositaire peuvent être adressées à :
OCDE, Bureau des Publications, 2 rue André-Pascal, 75775 PARIS CEDEX 16.
Orders and inquiries from countries where sales agents have not yet been appointed may be sent to:
OECD, Publications Office, 2 rue André-Pascal, 75775 PARIS CEDEX 16.

OECD PUBLICATIONS, 2, rue André-Pascal, 75775 Paris Cedex 16 - No.40.965 1978

PRINTED IN FRANCE